UNDERSTANDING EDUCATIONAL EVALUATION

UNDERSTANDING EDUCATIONAL EVALUATION

■■■ **NIGEL NORRIS** ■■■

St. Martin's Press
New York

All rights reserved. For information, write:
Scholarly and Reference Division,
St. Martin's Press, Inc., 175 Fifth Avenue, New York, NY 10010

First published in the United States of America in 1990

Printed in Great Britain

ISBN 0-312-05241-3

Library of Congress Cataloging-in-Publication Data

Norris, Nigel.
  Understanding educational evaluation/Nigel Norris.
    p.   cm.
  Includes bibliographical references and index.
  ISBN 0-312-05241-3
    1. Educational evaluation—United States. 2. Educational
  evaluation—Great Britain. I. Title.
  LB2822.75.N67 1990
  379.1'54—dc20   90-39558
                                                        CIP

Contents

Acknowledgements

More by luck than judgement, in 1976 I found myself with an opportunity to study evaluation at the Centre for Applied Research in Education at the University of East Anglia. I have remained at the Centre since then working on programme and policy evaluations and teaching various courses on applied research. This book is the product of that experience and of the many relationships that have contributed to my thinking. Over the years there have been a number of people who have made a significant contribution to my ideas. First and foremost I am indebted to Barry MacDonald for the many discussions we have had about evaluation, for his encouragement and support, and for his comments on the text. I have pursued many of the themes in this book through conversations with John Elliott, David Hamilton, Ernest House, Lawrence Ingvarson, Stephen Kemmis, Saville Kushner, Bev Labbett, Nick May, Clive Norris, Jack Sanger, Helen Simons, Lawrence Stenhouse, Ian Stronach, Harry Torrance and Rob Walker, and they have done much to improve my understanding of educational evaluation and applied research. Thanks are also due to Rob Fiddy for his help in locating material on TVEI and to Richard Davies and Rob McBride for commenting on various drafts. Finally, I would like to acknowledge the support of the ESRC, then the SSRC, without which the opportunity to write this book would not have existed.

Preface

. Let nothing be called natural lest all things be held unalterable.
(Bertold Brecht)

The belief that institutions and culture can be deliberately fashioned through experimentation and research is one of the hallmarks of twentieth-century social thought. Evaluation has emerged as the major practical expression of the application of theories and methods from applied social science to the problems posed by piecemeal social engineering. The last 30 years have seen a rapid growth in the scope and scale of evaluation activities to a point where it is often mandatory to evaluate the effects and effectiveness of expenditure on planned changed. As the proportion of research and development budgets devoted to evaluation has increased, so too has the number and kinds of organizations providing evaluation services. During the last 15 years, educational evaluation has expanded and diversified to such an extent that it is now extremely difficult to encompass the field as a whole. There has been, for example, a proliferation of methodological approaches to project and programme evaluation drawing from a wide variety of disciplines and sub-disciplines — psychology, psychometrics, sociology, social theory, sociometrics, epidemiology, demography, cultural anthropology, ethnography, economics, audit, jurisprudence, journalism, and literary criticism. Amid this bewildering diversity it is, however, possible to identify something of the common and recurrent problem structures that shape the theory and practice of evaluation.

This book is about educational evaluation and the key ideas that have shaped its theory and practice. It focuses mainly on the experience of evaluation in Britain and the USA, since it is in these countries that evaluation emerged as a major methodology for social planning and control. The aim of this book is to improve our understanding of educational evaluation by examining its origins, history and modern methodology and practice. I see the book as a number of related and overlapping stories — some practical, some methodological — that centre on how we think about evaluation.

Part 1 of the book offers a history of the development of educational evaluation in the USA and Britain. Like all histories it is, of course, partial and unfinished, and as such it is only one possible selection among the many that could have been made. It begins with an account of the social origins of the American tradition of educational evaluation — a tradition deeply influenced by progressivism, scientific management and the ideology of social efficiency.

Until very recently, the institutional or executive commitment to programme evaluation that can be found in the USA has not existed in Britain. By comparison with the USA, educational evaluation in Britain has been a modest activity, largely seen as an adjunct to educational research and development. Chapter 2 provides an account of the growth of educational evaluation in Britain, beginning with the influence of psychometrics and the small-scale studies of the effectiveness of the *initial teaching alphabet*, and tracing the development of project evaluation under the auspices of the Nuffield Foundation and the Schools Council.

The objectives model and the methodology of experimental design have had a significant and lasting impact on conceptions of curriculum development and evaluation on both sides of the Atlantic. When the objectives model was first advanced by Ralph Tyler it was a process of school-based curriculum planning. Tyler saw a focus of learning objectives as one of the ways that teachers could relate the curriculum to the changing opportunities and demands that students were encountering outside the school. By the 1960s, however, the objectives model had been transformed into a powerful technology of curriculum construction with experimental design providing the methodological standards for comparative studies of the effectiveness of different curricula or teaching methods. Taken together, the objectives model and experimentalism represent what is usually thought of as the traditional methodology of educational evaluation. Chapter 3 explores the mounting critique of experimentalist thought and the objectives model, and looks at the new approaches to the evaluation of educational innovation that emerged during the 1970s.

While evaluation theorists were advancing alternatives to traditional approaches, executive decision-makers were looking to measurement and testing to find ways of relating resource inputs to educational outputs in the name of both effectiveness and efficiency. As the mood of educational expansion in the 1950s and 60s gave way to concerns about accountability and cost-effectiveness, the steady and unremitting use of information systems and procedures for programme monitoring has become an integral part of social administration. In education this is clearly evidenced by the creation of the National Assessment of Educational Progress in the USA and the Assessment of Performance Unit and national testing in Britain. Part 2 of the book looks more towards the recent experience of programme evaluation in Britain. Chapter 4 examines the evaluation of three large-scale innovation programmes: the National Development Programme in Computer Assisted Learning, the Lower Attaining Pupils Programme and the Technical and Vocational Education Initiative. Chapter 5 charts the rise of a new cult of social efficiency and the impetus it has given to the technology of testing and measurement. Finally in this section, Chapter 6, examines the ways in which government contracts for funded research are threatening the conditions necessary for the independent evaluation of policies and programmes.

Part 3 of the book offers a critical exploration of the way we think about evaluation. The four chapters in this section examine a related set of problems and themes that describe current debates about the conception and conduct of educational evaluation. An enduring question for evaluation theorists has been whether there are significant differences between research and evaluation, and if so what they are? Those who do see research and evaluation as separate undertakings have faced problems in providing a convincing account of their differences. The question is an important one in at least two respects. First, if evaluation is essentially the same as research — if it is research by another name — then it is appropriate to judge it by the same criteria and methodological standards as we would judge research. Second, in so far as they are thought of as different activities, then it is important to be clear about the kind of questions that evaluation can address and the criteria appropriate for judging its success. Most definitions of evaluation suggest that its purpose is to provide information for decision-making of one kind or another. Within this broad conception of the role of evaluation there is a wide variety of practice and approach — for example, the logical theories of Michael Scriven, the pragmatic theories of Lee J Cronbach and others who emphasize the situational responsiveness of evaluation, the social epistemology of the Canadian theorists Walter Werner and Ted Aoki, and the political theories of Ernest House and Barry MacDonald. The way we think about evaluation is heavily conditioned by different conceptions of applied research and its relationship with the politics of educational administration and policy. Chapter 7 explores these different theories of, or ways of thinking about, evaluation.

In recent years it has been usual to describe evaluation in terms of competing paradigms for social inquiry — the naturalistic and the scientific. In many conversations and writings about evaluation the concept of paradigm is invoked in an attempt to elucidate different epistemologies for educational evaluation and the values they exemplify. Chapter 8 provides a critical analysis of the ways in which models, metaphors and paradigms are employed in our thinking about evaluation, and indicates that our understanding is not well served by a Kuhnian analysis and metaphysical interpretations of the concept of paradigm.

Historically the social sciences have been associated with social improvement and the maintenance of social stability. Educational evaluation is one expression of the deeply held belief that the methodology of science can be harnessed for the improvement and effective management of social affairs. Different conceptions of the methodology of evaluative inquiry imply different relationships between science and society. Chapter 9 examines the political implications of different views about the role of science and the methodology of evaluation in the management of innovation and change. It focuses on experimentalism, the applied science model of evaluative inquiry, case study and naturalistic inquiry.

One powerful solution to the problem of the relationship between evaluation, educational decision-making and improvements is to be found in the idea of the teacher as researcher which was originally articulated by

Ralph Tyler in the 1930s. In Britain the idea of the teacher as researcher is most closely associated with the work of Lawrence Stenhouse and his attempt to provide an integrated approach to curriculum development and evaluation. In both Britain and the USA there has been a marked shift away from curriculum evaluation for the classroom teacher and towards evaluation as an instrument of policy and accountability. As the locus of curriculum power has moved outside the classroom and the audiences for evaluation have changed, different conceptions of utility have come to the fore. Chapter 10 examines different theories of utilization of evaluation as a tool for public policy and attempts to re-conceptualize the problem of utility as one of the social purpose and responsibility of evaluation.

Part 1
The History and Social Context of Educational Evaluation

Chapter 1
The Origins of Educational Evaluation in the USA

Reflecting the nascent aspiration to harness the power of science to the social problems besetting America in the early twentieth century, Walter Lippmann wrote:

> We can no longer treat life as something which has trickled down to us. We have to deal with it deliberately, devise its social organization, alter its tools, formulate its methods, educate and control it. In endless ways we put intention where custom has reigned. We break up routine, make decisions, choose our ends, select means.[1]

These words could have been written as the prologue to the curriculum reform movement.

Educational innovations have usually been thought of as programmatic initiatives designed to improve education in a rational and planned way. For a number of decades the project has been the mechanism through which western societies have tried to force the pace of educational change and address the problem of curriculum renewal. Evaluation is one expression of the sentiments Lippmann voiced at the beginning of this century and it is part of the process of dealing deliberately with social life.

Naturally evaluation has developed rather differently on each side of the Atlantic and the story is different again in continental Europe. None the less, the underlying values and beliefs that gave rise to evaluation are very similar. The belief that the structure of society is not immutable, that the inherited order is not pre-ordained, that social systems can be rationally managed and are amenable to research and development — these are the beliefs that sustained evaluation and their roots are in the common experience of industralization, with its associated demographic and social upheavals.

From Frederick Taylor to Ralph Tyler

During the early part of the twentieth century a powerful alliance of business and professional élites led a drive towards the reform of American education in the face of the problems caused by rapid urbanization and political corruption. The 'administrative progressives', as David Tyack has called them, were notably successful at shaping the structure of urban education in their own image of rational efficiency. One of the aims of this movement was to shift the control of urban education from the politicians to the professional educators.[2] The publication of *The Principles of Scientific Management* by Frederick Taylor in 1911, marked the influence of the ideas of systematization, standardization and scientific method on industry and provided a methodology for the administration of education along progressive lines.[3] For example, in 1911 the US Office of Education began the movement towards more uniformity and specificity in school budgeting and accounting, and by 1915 30 or so large school systems had completed or were working on surveys of all phases of educational life.[4] A number of these surveys employed newly developed 'objective' tests to determine the quality of teaching.[5] Taylor's ideas were brought to the attention of educators and administrators through the Twelfth Yearbook of the National Society for the Study of Education — *The Supervision of City Schools* (1913) — and influenced the thinking of men like W W Charters and Franklin Bobbitt who were applying models of industrial efficiency to the construction of the secondary school curriculum.[6]

Educational evaluation is about social planning and control, and the key value is that of order. This may seem a strange argument in the light of House's observation that evaluation is essentially liberal in outlook. Yet as Ernest House argues, a central thesis of liberalism is that of an individualistic psychology in which each individual mind is presumed to exist prior to society.[7] Such a conception of the relationship between individual and culture suggests that a significant problem for liberal democratic societies is the problem of order — the management of individuals. The progressive educational reformers of the early twentieth century thought that the solution to this problem was to be found in the scientific as opposed to political administration of education and other social services. Such a conception of social progress relied on the growth of educational research and the technology of educational measurement to provide the blueprints for a new social order, and the feedback mechanisms for its effective maintenance.

Until Ralph Tyler's work in the 1930s, evaluation was virtually synonomous with measurement and testing. Many would regard Tyler as the founder of educational evaluation, indeed the invention of the term has been ascribed to him.[8] In 1929 Tyler was invited by W W Charters to join the Bureau of Educational Research at Ohio State University. Charters, who was director of the Bureau, wanted Tyler to assist the University in improving the instruction of undergraduates, and it was here that Tyler began to specify the importance of objectives in curriculum design.[9]

In 1934 Tyler was invited to direct the evaluation staff of the Eight-Year Study (1932–40) — a pilot programme to test the effectiveness of progressive education. The study was prompted by concerns over the relative merits of traditional and progressive secondary school programmes, concerns that had resulted in some colleges refusing to admit progressive-school graduates because they lacked credits in certain subjects. The effect of this, as seen from the perspective of the Progressive Education Association, was to stifle opportunities for changing the secondary curriculum in order that it should be more relevant to the needs of students.[10] In April 1930, the Progressive Education Association met in Washington DC to consider how secondary schools could better serve young people and 'develop their powers and equip them to assist in the rebuilding of [an] already profoundly disturbed national life.'[11] By the following October, as the Depression began to deepen, the Progressive Education Association established a 'Commission on the Relation of School and College'. The aim of the Commission was to 'explore possibilities of better co-ordination of school and college work and to seek agreement which could provide freedom for secondary schools to attempt fundamental reconstruction.'[12] In 1932 the Commission put forward a proposal for a 'sound experimental study of secondary education'. This proposal became known as the Eight-Year Study.[13] The rationale for the Study was ambitious. A small number of secondary schools were to develop educational programmes appropriate to the needs of their students, without regard to college entrance requirements or state accreditation regulations. The schools were to be responsible for collecting and reporting information on what students were learning so as to help colleges select candidates for admission.[14] According to Tyler:

> Most of the schools began their curriculum development with one or two ideas about what needed to be done, but they soon discovered that the problems were more complex than they had earlier conceived. Those who had become very conscious of the large gap between the needs and interests of the students and the content of the curriculum soon found that there was also a serious problem of relating the curriculum to the opportunities and demands of the changing situations that the students were encountering in life outside the school.[15]

The work of the evaluation staff was guided by three basic convictions: first, that evaluation and recording should be related to each school's purposes; second, that a school's evaluation programme should be comprehensive; and third, that teachers should participate in the construction of all the evaluation instruments and forms of reporting.[16]

In his report on appraising student progress, Tyler commented that the term 'evaluation' was used rather than 'measurement', 'test' or 'examination' because evaluation implied 'a process by which the values of an enterprise are ascertained.'[17] For Tyler and his colleagues one important purpose of evaluation was to make periodic checks on the effectiveness of schools and indicate points in the school's programme where improvements were necessary.[18] Another important purpose of evaluation which was stressed by Tyler was the validation of the 'hypotheses upon which the educational institution operates.'[19] Under Tyler's direction, the evaluation staff of the Eight-Year Study developed a theory of evaluation which was simple, powerful and so thoroughly integrated with the process of curriculum construction that it blurred the boundaries between development and evaluation. For Tyler education was essentially about changing the behaviour patterns of pupils; thus the curriculum could be constructed through the specification of desirable behaviours which were stated as objectives to be achieved. Evaluation then became a relatively simple matter which consisted of finding out whether the stated objectives were being met — a conception of curriculum evaluation that harked back to his work on course improvement with W W Charters at Ohio State University. Throughout the Study, curriculum specialists and the evaluators worked closely with the 30 pilot sites. Tyler and his colleagues devised summer schools for the Eight-Year Study participants. The rationale for the syllabus which guided the development activities in these workshops was later presented in Tyler's *Basic Principles of Curriculum and Instruction*, published in 1949.

Tyler's work shifted evaluation away from a focus on individual abilities and qualities towards a focus on curriculum design. He saw evaluation not as a technology for discriminating between individuals, but rather as a means of appraising the degree to which curriculum intentions were realized in practice. So for Tyler the process of evaluation was: 'essentially the process of determining to what extent the educational objectives are realized by the program of curriculum and instruction.'[20] While Tyler was reacting to the view that evaluation concerned the measurement of individual differences, he did not reject testing *per se*. He defined objectives as desirable changes in the behaviour patterns of students, so evaluation was the means by which educators could determine the degree to which predicted changes in behaviour were actually taking place, and testing was one of the ways to provide evidence of student behaviours. Indeed, in Tyler's early account of evaluation theory he appears to use the words 'appraisal' and 'evaluation' interchangeably, and by 'appraisal' he meant assessment. The idea that assessment data could be used for evaluating the effects and effectiveness of educational programmes was enormously persuasive. Tyler's approach to curriculum design and evaluation has attracted many imitators and remains influential even today.[21]

Although he was influenced by the progressive ideas of scientific management, much of Tyler's early work was closely tied to the classroom and what individual teachers could do.[22] It is now difficult to read Tyler's original formulation without reflecting on what followed as a result of his work. As the demand for evaluation grew, so the sensitivity of his approach, its emphasis on local initiatives and teacher participation, its radicalness, and the focus on community-based curriculum construction were lost. The objectives model was conceived in the context of university-based course improvement and school-based curriculum development. Its usefulness for evaluating social action programmes and a nationally funded system of innovation was always likely to be suspect. Nonetheless when these initiatives emerged a decade or so later, the idea of a systematic method of curriculum construction based on learning objectives and supported by a technology of testing had a powerful influence on the thinking of policy-makers and evaluators alike.

Federal investment in programme evaluation — Sputnik to Follow Through

There are two great landmarks in the growth of educational evaluation in the USA. The first is 4 October 1957, when the Russians launched Sputnik and the concept of the technological lag was reborn. The geopolitical implications of Sputnik committed the federal government to a programme of research and development to achieve the centrally defined goals of national security. To this end the National Science Foundation and the US Office of Education funded curriculum projects in physics, mathematics, chemistry, biology, English and social studies.[23] This massive increase in federal support for curriculum improvement was accompanied by a growing interest in evaluation, probably to support future budget requests as much as to monitor the process and progress of curriculum development.

The second and perhaps more important landmark was the Elementary and Secondary Education Act of 1965 (ESEA 1965), which was the first piece of social legislation to mandate project reporting. This unprecedented evaluation requirement was tied to Title 1 of the Act, which was a compensatory education programme of 1 billion dollars per annum allocated to meet the needs of disadvantaged children. The principal architect of the Title 1 evaluation requirement was Senator Robert Kennedy. He saw evaluation as a way of ensuring that federal dollars were actually spent on programmes for the disadvantaged, rather than on general aid for schools. His major concern was to protect the interests of the disadvantaged by furnishing parents with information which might enable them to have a say in how federal money was being spent in their school districts.[24] Others, notably William Gorham at the Department of Health Education and Welfare (HEW), saw evaluation as a means of gathering information which might yield evidence of the effectiveness of Title 1 projects, thereby leading to more efficient local practices and federal decision-making.[25]

The post-Sputnik curriculum development programmes and the reporting requirements of ESEA Title 1 created a demand for evaluation that was far in excess of the supply of social scientists with the requisite skills and experience. Furthermore, existing approaches to evaluation (the objectives model, the Planning Program-Budgeting-Systems (PPBS) of the Department of Defense,[26] the narrower forms of cost-benefit analysis which had become the stock-in-trade of welfare economics, and the social survey techniques developed by sociologists) were all to prove inadequately matched to the scale of federal intervention, the diversity of local initiatives and the needs of policy-makers and educationalists for a broad range of information about the nature and effects of innovation.

The early Title 1 evaluation efforts did not please the Assistant Secretary for Program Evaluation at HEW. Not only were state and local evaluations failing to comply with the spirit of the Kennedy reporting requirements (and were almost uniformly positive), but several national studies, for example Coleman's study of educational opportunity and the work of the US Commission on Civil Rights, were beginning to cast doubt on the widsom of investing federal money in compensatory education as an anti-poverty strategy.[27]

In 1967, HEW policy analysts at the Office of the Assistant Secretary for Program Evaluation began to take a serious interest in improving Title 1 evaluations. They commissioned TEMPO, a research division of the General Electric Company, to conduct an independent evaluation. The resulting study tried to identify successful practices within large-scale programmes using what they claimed were sophisticated analytical techniques. On the basis of anecdotal evidence of programme successes, the TEMPO evaluators selected a deliberately unrepresentative sample of 14 Title 1 projects. The projects were studied intensively using data collected by the school districts for the school years 1965–66. The Assistant Secretary for Program Evaluation hoped that the study would produce some hard evidence on the relationship between project characteristics and pupil performance, evidence which might then be used to improve the programme in other settings.[28] Yet a memorandum from Alice Rivlin (Deputy Secretary for Program Analysis at HEW) to Harold Howe (Commissioner of Education at the US Office of Education) indicates something of the growing but still private disillusion with systematic and scientific attempts to evaluate broad social action programmes:

> A couple of years of trying to assess what is known about the effectiveness of compensatory programs has convinced me of two things. (1) Not much is known yet. From the various evaluations and surveys no clear pattern emerges. (2) Neither present local evaluations nor sample surveys are likely to yield much insight into the what types of programs work best for particular types of children.[29]

In his introductory paper to the first of the American Educational Research Association's monograph series on curriculum evaluation published in 1967, Robert Stake indicated that the research community had been taken somewhat by surprise by the Title 1 evaluation requirement:

> The language of the Elementary and Secondary Act of 1965 . . . implies that the capability to evaluate is presently within our command. But the fluidity of our experiments and the bluntness of our tests deny that capability. Neither quantity nor quality of impact is measured.[30]

At the same time as Stake was describing the mismatch between legislative intent and evaluative capabilities, the Follow Through Programme was being planned as an extension to Head Start, with an anticipated $120 million appropriation.[31] Follow Through was thought of as a service programme to improve the schooling of disadvantaged children by building on and maintaining the *success* of Head Start.[32] The programme was the result of executive rather than congressional initiative and before it got underway the expected appropriation was slashed to $15 million for the first year.[33] Given the financial constraints and the difficulty of generating comparative evidence from the Title 1 projects, the US Office of Education agreed to convert Follow Through into a planned variation experiment which would compare pupils enrolled in different models of early childhood education to each other and to non-Follow Through classes.[34]

What distinguished Follow Through from many other social action programmes was the intention to provide systematic evidence on the relative effectiveness of programme variations. The authors of Follow Through believed that because social action programmes were not designed as experiments thay had little chance of yielding unequivocal results. The implication was that rather than recast the methodology of evaluation, programmes should be designed in ways which were commensurate with the assumed need of decision-makers for clearly defined and weighted policy option.

As House demonstrates, the history of Follow Through evaluations was not a happy one.[35] An initial evaluation contract was given to the University of Pittsburgh in 1967, but for some reason the Pittsburgh evaluators only managed to include pre-test scores in the final report.[36] In 1968 a large evaluation contract was hastily placed with the Stanford Research Institute by a procedure that was later criticized by the General Accounting Office.[37] The evaluation design envisaged the collection of a broad range of evidence on the impact of the programme with a focus on the community. Although the Stanford Research Institute saw the primary purpose of the evaluation as a description of the programme, they began their fieldwork by administering cognitive tests in 47 of the 91 trial sites. By October 1968, the evaluators and Follow Through administrators were faced with protests from minority groups who claimed that the evaluators had a biased and restricted view of the programme, and one which was insensitive to parental as well as community involvement.[38] As a result the Stanford Research Institute initiated a number of community case studies but these did not fare well. The problem from the perspective of the Stanford Research Institute was that each community was so different that it was difficult to make generalizations.

In 1970 the interim results of the impact of Follow Through showed no positive effects. The results were not made public. A serious problem for the advocates of social experiments was that while government agencies were willing to accept the idea of planned variation experiments, they found it difficult to accept the results. By 1971 the focus of institutional change which had been demanded by minority groups was quietly dropped.

After $12 million of federal money had been spent on Follow Through evaluation, the Office of Education had very little to show and were no nearer their goal of isolating effective practices. In the light of investigations from HEW and the General Accounting Office into the conduct of the Follow Through evaluation, the Office of Education appointed a new evaluation director and took greater control of the evaluation. A new evaluation contract was issued this time to the Huron Institute. An evaluation design emerged which the Institute claimed would seperate the effects of the models of early childhood education from the confounding effects of contextual site features.

Faced with mounting costs, Garry McDaniels, the newly appointed evaluation director, insisted that the evaluation should focus on a narrow range of programme goals.[39] In the meantime Abt Associates had been hired to deal with the complex problem of data analysis, while the Stanford Research Institute continued to be responsible for data collection. Predictably, at the 1972 annual Follow Through meeting parents once again began to voice their dissatisfaction with the evaluation. This time, however, there was no response from the Follow Through administrators and the by now even narrower evaluation design went ahead.[40]

The chequered story of the Follow Through evaluation was not atypical. In many respects similar problems were encountered by the evaluations of Head Start and the early studies of Title 1. In all these cases it seems that the technical difficulties of finding control groups, controlling for bias and measuring for a wide range of psychological and social effects proved difficult to overcome within the limits of experimental design and the prevailing technology of testing. The problems of these evaluations were not only methodological, however. In practice there is always likely to be a conflict between the conventions of experimental design (eg, randomization) and the established administrative procedures for determining access to social programmes. More significantly, perhaps, while experimental design and other means-ends approaches to evaluation call for clarity of purpose and careful control, innovation systems might well thrive on ambiguity of purpose and lack of control.

Although the evaluations of compensatory education were largely unhelpful, this did little to lessen the appetite of federal agencies for evaluation. Since the beginning of the 1970s programme, evaluations have become a matter of course and many arise out of congressional requests for information. Major educational evaluations mandated by Congress have included vocational education, bilingual education, special education and school finance.[41] There can be little doubt that the requirement for large-scale evaluation studies created a new social research industry. Evaluation is now big business. As Lee J Cronbach observed, evaluation activities mushroomed without plan during the 1970s, leading to a boomtown atmosphere. By 1974 federal expenditures for programme evaluation were six times higher than those in 1969. According to Cronbach, by 1977 HEW alone were spending $38 million per annum on programme evaluations and a further $264 million on policy-oriented research and development, some of which would have been clearly evaluative in purpose.[42] However, these figures give only a crude estimate of the scale of evaluation activities in North America. They exclude, for example, evaluations sponsored by charitable foundations or undertaken at state or local levels.

When we talk about the development of educational evaluation in the USA we are talking about a massive, ungainly and ill-defined enterprise that is as yet unclassified except in the most general way. Evaluations are often conducted by private rather than federal or public agencies and therefore questions of profitability may significantly affect evaluation designs. Educational evaluation in North America is predominantly quantitative in its methods and practices. It is a contribution to a liberal political philosophy favouring a gradualist approach to social change. Programme evaluation is intimately connected with government, both federal as well as local, and it could be argued that since the 1960s it has become the handmaiden of educational administration and bureaucratic control.[43]

Notes

1. Lippmann, W (1961) *Drift and Mastery*, Englewood Cliffs, NJ: Prenctice-Hall, p 147. First published by Mitchell Kennerly in 1914.
2. For a discussion of the administrative progressive movement in education see: Tyack, DB (1974) *The One Best System*, Cambridge, Mass: Harvard University Press, especially Parts IV and V, pp 126–98. Also see: Tyack, DB & Hanson, E (1982) *Managers of Virtue*, New York: Basic Books, especially Part II, pp 105–213.
3. Taylor, FW (1911) *The Principles of Scientific Management*, New York: Harper & Bros.
4. See James, HT (1971) The new cult of efficiency and education. In Browder, LH (ed.) *Emerging Patterns of Administrative Accountability*, Berkeley, Cal: McCutchan, pp 39–46.
5. See Madaus, GF, Stufflebeam, DL & Scriven, MS (1983) Program evaluation: a historical overview. In Madaus, GF, Stufflebeam, DL & Scriven, MS (eds) *Evaluation Models Viewpoints on Education and Human Services Evaluation*, Boston, Mass: Kluwer-Nijhoff Publishing, pp 3–23.
6. The title of the Twelfth Yearbook of the National Society for the Study of Education was *The Supervision of City Schools*. See: Hamilton, D (1977) Making sense of curriuclum evaluation: continuities and discontinuities in an educational idea. In Shulman, LS (ed.) *Review of Research in Education*, Vol 5, Itasca, Illinois: Peacock, pp 318–47.
7. House, E (1980) *Evaluating with Validity*, Beverly Hills: Sage, see in particular Chapter 3.
8. Madaus, GF, Stufflebeam, DL & Scriven, MS (1983) op. cit. p 8.
9. A personal account of Ralph Tyler's early career, from 1929 when he joined WW Charters at Ohio State University to 1943 when he became Director of the Examinations Staff of the US Armed Forces Institute, is given in: Tyler, RW (1983) A rationale for program evaluation. In Madaus, GF, Stufflebeam, DL & Scriven, MS (eds) *Evaluation Models Viewpoints on Educational and Human Services Evaluation*, Boston, Mass: Kluwer-Nijhoff Publishing, pp 67–78.
10. For an overview of the Eight-Year Study see: Aitken, WM (1942) *Adventure in American Education (Volume 1) The Story of the Eight Year Study*, New York: Harper & Brothers.
11. Ibid. p 1.
12. Ibid. p 2.
13. A proposal for better co-ordination of school and college work, May 1932. Detailed in: Aitken, WM (1942) op. cit., pp 140–46.
14. Smith, ER & Tyler, RW (1942) *Adventure in American Education (Volume 3) Appraising and Recording Student Progress*, New York: Harper & Row.
15. Tyler, RW (1983) A rationale for program evaluation. In Madaus, GF, Stufflebeam, DL & Scriven, MS (eds) *Evaluation Models: Viewpoints on Educational and Human Services Evaluation*, Boston, Mass: Kluwer-Nijhoff Publishing, p 73.

16. See Wilford M Aiken's Foreword to Smith, ER & Tyler, RW (1942) *Appraising and Recording Student Progress*, New York: Harper & Row, pp xvii–xix.
17. Smith, ER & Tyler, RW (1942) *Appraising and Recording Student Progress*, New York: Harper & Row, p 5.
18. Ibid. p 7.
19. Ibid.
20. Tyler, R (1949) *Basic Principles of Curriculum and Instruction*, University of Chicago Press, pp 105–6.
21. For a contemporary view of evaluation which is derivative of Tyler's objectives approach, see: Shipman, M (1979) *In-School Evaluation*, London: Heinemann.
22. See, for example, Waples, D & Tyler, RW (1930) *Research Methods and Teachers' Problems: A Manual for Systematic Studies of Classroom Procedure*. New York: The Macmillan Co.
23. Mary Waring suggests that while Sputnik underlined the concern about scientific and technological manpower, it did not engender the curriculum reform movement. However, although it is clear that curriculum projects in mathematics and physics were already established before 1957, Sputnik did focus attention on the problems of technical and scientific education. More importantly, it provided the justification for federal intervention in a decentralized education system. See: Waring, M (1979) *Social Pressures and Curriculum Innovation*, London: Methuen.
24. For an account of the origins of the evaluation requirements of Title 1 see: McLaughlin, M (1975) *Evaluation and Reform: The Elementary and Secondary Education Act 1965/Title 1*, Cambridge, Mass: Ballinger.
25. McLaughlin, M (1975) op. cit. p 7.
26. PPBS is a process of budgetary control and accountability based on systems theory and developed as the US Department of Defense by Charles Hitch. On 25 August 1965, President Johnson announced a plan to extend PPBS throughout the Federal Government. The basic elements of the system are: (a) five-year time horizons for agency planning; (b) the preparation of programme expenditures in a way which allows them to be compared with agency goals; and, (c) cost-benefit studies to determine the most effective allocation of agency resources among programmes. The advocates of PPBS say it is a comprehensive system for centralizing decision-making and rationalizing resource allocation among autonomous, self-interested and competing agencies. For an analysis of the effect which PPBS had on programme evaluation in education see: Elmore, R (1976) *Follow Through: Decision-making in a Large Scale Social Experiment.* Unpublished doctoral dissertation, School of Education, Harvard University.
27. See, for example, Coleman, J et al (1966) *Equality of Educational Opportunity*, Washington DC: US Government Printing Office. Also see: US Commission on Civil Rights (1967) *Racial Isolation in Public Schools*, Washington DC: US Government Printing Office.
28. McLaughlin, M (1975) op. cit., especially Chapter 3.
29. Quoted in Elmore, R (1976) Follow Through: Decision Making in a Large Scale Social Experiment. Unpublished doctoral dissertation, School of Education, Harvard University.
30. Stake, R (1967) Towards a technology for the evaluation of educational programs. In Tyler, R et al. *Perspectives on Curriculum Evaluation*, AERA Monograph Series on Curriculum Evaluation No 1, Chicago: Rand McNally.
31. House, E. et al. (1978) No simple answer: critique of follow through evaluation. *Harvard Educational Review*, **48**, 2, p 128.

32. Heat Start focused on pre-school children and took the form of enrichment projects. It began with the passing of the Economic Opportunity Act of 1964 and was administered by the now defunct Office of Economic Opportunity (OEO). In 1968 the Evaluation Division of the OEO awarded a contract to the Westinghouse Corporation with the University of Ohio to evaluate the impact of Head Start. See, for example, Cicarelli, V (1969). *The Impact of Head Start: An Evaluation of the Effects of Head Start on Children's Cognitive and Effective Development* (Ohio University Report to the Office of Economic Opportunity) Washington DC: Clearinghouse for Federal Scientific and Technical Information (EDO36321), and Datta, L (1983) A tale of two studies: The Westinghouse-Ohio Evaluation of Project Head Start and the Consortium for Longitudinal Studies Report, *Studies in Educational Evaluation*, Vol 8, pp 271–80.
33. House, E et al. (1978) op. cit.
34. Ibid.
35. House, E (1979) The objectivity, fairness, and justice of federal evaluation as reflected in the Follow Through evaluation. In *Educational Evaluation and Policy Analysis*, Washington DC: AERA, 1, 1, pp 28–42.
36. Ibid. p 30.
37. Ibid.
38. Ibid.
39. The cost of the Standford Research Institute's contribution to the Follow Through evaluation was $850,000 in 1968–69; $2.5 million in 1969–70; $3.5 million in 1970–71; and $5.4 in 1971–72. Figures cited in Elmore, R (1976) op. cit. p 238.
40. House, E (1979) op. cit.
41. See St Perre, RG (1983) Congressional input to program evaluation: scope and effects. *Evaluation Review*, 7, 4, pp 411–36.
42. Cronbach, LJ & Assoc (1981) *Towards Reform of Program Evaluation*, London: Jossey Bass, p 40.
43. Ibid. p 41.

Chapter 2
The Origins of Educational Evaluation in Britain

In Britain, the growth of social and psychological research has been closely related to the development of public policy. The Royal Commission on the Poor Law 1832–1834, is usually acknowledged as the beginning of applied social research in England.[1] From this time onwards the commission of inquiry became one of the main instruments of social investigation. The extent to which Royal Commissions and other committees of inquiry could be regarded as forms of evaluative research is a matter of debate. However, some commentators clearly see the origins of educational evaluation stretching back to the growth of political economy and public administration in the early part of the nineteenth century.[2]

Like America at the turn of the century, in Britain there was a concern among the professional middle classes for the promotion of efficient forms of social organization and governance. The Fabians, especially the Webbs, were influential advocates of national efficiency and came to see education as the key instrument to be used to achieve that end.[3] Inasmuch as this was a movement, it was one that emphasized the key role of intellectual élites and systematic inquiry in public policy and administration.[4] Martin Bulmer, commenting on the history of empirical social research in Britain, suggests that it was characterized by the absence of an institutional base; the key role of voluntary associations and private individuals in providing support; communications between a comparatively small élite drawn from the professional middle class; and the importance of reforming public servants who encouraged social inquiry.[5] By contrast, in America the social sciences developed early with a strong university base and stronger connections with state and federal governments.[6] Janet Finch, in her study of research and policy, describes the dominant tradition of social research in Britain as fact gathering through statistical methods and social surveys.[7] For those interested in educational evaluation, however, the development of a complementary but different technology, namely psychometrics, was perhaps more significant.

The influence of psychometrics

Earlier in this century, mental testing appeared to offer a scientific procedure for measuring ability that meant that judgements and actions based on that knowledge could be regarded as valid and uncontentious. Psychometrics was, in a certain sense, the methodology of the science of education.[8] In Britain the work of Galton, Pearson, Spearman and Burt; in France the work of Binet and Simon; and in America the work of men like Davenport, Cattell, Thorndike and Terman, contributed to the growth and international dissemination of the technology of mental testing and social classification.[9] Psychometrics has had a considerable influence on educational research and evaluation. The psychometric tradition had its origins in nineteenth century notions of social evolution and progress. For Sir Francis Galton psychological measurement offered the possibility of bringing 'the improvement of the natural gifts of future generations of the human race under control.'[10] For Stephen Wiseman, writing some 70 years later, the importance of psychometrics could not be underestimated 'in terms of its potentiality for the progress of mankind and the achievement of equality of opportunity.'[11]

The measurement of individual differences provided a technology of classification for the 'objective' allocation or exclusion of individuals to or from roles, treatments or forms of institutional provision. Psychometrics also promised a technology for relating inputs to educational outputs and for judging the effectiveness and efficiency of different teachers, schools, curricula, and forms of educational provision. Although the use of standardized test data in evaluation has been severely criticized, there continues to be a strong body of opinion and practice that regards pupil outcome data as persuasively indicative of teacher or school effectiveness.[12] Like sociometrics, psychometrics represented the political arithmetic for the simple social audit.

In his book *Hereditary Genius*, Galton argued that the mental characteristics of a population, like its physical characteristics, would follow a Gaussian distribution.[13] According to Donald MacKenzie, Galton followed the Belgian astronomer and statistician Quetelet in applying the basic technique of error theory to human data, but 'error theory' was primarily concerned with eliminating or at least controlling variability.[14] In psychometrics, however, variability was of particular interest as was the objective determination of normality.[15] Summarizing the shifts in the nomenclature of mental measurement, MacKenzie says that 'there was a gradual transition from the use of the term ''probable error'' to the term ''standard deviation'' (which is free from the implications that a deviation is in any sense an error), and from term ''law of error'' to the term ''normal distribution'' '.[16] Notions of normal distribution have played a central part in the technology of testing, providing a useful standard in the construction and analysis of tests. However, it is important to remember that the technology rests on the basic and questionable assumption that mental characteristics like intelligence are distributed throughout a population in the same way as physical characteristics are. Galton made such an assumption largely because his eugenic objectives necessitated the study of deviation.

Accurate classification and comparison require common forms of measurement, hence the concern in evaluation with standardization in many aspects of testing. William Angoff and Scarvia B Anderson, writing in 1963, suggested that the development and application of standardized tests represented one of the major contributions to educational progress of the last 50 years.[17] An important characteristic of standardized tests is that they are referenced to appropriate norm groups — frequently so called 'national norms' collected by age or age-related criteria like school grade or class.

The capacity to rank order and assign individuals to certain categories by apparently objective means provided, as Clarence Karier has argued, a convenient technology for maintaining social order, judging the relative effectiveness of different social treatments, and promoting both a meritocratic ideology and the goal of social efficiency.[18] The psychometric tradition was concerned with producing a technology for making scientific and therefore politically defensible forms of social classification and comparison. It embodied certain rigid methodological procedures and values that were adopted and adapted by those seeking to evaluate in education.

The early evaluation studies: learning to read

Many of the early evaluation studies in Britain focused on the effectiveness of the intital teaching alphabet (i.t.a.) in helping young children learn to read, and were steeped in the methodology of experimental design and the theory of mental testing. The promoters of i.t.a. argued that traditional orthography (t.o.) was a major cause of difficulty in learning to read and that the simplified and regularized orthography of i.t.a. should be used in the beginning stages. In 1958 James Pitman approached the Director of the NFER, Dr Wall, and the Director of the London Institute of Education, H L Elvin, to see if they would be interested in an experiment to test the advantages of his i.t.a.[19] To this end, and with a grant from Pitman and Sons as well as a personal financial guarantee from Sir James Pitman, a steering committee was established and a reading research unit was created as a base for the experiment.[20] The experiment attracted a considerable degree of political support, notably from the Minister of Education, the Association of Education Committees and Sir Ronald Gould of the National Union of Teachers. There was also keen international interest in the development.[21]

John Downing, a teacher and experimental psychologist, was appointed to the Institute in 1960 to conduct a field experiment under representative everyday classroom conditions to investigate the relative effectiveness of i.t.a. The first i.t.a. experiment attempted to address five instrumental questions:

1. Can children learn to read more easily with i.t.a. than they can with t.o.?
2. Can pupils transfer their learning in reading i.t.a. to reading in t.o.?
3. After the whole process of beginning with i.t.a. and transferring to t.o.,

are reading attainments superior to what they would have been without the intervention of i.t.a.?
4. Will children's written compositions be more fluent with the simpler i.t.a. code for speech?
5. How will children's later attainments in t.o. spelling be influenced by their earlier experiences of reading and writing different spellings on i.t.a.?[22]

The design included an experimental group of classes that began reading with i.t.a., a control group of classes that began reading with the same basic readers printed in t.o., and a special control group consisting of children one year older who had entered the control group schools one year before the experiment started. A comparison between the control group and the special control group was intended to provide a check on the Hawthorne effect. The experimental groups and the control groups were matched on intelligence tests, age, gender, social class, size of school, pupil:teacher ratio, urban/rural location, organizational variables and certain school amenities. Yet as Jack Holmes indicated in the *i.t.a. Symposium*, despite these efforts to reduce possible bias by matching there were inherent difficulties with the first experiment. One problem was that the rigorous attempts to adhere to broad-scale matching reduced the sample size and probably introduced a certain sampling bias. Rigidity on the part of administrators interfered with randomization. Downing was unable to randomly assign for each matched pair one class to his experimental group and the other to his control group, and this reduced the capacity to generalize from the experiment. Holmes was also critical of variability in the statistical decision rules for analysing the experiment.[23]

In the light of these difficulties and others that Downing had encountered, a second i.t.a. experiment beginning in September 1963 was conducted to provide more rigorous controls. One of the reasons why these had not been built into the first experiment was inadequate finance.

In 1965 the Schools Council commissioned an independent evaluation of the available evidence relating to the use of i.t.a. as a means of beginning reading with infants. The evaluation was undertaken by Professor Warburton and Vera Southgate from the University of Manchester.[24] Their evaluation had three strands. First, they conducted a questionnaire inquiry into the extent of the use of i.t.a. Second, they documented the views of 'knowledgeable people' who had been closely connected with the use of i.t.a. Third, they evaluated all the published research evidence on i.t.a. in Britain and the USA.[25] In all, research studies were reviewed by Warburton and Southgate including those undertaken by John Downing. Most of these studies suffered from similar methodological problems: inadequate statistical methods and analysis, failure to standardize independent variables, poor controls, and inadequate measures to deal with the Hawthorne effect.[26]

The i.t.a. experiments are a good example of the ways in which psychometrics have influenced educational evaluation. For example, the measurement programme involved a variety of standardized tests including: Raven's Coloured Progressive Matrices, the Crichton Vocabulary Test, the

Schonell Graded Word Reading Test, the Neale Analysis of Reading Ability, tests published by the NFER (A.R.$_{1c}$ and A.R.$_2$), and the Schonell Graded Word Spelling Test.[27] In particular, the use of intelligence tests for ability matching represented a major assumption derived from the psychometric movement.

With i.t.a., as with Follow Through, there was a conflict between the conventions of experimental design, and administrative and politically expedient procedures for determining access to the innovation. This is a problem which has serious consequences when it comes to the interpretation of the data and which undermines attempts at generalization. The theory of experimental design, for instance, requires randomization in order to transfer robust statistical generalizations from sample to target populations.

The essential factor which distinguishes the field experiment from other kinds of field study is the deliberate manipulation of conditions in order to determine causal relations. The i.t.a. experiments were field experiments employing a classic comparative input-output design where the process of innovation and the process of learning were treated as technical problems of productivity. The aim of the experiments was to provide unequivocal evidence of the superiority of i.t.a. in terms of measures of output. The social philosophy behind the experiments was one of social engineering and their guiding metaphor was industrial production.

Curriculum evaluation: Nuffield and the Schools Council

In Britain, like the USA, large-scale curriculum reform started in science education. During the 1950s there was considerable concern about the quantity and quality of students entering applied science or technology, as well as about the supply of science teachers in secondary schools.[28] On both sides of the Atlantic it was widely acknowledged that economic growth and national security depended on technological development, so the supply of technical labour was an important political issue fuelled by international competition for economic and military supremacy. In the USA it was the Democratic administrations of John F Kennedy and later Lyndon B Johnson who fully embraced the Keynesian programme of an economy managed for growth and full employment — the 'great society' made possible by deficit budgeting and engineered by the best and the brightest.[29] In Britain, although it was the Conservatives who represented the comfortable society of 1959, by 1964 it was the Labour Party who had captured the rhetoric of technological change and future prosperity sprinkled with the pepper of social equality. Like the Democrats, the Labour Party espoused the values of a modern society: the 'white heat' of technological change and the distribution of economic roles through achieved rather than ascribed status. Wilson too wanted the best and the brightest.[30]

The innovation movements of the 1950s and 60s were a response to two related but different problems; the first was curriculum obsolescence with its implications for manpower planning; the second was the persistence of poverty with its implications for social control. There was a growing belief that education could be used to influence and ultimately change the structure of society by redistributing life chances and providing the human resources for sustained economic growth. Yet in both Britain and the USA, the decentralized nature of schooling meant that governments found it difficult to intervene directly in education. In Britain a two-pronged policy emerged — compensatory education on the one hand and curriculum development on the other, and it is to this story that we now turn.

On 4 April 1962, David Eccles (Minister of Education) announced to Parliament the establishment of the Nuffield Foundation Science Teaching Projects. At first sight it might seem a curious testimony to the English commitment to education that philanthropy provided the financial stimulus for curriculum reform. But as Mary Waring's account of the history of the Nuffield Science Projects suggests, the relationship between government and the Nuffield Foundation was one of relative intimacy.[31] Moreover, Nuffield could intervene in the school curriuclum without raising suspicion about moves towards central control.

While the government was worried about the supply of scientific manpower, and had been so since the Barlow Committee reported in 1946, this concern did not find expression in the provision of public money. Barlow had predicted an escalation of manpower shortages unless the annual output of scientists could be doubled.[32] Ten years later a White Paper on technical education stated that other industrialized countries were making huge efforts to train more scientists and that Britain was in danger of being left behind, and although both parties promised, and the Conservatives created, a Ministry of Science after the 1959 election, governmental interest at that time did not extend to school science.[33] Industry, on the other hand, took a more forward-looking and obviously self-interested view. At the initiative of Jack Oriel of Shell International, a fund (the Industrial Fund) was established to provide help for school science. Eventually the Fund attracted support from 141 companies and was used to give financial assistance to independent and direct grant schools wishing to improve their science teaching equipment or their laboratories and buildings.[34]

The funding of the science projects by the Nuffield Foundation set the scene for, and the subsequent tone of, a national curriculum development movement. Nuffield saw themselves as providing the initiative but not the long-term investment. They had a policy of funding ventures with potential but where immediate success was in some doubt. However, once they had provided the innovation seed money, it was their policy to leave it to others to continue the development.[35]

In Britain in the early 60s evaluation was not a matter of general or even specialist concern. There is little to suggest that it was anything more than an extension of educational research, which itself was small albeit expanding.[36] The first wave of curriculum developers were largely confident of the eventual success of their projects. Tony Becher, who was for some time Assistant Director at the Nuffield Foundation, recalled that although there was considerable discussion at Nuffield Lodge about evaluation, the project directors were resistant to the idea. They argued that their projects were not concerned with measurable gains in factual knowledge but rather with changes in the attitudes of students towards science, and that evaluation was therefore inappropriate.[37]

The prevailing view at Nuffield Lodge was that the quality of a good project would be self-evident. Success depended on feedback from trial schools and the revision of materials to take account of criticisms and teething problems. Since it was thought impossible to mount an evaluation study which compared the Nuffield approach with other approaches to science education, the question of external evaluation was put to one side, only to be taken up later by the Schools Council. This was not the case, however, with Nuffield's investment in primary school French.

The Foundation's interest in foreign language teaching first found expression in 1960 when they funded two small experiments in the teaching of French to primary school children.[38] In 1963 the Foundation increased its support in this area. They jointly funded, with the Ministry of Education, a project to prepare a full range of teaching resources for an introductory course in French for children between the ages of eight and thirteen years old. The Foundation took responsibility for the preparation of materials while the Ministry organized the training of teachers and the selection of schools for the pilot scheme.[39]

Perhaps because of the direct involvement of the Department of Education and Science or maybe out of a desire to complement the planned HMI study, an external evaluation was included almost from the start. Funded by the DES and based at the National Foundation for Educational Research, the evaluation began in 1964. It was expected to consider not only the success of the project but also the effects of introducing French on the attainments and general development of children.[40] It comprised a longitudinal survey of two consecutive groups of pupils who were starting to learn French, from the beginning of their second year in the junior school to the end of their second year in the secondary school.[41] This study, like other evaluation projects of the time, relied largely on testing and questionnaires, generating both psychometric and sociometric data. But, unlike the evaluation of primary school science 5–13, the evaluation of primary school French was able to compare the perfomance of children who had started to learn French at the age of eight with various control groups who had started the language at eleven years old.[42] While this comparative element no doubt gave the study its evaluative flavour, by the time the full results were made public in 1974 it is questionable whether anyone had a serious need for them. In the words of David Hamilton: 'as time passed and the evaluation costs increased, the market value of its information declined.'[43]

Although the Nuffield initiatives had an enduring influence on the curriculum development landscape, it was the Schools Council that established evaluation as a familiar feature of curriculum development. The Council came into being on 1 October 1964, partly as a solution to the political problems caused by the creation of a Curriculum Study Group at the Ministry of Education. This had aroused fears that the Ministry were threatening teacher autonomy and eroding the responsibility of local government.

The Schools Council was formed as an autonomous agency jointly funded by central and local government with 73 nominated representatives, the majority of whom were teachers.[44] Within a year the Council had set up an Evaluation Advisory Committee under the chairmanship of Professor Kerr. The new committee was occasioned by a suggestion that the Council should evaluate the science materials produced by the Nuffield projects. It met for the first time in January 1966, and during that year considered various proposals for the evaluation of science and mathematics projects. Kerr, however, sought to broaden the role of the Committee and the Council's concept of evaluation. He was worried by the suggestion that evaluation might be limited to the measurement of project outcomes, so in a memorandum to the main business committee of the Council, the Co-ordinating Committee, he described what he saw as the role of the Evaluation Advisory Committee and its working definition of evaluation:

> The Evaluation Advisory Committee was formed as an *ad hoc* committee to put forward suggestions for the evaluation of the Nuffield Foundation Science Teaching Project. The O level biology, chemistry and physics sections had prepared all the draft materials and carried out extensive trials before the Evaluation Advisory Committee was asked to suggest means by which these courses could be evaluated. Under these circumstances, which were exceptional, evaluation could not contribute fully to curriculum development. Curriculum evaluation should be more than just a means of describing outcomes; it should be an integral and built-in part of the process of curriculum construction. The role of this committee should be to advise course development teams at what points in their work and in what ways evaluation can help. It should not be primarily concerned with setting up assessment exercises so that an appraisal of a finished product can be made. In relation to curriculum evaluation then, 'evaluation' is to be thought of as 'the collection and use of information to make decisions about an educational programme' at all stages of its development.

Kerr went on to delineate three 'decision areas' during the process of curriculum construction to which evaluation could contribute:

> (a) Decisions about the content of courses and the methods by which they should be taught. (b) Decisions about pupils' needs and achievements. (c) Decisions about the training of teachers.[45]

It is difficult to judge how influential Kerr's view of evaluation was, but it seems significant in two respects. First, it was clear from what he was saying that the Council ought to appoint evaluators from the beginning of projects, and in part this policy was gradually if unevenly adopted. Second, Kerr's definition of evaluation, and the main decision areas in curriculum construction, stressed the relationship between evaluation and decision-making.[46] This emphasis on decision-making was to find expression in most of the approaches to evaluation which were developed in Britain, while in the USA this was a view of evaluation that was extensively explored by Daniel Stufflebeam.[47]

According to John Banks (a member of the Council closely associated with the Evaluation Advisory Committee), the policy which emerged was that an evaluator should be assigned to each developemnt team. The ideal evaluator, Banks argued, was one who was both sympathetic to, but independent of, the project. Sympathy was needed to enable the evaluator to understand what the development team was aiming to do; and independence was required in order that the evaluator should have a free hand to challenge the formulation of objectives.[48] The degree to which this policy was implemented is, however, a matter of debate. While it seems that most projects paid some attention to evaluation, in many cases it was the responsibility of the whole team rather than a specific individual. More importantly, as the Evaluators Group (which replaced the Evaluation Advisory Committee in 1968) noted, few if any evaluators had any formal training in educational research or any experience of evaluation. In fact most were originally appointed to the development team and only subsequently switched to evaluation.[49] It is not surprising then that for many projects the distinction between evaluation and development roles was not clear-cut, and in circumstances such as these it was obviously difficult for evaluators to maintain the independent role which Banks suggested was ideal.

At roughly the same time as the Evaluation Advisory Committee was formed, a Working Party on curriculum evaluation was created, this time under the chairmanship of Professor Stephen Wiseman. The Working Party's terms of reference were to consider the problems and methods of curriculum evaluation, and to state them in a systematic way and in a form that was suitable for teachers and others.[50] The Working Party consisted of five professors, one HMI, a Divisional Officer from London, and assorted academics.[51]

On 26 April 1967, Stephen Wiseman wrote to the Chairman of the Co-ordinating Committee enclosing a draft Bulletin entitled *Curriculum Evaluation*. Wiseman's accompanying letter drew attention to the complexity of the principles of curriculum evaluation and the lack of British experience in applying them. Nonetheless, the recommendation from the Working Party was that the Council should publish the Bulletin since 'it would provide teachers with something to consider.' Both in tone and in substance, the draft Bulletin reflected the strong-mindedness of Scriven's work and the means-ends rationality of those who followed Tyler. The Bulletin had a distinctly American flavour and Wiseman, with his colleague Douglas Pidgeon (a member of the Working Party from the NFER), were in effect the leading advocates of the behavioural approach to curriculum development and evaluation. I say curriculum development and evaluation because it is clear that the objectives model is prescriptive about the way in which curricula should be developed. In a sense that was the legacy of Ralph Tyler's early work.

The Working Party thought that the need to evaluate arose out of the peculiar degree of freedom that teachers enjoyed in Britain. They argued that the price of teacher autonomy was an increase in responsibility and a concomitant duty to demonstrate the efficiency of teaching methods. Although they were aware that the issue of accountability was a sensitive one, they felt that the freedom to determine curricula content was not matched by a professional commitment to study the principles of curriculum development. They objected to the haphazard way in which curriculum development occurred and wanted to replace an *ad hoc* system, which they claimed was guided by fashion, fancy, hunch and political pressure, with a more rational approach guided by evaluation. Central to their argument was the belief that in the absence of clearly defined principles of evaluation, discussion about different kinds of curricula were reduced to battles of opposing judgements. The message seemed clear enough — evaluation was an instrument for determining rationally what was of value in the curriculum. However, it was also a mechanism for teacher accountability and professional development. In the event the Co-ordinating Committee decided against publication of *Curriculum Evaluation*. It was later published by the National Foundation for Educational Research.[52]

Why the decision went against the Working Party's recommendations is a matter of conjecture. However, some indication of why was perhaps evident at the Third International Curriculum Conference which was held at Oxford in September 1967. The conference was sponsored by the Schools Council, the Ontario Institute for Studies in Education and the National Education Association of Washington. From Stuart Maclure, who was the conference editor, we get a picture of a direct confrontation between the theoreticians and technocrats of North America (who were mainly from the universities and thought education was too important to be left to teachers) and the pragmatic and paternalistic British who were suspicious of detailed statements of objectives, and deeply committed to the ideology/myth of teacher autonomy.[53]

According to Maclure's account, it was Joslyn Owen, Joint Secretary of the Schools Council, who first spoke against the technocratic approach:

> The teacher is entitled to ask for a well-founded assurance that new work in the curriculum is properly co-ordinated. To that extent there has to be clarity and agreement about aims and methods of reform — and those have to be cast into something we call a strategy. But, if we preach a strategy it is one of partnership; we believe in and work towards the removal of conflict between the partners in innovation and towards the removal of what is irritational.[54]

At a later session it was Sir Alec Clegg who took up the challenge. 'The job of education' he said, 'was to strengthen the mind rather than fill it.' The task for innovators, Clegg argued, was to extend the range of options but the responsibility for choice must rest with the teachers. He went on, in aggressive style:

> I have no time for any system which recruits high powered thinkers to contrive and foist a curriculum on the schools. This cannot work unless we believe that the teacher of the future is to be a low grade technician.[55]

Maclure described Clegg's plea for the dominance of the teacher in the process of curriculum development as an expression of the English myth of teacher autonomy at its best and most vulnerable.[56] What seems important, however, is the influence that this myth exerted on those responsible for the management and funding of innovation; it was not just rhetoric, although it was as much an aspiration as a description of reality.

To return to Wiseman and Pidgeon, the question was why did the Council reject the recommendations of the Curriculum Evaluation Working Party? To begin with, the Bulletin could be read as an attack on the autonomy of the teacher and the funding policy of the Council. It was a call for greater accountability and a more systematic, coherent and rational approach to the management of curriculum renewal. At this point, at least two of the Joint Secretaries of the Council, Joslyn Owen and Geoffrey Caston, were worried about the political import of an aims and objectives model for curriculum development, and Education Officers like Clegg seemed to feel that such an approach was antithetical to the values of liberal education. Perhaps, however, there is more to it than this. The Curriculum Evaluation Bulletin could be read as a bid by the educational research establishment for a greater say in the curriculum development movement. The Working Party seemed to take a prescriptive view of what could count as an effective strategy for development and evaluation. They wrote of the principles of curriculum development and evaluation as if they were axiomatic, self-evident, beyond dispute and the only guidelines available. As such, they were making a case for the language in which curriculum issues should be discussed as well as for the methodology by which the value of curricula should be judged. For those schooled in the liberal tradition and for those who were more in tune with humanism and the humanities than with science and technology, the values of the objectives model were possibly too technocratic to assimilate. Moreover, the tone of the Bulletin was probably unpalatable to a Council which had strong teacher representation and was committed, at least rhetorically, to the principle of partnership.

Social action programmes: the case of EPAS

Both in Britain and the USA educational policy was not only directed towards the problem of curriculum reform but also towards issues of justice and equality, resulting in social action programmes and different applications of research and evaluation. In Britain, for example, the Plowden Committee focused to a large extent on the relationships between home and school, and the social factors affecting primary education. The Plowden Committee was appointed by Sir Edward Boyle as part of a regular process of review associated with the function of the Central Advisory Councils.[57] However, the Committee was unusual in certain respects: first, its Deputy Chairman was the Chairman of the previous Advisory Council, Sir John Newsom; second, it included an influential group of academics, among their number Professor A J Ayer, a leading exponent of logical positivism, David Donnison, Professor of Social Administration at the London School of Economics, and

Michael Young the sociologist and author of *The Rise of the Meritocracy*; third, the work of the Committee was supported by a large programme of research initiated by the HMI and the Department of Education and Science.[58]

Within a month of its publication in 1967, Volume One of the Plowden Report had sold 146,000 copies. Its recommendations urged a move away from selection at 11 years of age, and it was the first report of its kind to state the principle that 'public authorities should exercise positive discrimination in favour of the under-privileged.'[59] The emphasis the Committee placed on the correlation of social disadvantage and achievement at school, marked the growing influence of sociology on British policy-making and educational thought. Despite its somewhat tepid reception by the DES, the Secretary of State for Education, Antony Crosland, endorsed the idea of Educational Priority Areas (EPAs) with a related action research programme under the direction of A H Halsey, from the Department of Social and Administrative Studies at Oxford.

The Plowden Committee had made a plea for research to discover which of the developments in the proposed EPAs had the most constructive effects.[60] The educational priority programme was originally conceived of as action research rather than as a planned variation experiment like Follow Through. But here too the promise of applied research did not materialize. Although there was an intention to evaluate local EPA projects with a view to isolating successful features, as Halsey suggested at the EPA Conference at Oxford in 1969, there was a serious problem in trying to turn local studies into a single programme where resource inputs could be related to the effects of ameliorative action.[61] According to Halsey, the Department of Education and Science were primarily concerned with the action component of the programme, while the Social Science Research Council (SSRC), who contributed £75,000 of the £175,000 over three years, were more concerned with transforming action into action research.[62] As the programme developed, however, there was increasing pressure to strengthen the evaluation side and there was some divergence of opinion between local project directors and the national steering committee.[63] Not surprisingly, the Halsey report favoured the continuation of the EPA policy within the framework of action research. While Halsey and his colleagues acknowledged that there was sometimes a conflict between social research and policy interests, they argued for a more productive partnership between social scientists and educational administrators. However, Halsey failed to persuade the SSRC to continue their support for the action research programme beyond its initial three years and, to a large degree, the Halsey report was ignored and overtaken by economic events.[64]

In retrospect, the debate about national versus local aims was much more significant than it might have seemed at the time. The predilection of the project teams for a case study approach was understandable given the community-based nature of the programme. However, local initiatives and local systems of evaluation and review do not necessarily offer sufficient accountability for a central administration. The solutions and knowledge which local action research projects generate may well be too context-dependent to appear useful to a central government concerned with competing national priorities rather than local policies. So, for example, the conclusion of the Halsey Report that 'pre-schooling is the outstanding economical and effective device in the general approach to raising educational standards in EPAs' was never sufficiently endorsed by the Government to turn an essentially private operation into a public service.[65]

Since Britain did not have an institutionally established pattern of applied educational research and since there was little or no experience of project or programme evaluation, approaches to evaluation tended to evolve in diverse ways in response to immediate needs. The funding of programme evaluations, like the studies of Educational Priority Areas, was in fact unusual. The work of the EPA projects had little effect on the development of educational evaluation but it did reinforce a growing awareness of the importance of local factors in determining the content and implementation of innovation.

What characterized British educational evaluation in the 1960s and 70s was a focus on development, with a corresponding mistrust of summative or policy evaluation. It would be wrong to think of this as indicative of an explicit value orientation on the part of evaluators, rather it reflects the confluence of an innovation strategy and political context. It is important to remember that in Britain the existence of an independent inspectorate was probably seen to obviate some of the need to commission external programme evaluation. While the impetus for evaluation in the USA stemmed from legislation and was presaged by federal investment in large-scale social action programmes, in Britain it was the curriculum reform movement, which found expression in the curriculum project, that led to the growth of an evaluation community which by comparison with its American counterpart was very small indeed.

Notes

1. For a comprehensive account of the work of the Royal Commission of Inquiry see: Brundage, A (1978) *The Making of the New Poor Law*, London: Hutchinson, especially Chapter 2.
2. See, for example, Hamilton, D (1977) Making sense of curriculum evaluation: continuities and discontinuities in an educational idea. In Shulman, LS (ed.) *Review of Research in Education*, Vol 5, Itasca, Illinois: Peacock, pp 317–47.
3. Brennan, EJT (1975) *Education for National Efficiency: The Contribution of Sidney and Beatrice Webb*, London: Athlone Press.
4. See Finch, J (1986) *Research and Policy*, Lewes, Sussex: Falmer Press.
5. Bulmer, M (1978) Social science research and policy making in Britain, In Bulmer M (ed) *Social Policy Research*, London: Macmillan Press, pp 3–43.
6. See Sharpe, LJ (1978) The social scientist and policy-making in Britain and America: a comparison. In Bulmer, M (ed.) *Social Policy Research*, London: Macmillan Press, pp 302–12.
7. Finch, J (1986) op. cit. p 1.
8. It is interesting to note in this respect that Alexander Bain who is regarded as the first British psychologist, opened his book *Education and Science* (1879, 3rd

edn) with a consideration of the role of scientific method in the study of education. According to LS Hearnshaw (1964), Alexander Bain stood halfway between the mental philosophy of the eighteenth and early nineteenth centuries, and the scientific psychology of the twentieth century. In terms of the development of a science of education, Bain saw a crucial role for psychology. Bain's true successors, says Hearnshaw, were Throndike and the learning theorists who went on to develop the technology of testing in America.

9. See, for example: (i) Karier, CJ (1973) Testing for order and control in the corporate liberal state. In Karier, CJ, Violas, P. & Spring, J (eds) *Roots of Crisis: American Education in the Twentieth Century*, Chicago: Rand McNally; (ii) Gumbert, EB & Spring, JH (1974) *The Superschool and the Superstate: American Education in the Twentieth Century, 1918–1970*, New York: John Wiley & Sons, especially Chapter 3, 'Intelligence testing and the efficient society'; (iii) Curti, M (1935) *The Social Ideas of American Educators*, New York: Charles Scribner's Sons, especially Chapter XIV, 'Edward Lee Thorndike, scientist'; (iv) Hearnshaw, LS (1964) *A Short History of British Psychology 1840–1940*, London: Methuen, especially Chapter IV, 'Galton and the beginning of psychometrics'; (v) Flugel, JC (1951) *A Hundred Years of Psychology*, London: Gerald Duckworth, especially Chapter XI, 'Spearman and the "Factor" school'; (vi) Sutherland, G (1984) *Ability, Merit and Measurement: Mental Testing and English Education 1880–1940*, Oxford: Clarendon Press, especially Chapter 4, 'Measuring normality'; (vii) Torrance, H (1986) Assessment and Examinations: Social Context and Educational Practice. Unpublished PhD thesis, University of East Anglia, especially Chapter 2.

10. Galton, F (1892) *Hereditary Genius* (2nd edn) London: Macmillan. Quoted in: Wiseman, S (ed.) (1967) *Intelligence and Ability*. Harmondsworth, Middlesex: Penguin Books, p 17.

11. See Wiseman's introduction to Wiseman, S (ed.) (1967) *Intelligence and Ability*. Harmondsworth, Middlesex: Penguin Books, p 17.

12. For a review of the issues in the evaluation of teacher effectiveness through standardized testing, see: Glass, GV (1974) Teacher effectiveness. In Walberg, HJ (ed.) *Evaluating Educational Performance*, Berkeley, Cal: McCutchan, pp 11–32. It is interesting to note in this context that in February 1987, Mrs Rumbold, Minister of State for Education, suggested that teachers must expect some form of 'promotion by results'. See Lodge, B, Appraisal will gradually be linked to results — Rumbold. In *Times Educational Supplement*, 13/2/87, p 10.

13. See Sutherland, G (1984) *Ability, Merit and Measurement: Mental Testing and English Education 1880–1940*, Oxford: Clarendon Press, especially Chapter 4.

14. MacKenzie, DA (1981) *Statistics in Britain 1865–1930: The Social Construction of Scientific Knowledge*, Edinburgh University Press, p 58.

15. Ibid. p 59.

16. Ibid.

17. Angoff, WH & Anderson, SB (1963) The standardization of educational and psychological tests. In *Illinois Journal of Education*, February, pp 1923. Reproduced in Payne, DA & Morris, RF (1967) *Educational and Psychological Measurement*. Waltham, Mass: Blaisdell Publishing Co, pp 9–14.

18. Karier, CJ (1973) Testing for order and control in the corporate liberal state. In Karier, CJ, Violas, PC, & Spring, J (eds) *Roots of Crisis: American Education in the Twentieth Century*, Chicago: Rand McNally, pp 108–37.

19. Downing, J (1967a) *Evaluating the Initial Teaching Alphabet*, London: Cassel, p xi.

20. See HL Elvin's Introduction to *The i.t.a. Symposium*, Slough: National Foundation for Educational Research (1967), pp ix–xvi.

21. Ibid.
22. Downing, J (1967b) Historical background and origins of the i.t.a. research. In *The i.t.a. Symposium*, Slough: National Foundation for Educational Research, pp 1–2.
23. Holmes, JA (1967) Evaluation — 6. In *The i.t.a. Symposium*, Slough: National Foundation for Educational Research, pp 123–7.
24. Warburton, FW & Southgate, V (1969) *i.t.a. An Independent Evaluation*, London: John Murray and W & R Chambers.
25. Ibid.
26. Ibid., see especially Part 3, pp 182–286.
27. Downing, J (1967a) *Evaluating the Initial Teaching Alphabet*. London: Cassel, pp 121–47.
28. See for example: Todd, A The scientist — supply and demand. Presidential address to the Science Masters' Association, reported in: *School Science Review*, **38**, 1956–57, pp 106–7; and, Savage, G Presidential address to the Science Masters' Association. In *School Science Review*, **44**, **34**, 1952–53, pp 322–34; and also, Bowden, B Presidential address to the Science Masters' Association. *School Science Review*, 1962–63, pp 256–82.
29. Halberstam, D (1973) *The Best and the Brightest*, New York: Random House.
30. See, for example, National Executive Committee of the Labour Party (1961) *Signposts for the Sixties*.
31. Waring, M (1979) *Social Pressures and Curriculum Innovation*, London: Methuen, especially Chapter 4.
32. Cmnd 6824 (1946) *Scientific Manpower: Report of a Committee Appointed by the Lord President of the Council*, London: HMSO.
33. Cmnd 9703 (1956) *Technical Education*, London: HMSO.
34. Waring, M (1979) op. cit. p 68.
35. Ibid. p 81.
36. The Ministry of Education's research fund was £20,000 in 1962–63 but had expanded to £70,000 in 1963–64. See: Cmnd 2316 (1964) *Education in 1963*, London: HMSO.
37. This account of Nuffield evaluation policy is based on data from the SAFARI archive at the Centre for Applied Research in Education, University of East Anglia. SAFARI was a research programme which examined the impact of four national curriculum development projects, one which was Nuffield science. The archive includes an interview with Tony Becher.
38. Nuffield Foundation, *Sixteenth Annual Report*, 1960–61, pp 63–4.
39. Cameron, M (1970) Modern language teaching. In Butcher, HJ & Pont, HB (eds) *Educational Research in Britain 2*, London: University of London Press, pp 82–106.
40. Cmnd 2612 (1965) *Education in 1964*, London: HMSO, p 115.
41. Ibid.
42. For an account of the evaluation of the Science 5–13 Project see: Harlen, W (1973) Science 5–13 Project. In Schools Council Research Studies, *Evaluation in Curriculum Development: Twelve Case Studies*, London: Macmillan, pp 16–36.
43. Hamilton, D (1976) *Curriculum Evaluation*, London: Open Books, p 18.
44. Nisbet, J (1976) Contrasting structure for curriculum development: Scotland and England. *Journal of Curriculum Studies*, **8**, 2, November, pp 167–70.
45. Schools Council Memorandum SC/213/402/02. Quoted in Clift, P. Policy on Evaluation. Unpublished & undated paper, London: Schools Council.
46. Kerr's definition of evaluation and his outline of decision areas in curriculum construction was reminiscent of the influential early statement which Lee J

Cronbach made about evaluation. See: Cronbach, LJ (1963) Evaluation for course improvement. *Teachers College Record,* **64**, 8, pp 672–83.

47. Stufflebeam, D et al. (1971) *Educational evaluation and decision making,* Itasca, Illinois: Peacock.
48. Banks, LJ (1969) Curriculum developments in Britain, 1963–68, *Journal of Curriculum Studies,* **1**, 1968–69, pp 247–59.
49. Clift, P op. cit.
50. The Curriculum Evaluation Working Party was established by the Schools Council at its second meeting on 26 January 1965.
51. Details of the membership of the Working Party were included in a letter from Professor Wiseman to the Chairman of the Co-ordinating Committee — 26/4/67 — School of Education, Manchester University, Ref:D200C(b).
52. Wiseman, S & Pidgeon, D (1972) *Curriculum Evaluation,* Windsor: NFER.
53. Maclure, S. (1968) *Curriculum Innovation in Practice,* London: Schools Council, HMSO.
54. Ibid. p 15.
55. Ibid. p 25.
56. Ibid. p 28.
57. For a review of the origins and work of the Plowden Committee see: Kogan, M (1973) The Plowden Committee on Primary Education. In Chapman, RA (ed.) *The Role of Commissions in Policy Making,* London: George Allen & Unwin, pp 81–104.
58. The programme of research included work by HMIs, the Social Survey division of the Central Office of Information, the Research Division of the Ministry of Housing and Local Government, the NFER, the Unit on School Management and Government of Education at the London Institute of Education, the National Child Development Study, Professor Stephen Wiseman from Manchester University, and three other researchers from different universities who examined the social services affecting primary school children. Kogan (1973, p 93) notes that almost all of the research findings were received in time for drafting the report.
59. Kogan, M (1973) op. cit. p 86.
60. Central Advisory Council For Education (1963) *Children and their Primary Schools,* London: HMSO. (The Plowden Report.)
61. Halsey, AH (ed.) (1972) *Educational Priority Volume 1: Problems and Policies,* London: HMSO, p vii.
62. Ibid. p vii.
63. The Liverpool project, for example, tended to emphasize the action component of the programme. While the Steering Committee took a national perspective towards evaluation, the local projects tended to assert community aims and getting something done.
64. By 1974 the focus of educational policy was beginning to change from a concern with innovation to a concern for monitoring standards. A Government White Paper published in August 1974: *Educational Disadvantage and the Educational Needs of Immigrants* (Cmnd 570), established the Assessment of the Performance Unit and the Educational Disadvantage Unit, both of which were attached to the DES.
65. Van der Eyken (1977) *The Pre-school Years,* Harmondsworth: Penguin.

Chapter 3

Traditional Approaches Under Attack

The question of the degree to which evaluation studies should take account of local variation and context or work within a standardized methodological and often political framework, has evolved as a significant and discriminating issue for evaluators of social and educational programmes. It is significant because it is a question which has political consequences as well as epistemological implications. It is also significant because it is a question which divides the evaluation community into those who advocate pre-ordinate research designs and those who favour more responsive evaluation studies. Although the issue was not exposed sharply by Halsey's account of the evaluation of Educational Priority Areas, it is revealed in the tension he describes between action and research. The social action programme by its very nature aimed to respond to community aims and local conditions whereas the evaluation/research programme was directed, at least in its conception, towards questions of generalization and national policy.

Evaluation as illumination

In the same year that Halsey's report was published, Parlett and Hamilton examined this issue from a somewhat different perspective. Published as an occasional paper by the Centre for Research in Educational Sciences at Edinburgh, *Evaluation as Illumination: A New Approach to the Study of Innovatory Programmes*, is probably one of the best known evaluation papers to be published in Britain. By many accounts, Parlett and Hamilton's paper was disseminated very quickly and it would be easy to underestimate its influence. What this paper managed to do was encapsulate something of the disquiet which many evaluators and educators felt about the traditional approaches to the study of educational innovation. More than this though, it provided the impetus and the legitimation for those who wished to broaden the methodological scope of evaluation.[1] In many respects the paper should be read as a rejection of the psychological tradition of educational research. The significance of this shift away from a psychological and towards a more sociological focus was the emphasis it gave to the cultural as opposed to the technological features of an innovation. The humanist values of this approach are probably best captured by a crusading phrase from Parlett: 'a paradigm for people not plants.'[2] Illuminative evaluation has been criticized for not providing sufficient safeguards on the 'subjective' and personal interpretations of the evaluator.

Some commentators have argued that illuminative evaluation concentrates too much on method and too little on theory, and that as a result it lacks a sound theoretical position.[3] Such criticisms, however, really miss the point. Illuminative evaluation was a reaction to the psychometric tradition and it was a paper of advocacy that crystallized a schism in educational evaluation.

The naturalistic fallacy

As Stephen Kemmis has observed, writing in the context of the evaluation of computer-assisted learning, the distinction between nomothetic and idiographic methodologies in psychology is a venerable one.[4] Nomothetic approaches are concerned with establishing laws and statistical generalizations. Idiographic approaches, by contrast, are concerned with the intensive study of individuals or particular cases. In the social sciences there has been a long debate between those who argue for the unity of scientific method and those who claim that the objects of social science are different in kind from those of the physical sciences, and as such require different methodological procedures. While this debate has taken many forms at root, it revolves around a single question: *To what extent can social life be studied in the same way as nature?* The thesis that there is an essential unity of method between the natural and the social sciences is usually referred to as 'naturalism'. It is useful, however, to make a distinction between the two species of naturalism. The first we can call 'reductionism' — this asserts that there is an identity of subject matter as well as of method. The second we can call 'scientism' — this simply denies that there are any significant differences in the methods appropriate to the study of social and natural objects, but stops short of the reductionist position.[5]

In 1963, as a major contribution to AERA's first *Handbook of Research on Teaching*, May Brodbeck outlined a model (rational reconstruction) of scientific method for the social sciences. Brodbeck's exposition was in effect commending to students of educational research the epistemological virtues of empiricism.[6] The essence of Brodbeck's claim (like that of John Stuart Mill in his *System of Logic*) was that the logical properties of an adequate explanation were the same throughout the sciences and that any methodological requirements in the natural sciences would be equally valid in the social sciences. Brodbeck's position represented the orthodoxy of an educational research community which at its most dogmatic was reductionist.

The model of science which Brodbeck also outlined well described the epistemological orientation of educational evaluation. She stressed the importance of a clear and unambiguous operational language for research, stating that concepts had to be defined in terms of their observable characteristics and that to be useful they had to be related to general laws. She argued that social phenomena should always be understood as resulting from the behaviour of individuals. The position she commended to her colleagues was one of 'methodological individualism', as opposed to what she called 'metaphysical holism'.[7] Explanation and understanding in the social sciences was, according to Brodbeck, deductive, statistical and nomological in nature — to explain was to predict and to predict accurately was to confirm a generalization. If we take the objectives model as an example, it is not difficult to see how this form of empiricism found expression in the methodology of evaluation. The objectives model requires curricula (the language of education) to be expressed as observable and measurable predictions of student behaviour. As educational processes are described by aggregating individual performances, the model is consonant with the principle of methodological individualism. The correlate of explanation in the objectives model is the validation of curricula by comparing logically deduced predictions (objectives) with observed results (test scores). Finally, experimental design provided the methodological standards which offered evidence that was reliable enough to confirm the technical superiority of one curriculm or teaching instrument over another.[8]

The thesis of the unity of science has come under increasing attack, the more so since European social theorists, especially the German idealists, found sympathetic ears in both Britain and the USA.[9] Of equal importance, though, is the fact that empiricism has been found wanting as an adequate account of science.[10] Yet, for many evaluators schooled in the values and procedures of behaviourist psychology, the mantle of positivism was, no doubt, difficult to cast aside. As evaluation had become institutionalized so too had its methodology, and not only were reputations and incomes at stake but also institutional practices. Nonetheless, some very substantial cracks in the edifice were apparent.

The objectives model and its critics

From the perspective of the curriculum developer, the objectives model of evaluation offers a rational approach to curriculm planning that is very persuasive both in education and training. The objectives model, however, is more than a technology for evaluation, it is also prescriptive as to the nature of knowledge and its acquisition. While acknowledging the benefits of evaluation, some curriculum and evaluation theorists felt that it was limiting the scope of curriculum reform and that at times it trivialized the nature of learning.[11] Others have been sceptical about the claim that educational objectives can be applied to any domain of knowledge. For Elliot Eisner, for instance, some domains of knowledge, particularly art, are unsuited to the prior specification of outcomes since by its nature creativity is unpredictable.[12]

In the USA criticism, of the objectives model had been mounting since Lee J Cronbach's *Course Improvement Through Evaluation* was published in 1963. Cronbach argued that evaluation had become too dependent on the routines and rituals of testing. Like Tyler, whom he studied with, Cronbach emphasized the role that evaluation could play in course improvement rather than terminal judgement. For him the outcomes of instruction were always multi-dimensional and therefore inadequately described by studies that aggregated different types of performance into single test scores. His concern was twofold. First, he wanted to extend the range of evidence which an evaluator might collect to describe an educational programme; and second, he wanted evaluation to pinpoint features of an education programme which required further attention and revision.[13]

Building on, yet also taking issue with, the work of Cronbach, Michael Scriven in his now classic and justly praised paper *The Methodology of Evaluation*, reasserted the importance of rational (scientific) judgement in the evaluation of innovation.[14] Scriven took issue with Cronbach's 'tender-mindedness' an attitude which he thought devalued the significance of summative judgements. In making a distinction between the roles and the goals of evaluation, Scriven was at pains to stress the obligation of evalutors to estimate worth or merit. He reasoned that the widespread confusion between roles and goals was tolerated and even encouraged because it tended to allay anxiety and emphasize the constructive part evaluation could play in programme improvement. In an uncompromising argument, relying on an analogy between effective business practices and effective educational practices, Scriven stated that anxiety about evaluation could not be tackled by 'ignoring its importance or confusing its presentation'. The loss of efficiency was, according to Scriven, too high a price to pay for the dubious benefit of not offending people's sensibilities.

Yet while Scriven was attracted by the metaphor of industrial efficiency, he was scornful of those evaluations which relied exclusively on the estimation of goal achievement. His main argument against the objectives model was that it represented an extreme relativization of evaluation since there were no procedures for judging the worth of the goals themselves. At the root of Scriven's position was the belief that facts and values could be adequately separated to allow for reliable knowledge that was independent of human interests. The objectives model could be seen as an attempt to sidestep the problem of determining the efficiency or righteousness of particular value orientations. You might argue, for example, that since science is unable to tell us what ought to be but should properly tell us what is, then goals should be taken as given and the only remaining question is the degree to which these goals are realised. Scriven, however, argued that there was and should be a moral consensus based on the principle of equality, and that within this normative framework value orientations would be open to rational criticism and hence objective determination.

In the same year (1967) that Scriven's contribution to the methodology of evaluation was published, another, and in retrospect more significant, reassessment of educational evaluation appeared. Robert Stake's *The Countenance of Educational Evaluation* is now recognized as one of the most persuasive yet coded criticisms of conventional evaluation practice. The countenance model, as it came to be known, addressed the question of the kind of evidence that an evaluator should collect.[15] Stake was mindful of the mistrust that educators felt towards evaluation and he was also aware of the political friction which the reporting requirements of ESEA Title 1 had caused. State and local administrators as well as teachers were suspicious of the growth of federal evaluations. They felt that evaluation studies would presage federal control and permit harmful comparisons to be made between different schools, school districts and states. Stake felt evaluation was not addressing the questions educators were asking. The countenance model articulated a view of evaluation that reflected the complexity and particularly of educational programmes. The key to the model was an extension of the range of relevant data an evaluator should collect. Stake's concern was that evaluation should not only contribute to short-term judgements about programme effectiveness, but that it should also improve understanding of the process of innovation. 'The countenance of evaluation', wrote Stake, 'should be one of data gathering that leads to decision making, not trouble making.'[16]

Perhaps the best critique of the objectives model was offered by Lawrence Stenhouse in his book *An Introduction to Curriculum Research and Development*.[17] The objectives model is the clearest expression of an approach to curriculum construction that integrates development and evaluation, but it is the technical demands of evaluation that determine the form and scope of curricula. Stenhouse argued that the relationship between development and evaluation should not be this kind. His reasons were twofold. The main argument he put forward was that the objectives model leads to a mistaken view of education and knowledge. For Stenhouse education was concerned with the development of personal autonomy. 'Education', he wrote 'enhances the freedom of man by inducting him into knowledge of his culture as a thinking system.' The argument continued:

> The most important characteristic of the knowledge mode is that one can think with it. This is in the nature of knowledge — as distinct from information — that it is a structure to sustain creative thought and provide frameworks for judgement.[18]

In conclusion, Stenhouse articulated a definition of education and its success which was unusual in acknowledging the contradiction between the goal of autonomy and the demands of predictability: 'education as induction into knowledge is successful to the extent that it makes the behavioural outcomes of the student unpredictable.'[19]

For Stenhouse there could be no curriculum development without teacher development and this axiom formed the basis of his second, yet related, reason for rejecting the objectives model. Stenhouse argued that the objectives model attempted to improve educational practice by increasing clarity about ends but, 'even if this was logically justifiable in terms of knowledge — and it is not — there is a good case for claiming that it is not the way to improve practice.'[20] Stenhouse reasoned that the most effective way of improving practice was through teachers criticizing practice. What he offered was a strategy based on the teacher as researcher, rather than external evaluation as an instrument of curriculum renewal and quality control.

Alternative approaches

By the mid-1970s, documented alternative approaches to the objectives model and experimental design were beginning to emerge. The specific origins of what some called a 'counter-culture'[21] and others a 'new wave'[22] in evaluation are now not easy to tease out, but it is clear that a major impetus for change arose from a series of small but influential conferences held in Cambridge during the 1970s.

In December 1972, Parlett and Hamilton were invited to attend a working conference at Churchill College, Cambridge. The conference was financed by the Nuffield Foundation and aimed to explore non-traditional approaches to educational evaluation and set out guidelines for its future development. The impetus for convening such a conference was given by Tony Becher, who was still at Nuffield Lodge and as we have noted was a prominent figure in the early curriculum development movement. This first Cambridge conference drew together evaluators from Britain, the USA and Sweden, as well as administrators from the Department of Education and Science, and people from the Centre for Research and Innovation in Education, OECD. The discussion at the conference reflected dissatisfaction with the objectives model and the values of social engineering. At the conclusion of the conference the participants drew up a statement criticizing past practice and presenting a manifesto for the future. The participants agreed that evaluation should be:

> (a) responsive to the needs and perspectives of differing audiences; (b) illuminative of the complex organizational, teaching and learning processes at issue; (c) relevant to public and professional decisions forthcoming; and (d) reported in language which is accessible to their audiences.

Specifically, they recommended that:

> observational data, carefully validated, be used (sometimes in substitute for data from questioning and testing); evaluation be designed so as to be flexible enough to allow for response to unanticipated events (progressive focusing rather than pre-ordinate design); and that the value positions of the evaluator, whether highlighted or constrained by the design, be made evident to the sponsors and audiences of the evaluation.[23]

The first Cambridge conference brought together evaluators who were thinking about new ways to study educational innovations. The conference was part of the process of justifying alternative methodological practices and political roles for evaluation and it is significant, therefore, that two of the participants were from the Department of Education and Science. One of the major outcomes of the conference was the influential and widely read publication *Beyond the Numbers Game* — 'a book charting a paradigm shift from an evaluation methodology valuing numeracy to one valuing literacy.'[24] The ambience of the first Cambridge conference was optimistic and foward-looking. It had a feel to it of breaking the mould by challenging traditional assumptions and approaches, and creating alternative yet legitimate possibilities. The talk about paradigm shifts was, of course, suggestive of a social movement drawing strength from more humanistic research traditions outside of psychometrics, experimentalism and the social survey. There was also an element of hyperbole about such discussions; this is not, however, to underestimate their influence but merely to suggest that the significance of the Cambridge conferences and the movement they represented fall somewhat short of revolutionary scientific change.

Following the success of the first Cambridge conference three more were organized. The second met in 1975 and focused on the methods of case study research. A third was organized in 1979 to examine the use of naturalistic methods in evaluation and, most recently, a fourth conference was convened to consider performance appraisal and the evaluation of different approaches to assessing teachers and pupils.

Given the continuity of people and themes, taken together these conferences are an important source of evidence about the changing climate for evaluation. The optimism of the first conference was soon overshadowed by the problems of practice and a rapidly changing political climate. By 1979 the political importance of accountability and the growth of managerialism were proving serious obstacles to the formative and democratic intentions of those evaluators who had met at Cambridge seven years earlier. At the third conference it was agreed that educational evaluation shared many of the problems of more general policy-related research. A number of problems captured the experience of those present: the inadequacy of theories of policy and policy-making processes; the usual emphasis on programme evaluation as opposed to policy evaluation; the deterioration in the relationships between evaluators and their sponsors, clients and other audiences often because of the overtly political nature of innovation; the difficulty of matching the information needs of decision-makers and serving multiple audiences within the timescales set by programme managers; a history of rejected products, rejected especially by those busy administrators who expected reports to simplify rather than complicate their tasks; the problem of maintaining independence; the personal and institutional vulnerability associated with naturalistic forms of evaluation employing the portrayal of persons and the extensive description of institutional climate and context; and the conservative nature of naturalistic inquiry favouring, as it was thought, description over analysis.[25]

Broken promises

It could be argued that evaluation in both Britain and the USA has had little direct impact on education policy, and that where it has had impact it may well have served to complicate rather than rationalize the policy-making process.[26] The large-scale educational evaluations of the 1960s and 70s were generally unsuccessful at providing unequivocal evidence about programme effectiveness. The conventions of experimental design meant that there was often a conflict between reliability and relevance, while the cost and complexity of evaluating social experiments suggested a similar conflict between the needs for timeliness and fairness. Some evaluators interpreted the problem as one of programme design rather than evaluation methodology.[27] However, even where educational programmes were ostensibly designed to yield clear-cut policy options — as with Follow Through — the evaluators still failed to deliver the promise of useful and reliable information. The upshot of this failure was a good deal of cynicism and disillusion with large-scale quantitative evaluation studies and institutionalized evaluation procedures. Milbrey McLaughlin, for example, reports a former Bureau of Elementary and Secondary Education evaluator as saying:

> Evaluation at the US Office of Education is prostituted to such an extent now that it can't possibly have an impact because everyone knows it is just fun and games.[28]

And equally damning, Representative Edith Green, who conducted an inquiry into federal evaluation practices, concluded that the hundreds of millions of dollars spent on evaluation was absolutely worthless.[29] Criticism of this kind resulted in an increase in research devoted to the study of utilization and the factors which enhance the impact of applied research on policy-making.[30] There were also a number of attempts to fund the systematic development of new evaluation methods and approaches. For example, in 1978 the National Institute of Education (NIE) began funding research to develop alternative evaluation methods for use in local school districts and state departments of education[31], and othe federal agencies have engaged in similar efforts, reflecting a more general concern for the quality and usefulness of evaluation.[32]

Evaluation is thought of and funded as a utilitarian enterprise. It is usually justified in terms of the political or administrative need for the information it produces and its capacity to rationalize social policy-making. For those interested in educational reform, evaluation can be seen as a way of generating feedback for the purposes of programme or policy improvement. Those concerned with political reform or the realization of democratic and constitutional values, might see evaluation as part of the process of creating and informing public debate. For those concerned with accountability and the efficiency of resource allocation and use, evaluation, it could be argued, provides evidence of programme effects and effectiveness so as to improve policy implementation and the delivery of services. Irrespective of the way evaluation is seen, however, it is precisely the utilitarian values inherent in all its expressions that makes evaluation so political in nature.

The basic beliefs which have informed the practice of evaluation and its relationship to policy could be summarized in the following way:

1. research is more authoritative and trustworthy than common-sense judgement;
2. policies consist of discrete decisions;
3. better knowledge results in better decisions; and
4. evaluation affects policy by influencing defined choices among competing options.[33]

As Cohen and Garet have argued, traditional beliefs about the relationship between applied research and policy are seriously inadequate because they do not take account of the political, incremental and relatively undisciplined nature of policy-making.[34] Conceptions of policy-making as a rational step-by-step process consisting of defined decision points which can be informed by evaluation reports, do not reflect the reality of political or administrative systems. Even if this was an adequate account of policy-making, contentious programmes, different conceptions of methodology and validity, and different value positions and political interests, mean that there are conflicting interpretations of the results of applied research.

In the USA much of the work directed towards improving the utility of evaluation has centred on technical rather than conceptual problems — problems of performance rather than purpose. Although there has been a general acknowledgement of the political nature of applied research, this has not led to the development of political approaches to evaluation practice. In Britain questions about the utilization of evaluation have not resulted in much empirical research. However, the work of Barry MacDonald, in particular, has focused attention on the political context of educational evaluation.[35]

Responsive evaluation

An increasing number of evaluation theorists are taking a pragmatic view of the design and conduct of evaluation; pragmatic, that is, as opposed to methodologically dogmatic. As Helen Simons has indicated, most descriptions of programme evaluation now refer to the fact that evaluation focuses on the particular.[36] A focus on the particular and attention to the questions, concerns, issues and information needs of 'stakeholders' and decision-makers is the touchstone of many contemporary accounts of evaluation, and can be seen as a rejection of the evaluation research tradition. Michael Patton, for example, argues that there has been a shift away from the hypothetico-deductive paradigm towards 'a paradigm of choices emphasizing multiple methods, alternative approaches and . . . the matching of evaluation methods to specific evaluation situations and questions.'[37] Patton has described this 'paradigm of choice' as situational responsiveness, stressing, like others, the creative rather than the rule-governed aspects of evaluation design.

Echoing the need for evaluators to be responsive, Guba and Lincoln define the major purpose of evaluation as 'responding to an audience's requirements for information, particularly in ways that take account of the several value perspectives of its members.'[38] While Robert Stake, who coined the term responsive evaluation, says that it is an approach that 'sacrifices some precision in measurement to increase the usefulness of the findings.'[39] He contrasts a responsive with a pre-ordinate approach, writing:'

> many evaluation plans are more pre-ordinate, emphazing statement of goals, use of objective tests, standards held by programme personnel, and research type reports. Responsive evaluation is less reliant on formal communication, more reliant on natural communication . . . An educational evaluation is responsive evaluation if it orients more directly to program activities than to intents, if it responds to audience requirements for information, and if the different value perspectives of the people at hand are referred to in reporting the success and failure of the programme.[40]

There is little doubt that evaluation theory is moving away from refining and adapting a single methodology towards a greater concern for situational responsiveness and, as Simons points out, this represents an important change in our thinking about programme evaluation.[41] The importance of situational responsiveness can, however, be overstated both as guide to the design of evaluation and as a description of good practice. There are a number of reasons to doubt the adequacy of situational responsiveness as a rallying call and standard for modern evaluators. As Cronbach has suggested, underlying any attempts to make evaluation more functional and responsive there needs to be a broad theory of both validity and utility.[42] Situational responsiveness is not a political or moral principle but a functional one and is, therefore, an insufficient guide to action. Except in a very general sense, the idea that the choice of design and methods of investigation should be seen as a function of the object and circumstances of evaluation, suggests that we can comprehend and grasp these things independently of our theories of innovation and methodological presuppositions. Finally, situational responsiveness represents an inadequate description of practice since it does not indicate how actual methodological choices are made or conflicts resolved.

Different evaluation theorists underline different aspects of responsiveness. Patton, for example, stresses the need to identify relevant decision-makers and information users in concrete terms, and to work with them in a collaborative way.[43] Cronbach argues that merit lies not in the form of inquiry but in the relevance of information for policy.[44] Guba and Lincoln write of the evaluator's duty to identify all the audiences who have a stake or interest in the enterprise and to determine what their concerns and issues are. From their perspective, justice and fairness require that everyone with a stake also has a voice[44]; they say that naturalistic responsive evaluation uses as its organizer the concerns and issues raised by 'stakeholders'. Yet they also write of evaluation as a service to the client or commissioning agency, emphasizing that:

> since he who pays the piper calls the tune, the evaluator must have a firm understanding with the client about what the evaluation is to accomplish, for whom, and by what methods.[46]

Alkin and his associates take a much more restrictive view of responsiveness and like Patton stress the need for decision-makers or administrators to be linked at every stage of an evaluation. Indeed, Alkin sees evaluation as an administrative tool.[47]

Some evaluation theorists like Alkin think that the cause of social utility is best served by providing a technical service to those who are charged with the formal responsibility of making decisions and implementing programmes. The socially useful evaluator works hand-in-hand with specific decision-makers to improve the operation of an administrative system. Patton in many ways takes a similar view and, although he sees evaluation as partly a political process, his primary concern is with improving the utility of evaluation for those individuals who can make a difference. For Patton, the socially useful evaluator identifies specific key decision-makers and addresses the questions to which they want answers. According to Patton, evaluators must be prepared to find 'the strategically located person or persons who are enthusiastic, committed, competent, interested and aggressive' and speak directly to their concerns.[48] In Patton's view, a 'utilization focused evaluation' also avoids questions that decision-makers do not want answered because these will limit the impact of the evaluation.[49] Taken to the extreme, it could be argued that both Patton and Alkin want evaluation to be a direct information service to named individuals occupying positions of authority, and that the evaluator is in some way analogous to a personal and private secretary.

Other evaluation theorists like Guba and Lincoln, think that the cause of social utility is best pursued by oiling the mechanisms of democracy with information that has been carefully construed to represent the information needs and preferred style of reporting of different groups. Yet, to write, for example, as Guba and Lincoln do, of evaluation representing the concerns, issues and questions of *everyone* who has a stake or interest in the programme, is simply naive or disingenuous. Such a view of evaluation, based on an image of the political process as a small-town rural democracy, looks more than a little fanciful in downtown Detroit or Greater London. The aspiration to address the concerns of different groups and individuals with different reports tailored to meet their specific needs, presents the evaluator with two problems — the first of these is practical and the second, political or ethical. In the world of limited time, specific contracts and finite budgets, choices have to be made to include some things and exclude others. In practice, it is difficult enough to prepare accurate, relevant, fair and timely reports for a single person, let alone to prepare separate reports for all probable audiences. Even if it were possible, it is doubtful whether it would be desirable — providing different reports for different groups could easily look like secret reporting. Ensuring that everyone has access to the same reports would overcome this problem but lessen considerably the advantages of providing different information to different interest groups. The problem, however, is likely to remain an academic one. It is because an evaluation cannot address directly all the issues and questions of all those concerned with a programme that it is important to consider such questions as: Whose definition of the situation should an evaluator respond to? To whose concerns and issues should an evaluator be responsive? How should the boundaries of the programme or policy be drawn? Which audiences will the final report be directed towards? It is important to be aware that these are political or moral questions, rather than simply functional ones.

Situational responsiveness is often used to mean two rather different things. Sometimes it is used to mean that methodological choices should reflect the nature of the beast — that is, the kind of programme it is and the kinds of questions that can be asked of it. This is what Parlett and Hamilton seemed to have in mind when they argued that problems should define methods, rather than the other way around.[50] Largely, however, situational responsiveness is used in the sense of responding to the social and administrative circumstances of a programme — in effect, responding to the different information needs and different values of the people in and around the programme. In either sense the principle of situational responsiveness is an important reminder of the particularity of programmes, but by itself it does little to address the problem of the proper relationship between evaluation and decision-making, audiences and public policy.

Notes

1. Parlett, M & Hamilton, D (1972) *Evaluation as Illumination: A New Approach to the Study of Innovatory Programmes*, Occasional Paper 9, Centre for Research in Educational Sciences, University of Edinburgh. Also published in: Hamilton, D et al. (eds) (1977) *Beyond the Numbers Game*, London: Macmillan.
2. Parlett, M (1970) *Evaluating Innovations in Teaching*, Mimeo, Research Unit on Intellectual Development, Department of Educational Sciences, University of Edinburgh.
3. Parsons, C (1976) The new evaluation: a cautionary note, *Journal of Curriculum Studies*, **8**, 2, pp 125–38.
4. Kemmis, S (1977) Nomothetic and idiographic approaches to the evaluation of computer assisted learning. In Kemmis, S with Atkin, R & Wright, E *How do Students Learn?* Centre for Applied Research in Education Occasional Publications No 5, Norwich: University of East Anglia.
5. This distinction is made by Roy Bhaskar in his critique of naturalism in the contemporaty human sciences. See: Bhaskar, R (1979) *The Possibility of Naturalism*. Sussex: Harvester Press.

6. Brodbeck, M (1963) Logic and scientific method in research on teaching. In Gage, NL (ed.) *Handbook of Research on Teaching*, Chicago: Rand McNally, pp 44–93.
7. Ibid.
8. Campbell, DT & Stanley, JC (1963) Experimental and quasi experimental designs for research on teaching. In Gage, NL (ed.) *Handbook of Research on Teaching*, Chicago: Rand McNally, pp 171–246.
9. For an account of the social philosophy of the German idealist tradition see: Habermas, J (1978) *Knowledge and Human Interests* (2nd edn) London: Heinemann. For a more general review of those social theorists antithetical to the empiricist thesis of the unity of science see: Outhwaite, W (1975) *Understanding Social Life*, London: Allen and Unwin.
10. See, for example, Lakatos, I (1978) *The Methodology of Scientific Research Programmes*, Cambridge University Press.
11. Atkin, JM (1963) Some evaluation problems in a course content improvement project, *Journal of Research in Teaching*, **1**, pp 129–32.
12. Eisner, EW (1967) Educational objectives: help or hindrance? *School Review*, **75**, 3, pp 250–60.
13. Cronbach, LJ (1963) Course improvement through evaluation, *Teachers College Record*, **64**, May, pp 672–86.
14. Scriven, M (1967) op. cit.
15. Stake, RE (1967) The countenance of educational evaluation, *Teachers College Record*, **68**, April, pp 523–40.
16. Ibid.
17. Stenhouse, L (1975) *An Introduction to Curriculum Research and Development*, London: Heinemann.
18. Ibid. p 82.
19. Ibid.
20. Ibid. p 83.
21. Parsons, C (1976) The new evaluation: a cautionary note, *Journal of Curriculum Studies*, **8**, 2, pp 125–38.
22. Galton, M (1980) Curriculum evaluation and the traditional paradigm. In Galton, M (ed.) *Curriculum Change the Lessons of a Decade*, Leicester University Press, pp 51–63.
23. For a more detailed account of the first Cambridge conference see: MacDonald, B & Parlett, M (1973) Re-thinking evaluation: notes from the Cambridge conference, *Cambridge Journal of Education*, **3**, 2, Easter Term.
25. This account of the Cambridge conference is based on: (i) MacDonald, B & Parlett, M (1973) Re-thinking evaluation: notes from the Cambridge conference, *Cambridge Journal of Education*, **3**, 2; (ii) Adelman, C, Jenkins, D & Kemmis, S (1967) Re-thinking case study: notes from the second Cambridge conference, *Cambridge Journal of Education*, **6**, 3; (iii) Jenkins, D, Simons, H & Walker, R (1981) Thou nature art my goodness: naturalistic inquiry in educational evaluation, *Cambridge Journal of Education*, **11**, 3; (iv) Bridges, D, Elliott, J & Klass, C (1986) Performance appraisal as naturalistic inquiry: a report of the fourth Cambridge conference on educational evaluation, *Cambridge Journal of Education*, **16**, 3.
26. For example, Clarke Abt, generalizing from an overview of approximately 1,000 evaluation studies of American social action programmes completed each year for the federal bureaucracy, concluded that less than one per cent of evaluation research reached the potential pay-off of policy application. See: Abt, C (1976) Supply, Demand, Motives and Constraints of the Evaluation Producing Community. Paper presented to the annual meeting of the AERA, San Francisco.

27. For example, see Rivlin, A (1972) *Systematic Thinking for Social Action*, Washington DC: Brookings.
28. McLaughlin, M (1975) op. cit., p 118.
29. Ibid.
30. See, for example, (i) Patton, MQ (1978) *Utilization Focused Evaluation*, Beverly Hills, Cal: Sage; (ii) Alkin, MC, Daillak, R & White, P (1979) *Using Evaluations: Does Evaluation Make a Difference?* Beverly Hills: Sage; (iii) Smith, NL & Caulley, DN (1982) *The Interaction of Evaluation and Policy: Case Reports from State Education Agencies*, Portland, Oregon: Northwest Regional Educational Laboratory.
31. In 1980 NIE spent $1,317,100 on research to develop new approaches to evaluation. See: Smith, NL (1981) Creating alternative methods for educational evaluation. In Smith, NL (ed.) *Federal Efforts to Develop New Evaluation Methods*, San Francisco: Jossey Bass, pp 77–94.
32. For instance the US Department of Justice. See: Silberman, G (1981) New methods in criminal justice evaluation. In Smith, NL (ed.) *Federal Efforts to Develop New Evaluation Methods*, San Francisco: Jossey Bass, pp 25–40.
33. Cohen, DK & Garet, MS (1975) Reforming educational policy with applied social research, *Harvard Educational Review*, **45**, 1, February, pp 17–43.
34. Ibid. p 21.
35. See, for example, MacDonald, B (1976) Evaluation and the control of education. In Tawney, D (ed.) *Curriculum Evaluation Today: Trends and Implications*, London: Macmillan, pp 125–36.
36. Simons, H (1987) *Getting to Know Schools in a Democracy: The Politics and Process of Evaluation*, London: Falmer Press, p 9.
37. Patton, MQ (1981) *Creative Evaluation*, Beverley Hills, Cal: Sage, p 270.
38. Guba, EG & Lincoln, YS (1982) *Effective Evaluation*, San Francisco: Jossey-Bass, p 36.
39. Stake, RE (1983) Program evaluation, particularly responsive evaluation. In Madaus, GF, Stufflebeam, DL & Scriven, MS (eds) *Evaluation Models: Viewpoints on Educational and Human Services Evaluation*, Boston, Mass: Kluwer-Nijhoff, pp 287–310.
40. Ibid. p 292.
41. Simons, H (1987) op. cit.
42. See Cronbach, LJ (1982) *Designing Evaluations of Educational and Social Programs*, San Francisco: Jossey-Bass, p 5.
43. Patton, MQ (1978) *Utilization-focused Evaluation*, Beverly Hills, Cal: Sage, p 284.
44. Cronbach, LJ (1980) *Toward Reform of Program Evaluation*, San Francisco: Jossey-Bass, p 7.
45. Guba, EG & Lincoln, YS (1981) op. cit. p 306.
46. Ibid. p 271.
47. Alkin, MC and Assoc (1985) *A Guide for Evaluation Decision Makers*, Beverly Hills, Cal: Sage.
48. Patton, MQ (1978) op. cit. p 71.
49. Ibid. pp 85–6.
50. Parlett, M & Hamilton, D (1976) op. cit. pp 84–101.

Part 2

The Control and Purview of Evaluative Inquiry

Chapter 4
Managerialism and Categorical Funding

The National Development Programme in Computer Assisted Learning

With the demise of the Schools Council, other agencies and innovation programmes prompted different kinds of evaluation and different kinds of relationships between applied research and educational development. In Britain, as in the USA some 15 years earlier, a major impetus to the spread of evaluation was the emergence of categorically funded programmes with the associated tendency to bureaucratize and centralize curriculum initiatives. The origins of these changes in the organization of curriculum development can be traced back to the early 1970s, when central government invested in the development of computer-assisted learning and started to evolve new administrative structures for the management of innovation. The Schools Council thought of educational change in terms of subject-based, semi-autonomous national curriculum projects providing good materials, ideas and practices that would enhance the range of choices available to the teacher. By contrast, the National Development Programme in Computer Assisted Learning (NDPCAL) had a theory of innovation that placed more emphasis on central direction and institutionalization.

In the Spring of 1972, following discussions among interested government departments, Mrs Thatcher, Secretary of State for Education and Science, approved the setting up of a five-year programme in computer-assisted learning with a budget of some £2,500,000. The main aim of the programme was to 'develop and secure the assimilation of computer assisted and computer managed learning on a regular basis at a reasonable cost.'[1] The programme was controlled not by a steering group representing relevant interests, but by an executive committee of civil servants drawn from the seven sponsoring government departments. This committee (called the Programme Committee) was supported by a full-time directorate headed by Richard Hooper, formerly of the BBC. The directorate were responsible for recommending project investments, monitoring development and reporting to the Programme Committee on progress and problems. The host institutions involved in NDPCAL had to match the funding provided, and projects had to agree to evaluate their own work and report at stipulated points of review. Stepped funding was introduced and in the first instance projects were funded for only two years. Decisions about further funding were made on the basis of periodic external evaluations and in theory, at least, projects could be substantially revised or even terminated.[2]

NDPCAL was a departure from established practice and expectation. The decision not to fund the programme through the Council for Educational Technology was itself unusual and perhaps indicative of a desire for closer bureaucratic control than was customary. The principle of matched funding suggested a concern with the impact and institutionalization of innovation, something to which the Schools Council had given little attention. From the start there was also a concern to invest in both education and training, including projects in the military and industrial sectors. The direct presence of the sponsoring departments provided for a more managerial climate than that of the Schools Council, and suggested a growing concern for accountability in temporary innovation systems. This was also reflected in the scale of evaluation activities associated with the programme. By British standards the resources devoted to evaluation were considerable — internal project evaluation, educational and financial evaluations, as well as technical evaluation, all played a part in the overall strategy.

In 1973 the Programme Committee commissioned two independent evaluations of NDPCAL — one financial, the other educational. The financial evaluation was undertaken by John Fielden, a management consultant specializing in Education from Peat, Marwick, Mitchell and Co, and indicated the growing importance of audit and financial planning to a cost-conscious government.[3] The educational evaluation (called UNCAL — Understanding Computer Assisted Learning) was based at the Centre for Applied Research in Education of the University of East Anglia, and was under the direction of Barry MacDonald.[4]

Unlike the Schools Council, there was a recognition on the part of the NDPCAL directorate, though not the executive, of the need for policy evaluation at the programme level. In an interim report, Richard Hooper outlined two reason why evaluation was important to the National Programme. First, NDPCAL was, in educational terms, a costly undertaking and it was important to establish the value of the product. Second, given the concentration on development and application rather than on research, there was a need for 'the fullest possible information on the results of actions, especially unexpected results, to create a base for adaptive decision-making.'[5] Given the pressures for more central control of innovation, the fact that the Programme Committee accepted a proposal for an independent evaluation from Barry MacDonald was somewhat surprising. UNCAL could be seen as an operational test of MacDonald's conception of democratic evaluation and was not, therefore, likely to be an attractive proposition to an executive committee of civil servants. It was in March 1973 that Richard Hooper recommended to the Programme Committee that they fund a three-year educational evaluation directed by MacDonald. The recommendation was referred to a sub-committee for further consideration. The sub-committee expressed three reservations about Hooper's recommendation:

1. MacDonald's unfamiliarity with the field of computer-based learning.
2. Committee members' unfamiliarity with some of the newer techniques of evaluation which MacDonald planned to employ.
3. The dangers of making a large, non-retractable evaluation funding before the substantive shape of the Programme had developed.[6]

A decision was reached to offer MacDonald a nine-month consultancy to plan and design an evaluation study, thus allowing the Programme Committee more time and information on which to make a judgement. In November 1973 the Programme Committee considered a formal evaluation proposal from MacDonald and decided to fund the study from January 1974.

Part of the reason why the UNCAL evaluation was funded by the Programme Committee was that MacDonald enjoyed the support of the Director, Richard Hooper. Another reason was that the Programme Committee undoubtedly did not understand the implications of commissioning a democratic evaluation, and this was not spelled out fully during the period of consultancy nor in the original proposal. In a companion volume to Hooper's *Two Years On*, MacDonald and his colleagues acknowledged that UNCAL was commissioned amid a certain amount of unease.[7] Hooper also commented that while the UNCAL team had reported on various programme issues, rather than stimulate discussion, the main effect had been to reinstate earlier difficulties regarding the purpose of evaluation and the procedures it should adopt.[8]

Concern about the role of independent evaluation surfaced as a specific issue at a meeting of the Programme Committee in September 1974. Here Professor Annett and an HMI, Mr JG Morris, presented a paper questioning the function of the UNCAL evaluation and the nature of its independence. Annett and Morris argued that while the programme as an educational phenomenon merited investigation and interpretation by educational sociologists, this was not the prime concern of the sponsors. They also argued that although the Programme Committee had a responsibility to judge the performance of the directorate, the UNCAL team were not 'required to evaluate Hooper', and were not independent of the directorate of the Committee but of the projects.[9] Annett and Morris saw the role of the UNCAL team as assisting:

> the decorate and the committee to reach conclusions on the conduct and outcome of the individual projects by virtue of their expertise in matters of data collection, the sifting of evidence and the processes of scientific inference.[10]

In response to these concerns the UNCAL team prepared a short paper dealing with each of Annett and Morris' points. MacDonald argued that his proposal had made it clear that the evaluation would not be restricted to the constituent projects, and that to exclude from purview the circumstances of the programme would prejudice any fair evaluation of the educational viability of computer-assisted learning. In particular, MacDonald was keen to defend and define the independence of the UNCAL evaluation and, referring back to the original proposal, wrote:

> The opening statement of the proposal called 'The Meaning of evaluation', stipulates that the evaluator has 'many audiences who will bring a variety of perspectives, concerns and values to bear upon his presentations'. The statement is not compatible with the view of the evaluation project as the instrument of central management, subject to its control and direction. If the concept of 'independence' were accorded the restricted interpretation suggested by Annett and Morris, it would cease to have any meaning, since it is impossible to envisage a 'dependent' alternative.[11]

MacDonald and his colleagues defined the UNCAL evaluation in terms of its goals , roles, and principles of procedure. They identified four main goals:

1. assisting individual projects to develop evaluation strategies which would be worthy of adoption by future users of computer-assisted learning;
2. providing feedback to the programme directorate about the effects of its actions;'
3. rendering the work of the programme accessible to a range of relevant audiences; and
4. identifying the educational issues raised by the programme and encouraging constructive thinking around them.

Associated with these goals were the following four roles:

1. A documentation role to establish a history of the programme leading to a narrative account of its experience.
2. A responsive role attempting to orient evaluation activities more towards action than intention and focus on the information requirements of various audiences.
3. A development role providing consultancy to individual projects on their internal evaluation plans.
4. A dissemination role seen in terms of mediating between the producers and consumers of information about the programme.[12]

According to some members of the UNCAL team, in practice the decision to pursue multiple goals and roles 'resulted in widespread misunderstanding, uncertainty and mistrust.'[13]

In view of the bureaucratic nature of the programme the UNCAL team faced considerable problems resolving the conflict between a development role and providing the directorate with disinterested feedback on the operation of the programme. A major distinguishing feature of the UNCAL evaluation, however, was not its multiple goals and roles but the concern with the distribution of power and knowledge within the programme and between UNCAL and programme participants. In the original proposal MacDonald stated that the 'crucial procedural problem' for the evaluation team was 'how to provide the National Directorate with information about the projects and at the same time avoid a "centre spy" role which would seriously reduce its access to the work of the projects and jeopardize its relationships with them'.[14] In response to these concerns the UNCAL team developed principles of procedure to guide its work with programme participants, and in particular for negotiating arrangements for access to and the distribution of evaluation data.[15]

While it would be wrong to see NDPCAL as a test-bed for establishing and refining a new change strategy, it *was* indicative of a stronger central voice in the promotion and management of innovation. NDPCAL also encapsulated the increasing emphasis placed by central government on evaluation — a trend which was broadly in line with renewed efforts by senior civil servants (finding sympathetic ears in the Conservative administration under Edward Heath) to improve the effectiveness of government planning and the control of resource allocations through systems analysis and policy research. Other and related trends have also increased the importance and scope of evaluation in Britain; in particular, the development of categorically funded programmes which like NDPCAL are reliant on evaluative feedback for their effective operation.

Categorical funding

The domestic politics of Britain have, since local government reorganization in 1974, been marked by tensions in the relationship between central and local authorities — this has been most manifest in the financing of local services and especially of education.[16] Since 1967 the main financial instrument for determining expenditure on education left the DES with very little direct influence on the education system for which they are accountable. After the general election of 1979, when stricter control of local government expenditure became an important part of the new Thatcher administration's monetary policy and LEAs faced serious financial problems further exacerbated by falling rolls, central government, largely through the power of the purse, increased its capacity to shape educational policy in line with national priorities. While the innovative programme or project remained as one of the main strategies for promoting educational innovation, an important point of departure was the emergence of categorical funding which in times of fiscal constraint can prove a powerful lever for change. Indeed, one of the defining features of categorical funding is that it is a financial instrument which can, under the right circumstances, achieve the effect of a statutory instrument when one does not exist. Categorical funding afforded the DES more purchase on the education system, especially through its control of in-service training grants and the introduction in 1984 of Education Support Grants.

The development of categorical funding was significant in a number of respects. It represented a change in political relationships and a shift in the balance of power, tilting the system more towards the centre. In this respect categorical funding could be seen as an aspect of the continuing struggle to shape the school curriculum in line with assumed economic needs. Because categorical funding leads to an increase in monitoring and evaluation (monitoring to ensure that contracts are being met, criteria are adhered to, and expenditure correctly targeted and accounted for; evaluation to identify good practice and improve the processes of implementation so that programmes can be replicated), it also alters existing patterns of management, accountability and control. Categorical funding can both make the operation of the education system more visible and lead to increased efforts at impression management and creative accounting.

In addition to the in-service and education support grants, two other major programmes of categorical funding have emerged under the Conservative administrations of the 1980s: the Lower Attaining Pupils Programme funded by the DES and the Technical and Vocational Education Initiative funded by the Manpower Services Commission.

Lower Attaining Pupils Programme

In July 1982 the Secretary of State for Education announced plans for a programme of development projects for lower attaining pupils in the fourth and fifth years of secondary schooling. Local authorities were invited to submit proposals in line with criteria specified by the Secretary of State.[17] Sixty-three LEAs submitted bids to take part in the Lower Attaining Pupils Programme (LAPP) and thirteen were selected for funding beginning in the September of 1983.[18] LEAs were required to fund 25 per cent of project costs from their own resources and to make arrangements for local evaluation. Some six months after the official start of the programme, in March 1984, the DES commissioned the National Foundation for Education Research to conduct a central evaluation under the following terms of reference:

> To evaluate the operation and the results of the programme in relation to its overall objectives and with reference to particular themes; to observe the projects on the ground, and to consult, advise and co-operate with those concerned with local monitoring and evaluation; to advise the DES and LEAs on outcomes suitable for wider dissemination and replication and other matters as appropriate; to produce interim reports at agreed intervals and at such times as requested by the Department and produce a final report by the end of 1987.[19]

As the DES terms of reference suggest, the national LAPP evaluation team were expected to work collaboratively with the local project evaluators to create a coherent and integrated strategy for evaluation. One immediate problem for the NFER team was that arrangements for local evaluations, like the projects themselves, varied enormously and some project teams already had their own formative evaluation strategies.[20] In five of the LEAs local evaluators were appointed or commissioned from institutions of further or higher education; in six of the LEAs the evaluator was based within the authority and often had advisory status; and in the remaining two authorities one evaluator was from the Further Education Unit of the DES and the other, a former HMI, worked from home.[21] Some projects then had external local evaluators while others had internal LEA evaluators, some of whom were or became members of the project teams.

Although their approach to evaluation was described as co-operative and formative, the NFER team had a clear responsibility to evaluate the programme as a whole and address issues like replication. No doubt there was an expectation that local evaluators would feed the central evaluation team with information, but there was no effective co-ordination of local evaluation efforts. The NFER team, therefore, had to create their own primary database by collecting snapshots of the projects and cohorts of pupils over time, and could not act simply as a meta-evaluation. In addition to national and local evaluation, HMI had been asked to evaluate LAPP as part of their general responsibilities and European Community evaluators also had an interest in the programme.[22]

A coherent strategy for evaluating LAPP never really emerged and it seems as if little thought was given to the organization and co-ordination of its various components.[23] It is arguable too that the idea of a programme was a convenient umbrella under which to fund 13 separate initiatives and get something going. While categorical funding appeared to afford the DES a mechanism through which to influence the school curriculum, in practice the Secretary of State's criteria were open to such wide interpretation, the resulting projects were so diverse, the size of the intervention so small and dissipated by comparison with the scale of the problem, and the initial planning for evaluation so chaotic, that it is difficult to see how the programme could produce anything other than temporary and highly localized opportunities for change. When announcing the initiative, Sir Keith Joseph had stressed the need to look for 'lessons' that were not dependent on 'charismatic personalities or unique school characteristics for success.'[24] From this perspective LAPP could be viewed as a pilot programme of experiments from which to learn how to improve educational provision for specific children. The original evaluation brief suggested that the DES had aspirations towards replicating good LAPP practice, and later on in the life of the programme the Department stated that it would not have succeeded in its aims unless the lessons emerging from the projects were passed on to all remaining LEAs.[25] Leaving aside the important question of how such a dissemination exercise could be achieved, the idea that LAPP could produce 'lessons' capable of being transferred from one setting to another without the additional resources which produced them was highly questionable. Even if there was a chance of reliable evidence from the evaluation team that these lessons were worth while and could be sustained, indications from HMI suggested that the DES were disinclined to wait for the NFER team to report before making arrangements to disseminate and extend the programme. Speaking in July 1986 at a LAPP open day, a Staff Inspector for Secondary Schools stated that the system could not wait until the final, summative evaluation report was published before assessing 'value for money' and looking for 'signs of appropriate replicability.'[26]

The Technical and Vocational Education Initiative

On 12 November 1982, the Prime Minister, Mrs Thatcher, announced to the House of Commons that a new scheme of technical and vocational education for the 14 to 18 age group was to be launched by the Manpower Services Commission (MSC) — now the Training Commission. The announcement was so unexpected that it even took the DES by surprise. Initial reactions from the local authorities were sufficiently hostile to make David Young, then Chairman of the MSC, talk about the Commission setting up its own technical schools.[27] As the consultative machinery started working again, the familiar rhetoric of representative and consensus planning helped paper over the more obvious cracks in the principle of partnership.[28] More importantly, perhaps, the possibility of MSC funding was no doubt a palatable if not attractive proposition to chief education officers facing tight budgets, falling rolls and pressures from conservative councillors to participate in the scheme.

The Technical and Vocational Education Initiative (TVEI) shared many of the organizational features of LAPP: requests for project proposals from LEAs wishing to enter the initiative; a complex selection process relying on the interpretation of pre-specified criteria and sometimes involving lengthy negotiations between LEA and government department; the establishment of steering groups or management committees having a general overview of the project; the appointment of LEA-based project co-ordinators responsible for day-to-day management and the designation of school-based co-ordinators responsible for the development of the iniative within a particular school; considerable variety in the project designs, patterns of provision and curricular initiatives adopted by the LEA; and a mixture of national and local evaluation including the active participation of HMI. The TVEI was planned as a complementary programme to the proposed £1,000 million Youth Training Scheme.[29] It was funded and administered by the MSC and guided by a National Steering Group made up of representative bodies. Initially considered as a five-year programme involving about 10,000 students in ten LEAs, the pilot scheme was to test ways of organizing courses and developing content and methods for technical and vocational education in schools, colleges and industrial training centres.

The TVEI was a major programme of categorical funding and a significant departure from previous patterns of curriculum development and planning in education. To participate, LEAs were invited to submit proposals in line with criteria set out by the MSC. According to McCulloch, 68 proposals were offered by 66 LEAs out of the 104 in England and Wales, and 14 were eventually chosen to run pilot schemes.[30] By September 1983 about 3 per cent of young people in the TVEI age group, drawn from 8 per cent of secondary schools, were involved in the initiative.[31]

In 1984 the MSC invited a second round of proposals. In the September of that year another 48 LEAs joined the scheme, and in 1985 a further 12 projects were added so that by 1986 there were 74 projects operating in 73 authorities. In that year a joint White Paper that was presented to Parliament by the Department of Employment and the Department of Education and Science, recommended the national extension of the TVEI to cover all schools in Britain from Autumn 1987; this was to be funded (building from £12 million in 1987–88 to £84 million in 1989–90) from within the MSC's planned provision for young people.[32] Somewhat unusually, the White Paper promised that such a policy would be 'fully evaluated to ensure value for money', and that agreed performance indicators would be developed for non-advanced further education.[33] In November of 1986, Kenneth Baker, the new Secretary of State for Education coming to the DES from the Department of Trade and Industry, proclaimed the successful introduction of the pilot projects and formally announced the national extension of the TVEI to all LEAs, claiming that the scheme represented a 'dramatic force for change' bringing 'industry and commerce right into the heart of the work of schools and colleges'.[34]

In line with their policy of categorical funding, the TVEI Unit of the MSC had a strong commitment to both national and local evaluation.[35] The overall programme of evaluation associated with the TVEI had the following four main components:

1. two national initiative-wide summative evaluations based at the NFER and Leeds University respectively, and commissioned by and reporting to the TVEI Unit;
2. special studies commissioned by the TVEI Unit to examine particular issues like equal opportunities, profiling and financial feasibility;
3. national monitoring aimed at establishing a database on curriculum, student/teacher characteristics, and financial information for operational purposes;
4. local evaluations commissioned or undertaken by LEAs and that were largely formative in character.[36]

In January 1985 the NFER was commissioned to undertake a three-year evaluation of the organization and operation of the TVEI. The NFER were asked to document and evaluate the introduction, organization, management and functions of TVEI schemes throughout England and Wales, exploring questions relating to:

- the replication of different TVEI projects or courses and the innovative practices and provision identified with them;
- the resource implications of implementing the various schemes;

- the reactions, to and perceived relevance of, the schemes by various parties involved; and,
- the impact of the projects on young people.[37]

The design of the NFER evaluation was based on a blend of quantitative and qualitative research involving questionnaire data, interview data and selected thematic case studies.[38] According to their in-house *Research News* at the centre of their research was 'a commitment to document the experiences of the students who take part in TVEI schemes'.[39] To this end the NFER team planned to survey students' responses to the schemes and their intentions for future education and employment at 13+, 15+ and 17+ years. They also planned to undertake complementary studies focusing on the views of parents, unions and trade associations, as well as a major interview programme directed at some 200 employers.[40]

The Leeds evaluation team had a different remit and methodological orientation. They were responsible for evaluating the curricular aspects of the pilot projects, focusing on content, organization, learning and teaching methods, assessment, and guidance and counselling.[41] Their methodology was qualitative and ethnographic, utilizing direct observation, interviews and the analysis of written materials. Their design envisaged a series of two-week evaluation studies of 26 TVEI schools that were selected as a representative sample from projects funded in rounds one, two and three of the initiative, covering different geographical areas and employment markets, and taking account of special curriculum features and types of schooling. Like the NFER evaluation, the Leeds evaluation included a major focus on the attitudes and perceptions of students towards the TVEI. However, unlike the NFER studies which aimed to collect various kinds of frequency data and organizational statistics, the Leeds evaluation was more concerned with emergent issues derived from case studies of TVEI schools.[42] In a first interim draft report on methodology and procedures compiled early in 1987, the Leeds team drew attention to the effects of the long-running dispute between central government and the teacher unions, which in their view had 'massively influenced the way in which schools, teachers and students coped with the normal pressures of teaching and learning', and no doubt had an effect on the capacity of the evaluation team to implement their case study plans.[43]

As might be expected, TVEI local evaluations were characterized by diversity. According to Ruth Tenne of the TVEI Unit (Section A4), the aim of local evaluation was to aid development at the local level and help in the dissemination of the scheme across the LEA.[44] An LEA commitment to evaluation was a condition of TVEI funding and authorities had to include plans for evaluation in their submissions to the TVEI Unit.[45] The result was a proliferation of local TVEI evaluation projects; these were usually located in university or polytechnic departments of education, funded either by single LEAs or by a consortium of TVEI authorities, and accountable to a steering group or management committee.[46] The MSC specified that a minimum of £4,000 each year should be dedicated to evaluation though authorities were free to devote to it more of their MSC funds if they wished.[47] In practice, LEAs tended to devote about 1 per cent of their annual TVEI budget to project evaluation, making consortium funding an attractive proposition if the resources to employ a full-time external evaluator were to be found. One of the largest consortia comprising 13 LEAs was organized by Lancaster University yet still only provided sufficient resources to fund two full-time experienced researchers. The Lancaster consortia evaluation was based on a programme of interviews with project and school personnel and comparative surveys of TVEI and non-TVEI students through the four years of the course and into employment, unemployment, higher education or the Youth Training Scheme.[48] Another consortium, centred on the University of East Anglia, comprised three LEAs providing for one full-time evaluator working largely through interview and observation. By contrast, a number of LEAs chose to appoint seconded teachers as evaluators rather than use an external agency or institution.

An important element of the TVEI Unit's evaluation strategy was a financial evaluation to calculate inputs and outputs so that the costs and benefits of different kinds of projects could be judged. To this end the TVEI Unit set up a Financial Evaluation Steering Group (FESG) consisting of representatives from the MSC, HMI, the DES, and the Department of Employment, as well as educational economists.[49] The Steering Group decided it was necessary to conduct a feasibility study before implementing a full financial evaluation exercise. A small working sub-group was thus created to draw up a specification for the study which was estimated to take two evaluators 36 days spread over four months.[50] The feasibility study was done by John Mills from Surrey Local Education Authority and Margaret Powell from the TVEI Unit. Their work began at Solihull in January 1986 and short follow-up studies took place in Northamptonshire and Surrey.[51]

The FESG argued that in any decision to extend the TVEI to cover a wider group of pupils and curriculum arrangements, the resource implications and putative educational benefits of competing or different patterns of organization, management and curricular approaches would have to be computed if efficient and effective alternatives were to be chosen either at a national or local level.[52] There were a number of serious difficulties facing the financial evaluation team: enormous variation in the organizational and administrative arrangements for projects: markedly different curricular approaches and subject areas: wide variation in the sources of direct funding: unquantifiable inputs to projects often starting from different resource bases: uncertain and unmeasurable outcomes: confounding of the effects of the TVEI because of the presence of other programmes and initiatives; and the lack of useful financial information. The feasibility study concluded that a full financial evaluation would be neither practicable nor worth while, largely because outputs could not be quantified. Instead the evaluators recommended that future work be confined to comparative financial evaluations focusing on specific aspects of the programme — for example, different types of TVEI organization. One firm recommendation they did make was that 'any consideration of the replication of TVEI activities must take account of total resource inputs, not just those of the MSC.'[53]

When the national extension of the TVEI was announced, neither the Leeds nor NFER team had reported and it appeared that the decision to extend the initiative had been taken irrespective of any evaluation findings, and with little knowledge of the actual cost of the initiative to participating LEAs. The success of the TVEI was simply proclaimed and the Government made it clear that it was its intention that every LEA should take part in the extension.[54]

The political aspirations that gave rise to the TVEI have a long history and in this respect there is a degree of continuity between it and earlier forms of curriculum development. Ideas about manpower planning have, since before the First World War, had a significant effect on the education system as a whole and they have usually been associated with concerns about the international competitiveness of the British industrial/military economy. Recent government thinking has reasserted the doctrine that international competitiveness is the key to national prosperity and that training is a critical variable in providing a sound and responsive economy. The political rhetoric of the TVEI accentuated the importance of producing a technically competent labour force with appropriate skills and attitudes to make their way in a modern and rapidly changing labour market. The TVEI also helped to suggest that the problem of unemployment should be seen not as a product of poor economic management but as a consequence of individual behaviour and outmoded institutions.

Unlike the earlier curriculum development movement, the TVEI emerged at a time when political circumstances favoured the already established trend towards the central control of education. Reflecting this trend, the TVEI was in many ways a highly bureaucratic innovation system; looked at as a whole, it was characterized by a considerable amount of pencil and paper planning and pre-specification at every level, giving the appearance of a consensual, well-ordered and coherent pilot programme that was centrally monitored and managed while being locally devised and delivered. However, with the successive addition of the more LEAs it looked less and less likely that the pilot status of the programme could or would be sustained. This is to assume, however, that the TVEI was seen as a policy experiment. It was not. As Donald Campbell has observed, 'specific reforms are advocated as though they were certain to be successful'.[55] The TVEI was a statement of political to the political and methodological obstacles facing any evaluation of the policy or even the programme but factors such as the following: operating questions, implementation and change strategies, uptake among young people, the cost-effectiveness cf alternative forms of provision, the responsiveness of teachers and local administrators to a reordering of curriculum priorities, and the capacity of the education system to develop links with industry and courses that related to local and national employment opportunities.[56] Like the Lower Attaining Pupils Programme, it is also questionable whether the TVEI should be thought of as a curriculum development programme operating in line with national priorities. The TVEI was characterized by a enormous variety of projects. The programme, if there was one, was given by similar starting points, common but broad criteria, common patterns of funding and management, and common requirements for monitoring and evaluation. In this respect it appears that innovation was in the programme infrastructure rather than in the specific nature of course provision.

The TVEI has been subject to a vast array of evaluation projects and monitoring exercises, making it the most heavily researched and evaluated curriculum innovation ever in the UK. Whatever else the TVEI achieved, it resulted in a significant increase in the number of people and institutions with some experience of evaluating or being evaluated. Yet for all this evaluation activity, proper policy evaluation was largely absent.

One practical problem was the capacity of policy-makers to consider, let alone use, the variety and quantity of information that TVEI monitoring and evaluation produced. An associated and more political problem was the reliance of policy-makers on the TVEI Unit to sift and sort the mass of information available and to select that which was relevant and usable. Clearly, the TVEI Unit and its evaluation section had a direct interest in the success of the initiative. This alone suggests that the credibility of their monitoring and evaluation exercise was in some doubt. Even if this was not the case (and in their defence the TVEI Unit would surely claim that they commissioned two national external evaluations ensuring impartiality and independence of judgement), there must be serious reservations about the technical feasibility of the TVEI evaluations and their relationship to policy.

At the outset of TVEI, before the national evaluators had been commissioned, Professor Ted Wragg from Exeter University drew attention to the political and methodological obstacles facing any evaluation of the programme, and outlined a five-point plan for a feasible evaluation strategy. Wragg argued that the national evaluation of TVEI should:

1. be democratic in MacDonald's use of the term;
2. be formative but not collusive;
3. make judicious use of quantitative methods though not experimental design;
4. check the extent to which implementation matches intention as well as measure learning, attitude change, behaviour and the acquisition of skills;
5. employ ethnographic approaches that would involve careful record-keeping by both participants and evaluators, with proper verification of one view against another.[57]

In the event, the arrangements for the national evaluation were more bureaucratic than Wragg would have hoped. Given the dependence of the NFER on central government contracts they were unlikely to be offering anything other than a bureaucratic information service.[58] For their part, the Leeds team were new to evaluation and constrained contractually in terms of their reporting.

Ernest House has argued that the practice of evaluation is properly seen as a social decision procedure, and that each evaluation has a logic of its own permitting different forms of persuasion and different aspects of reality to be constructed and disclosed.[59] Such a view of evaluation might equally well apply to pilot programmes and innovation systems. For example, Rob Fiddy has described the TVEI as a kind of economy involving trading between the power brokers at different levels in the system and the marketing of different conceptions of the innovation.[60] Like others he has noted the strong tendency for the take-up of the innovation to be based on the need for extra resources rather than a commitment to particular kinds of change. Both nationally and locally the TVEI had a carefully presented profile and the trappings of an evaluation strategy formed part of that presentation. The TVEI Unit, for example, went to considerable lengths to describe and publicize their evaluation strategy, using glossy brochures creating an image of rational planning and control.[61]

Part of the problem structure of any evaluation arises from the politics of innovation and the realities of the policy-making process. Evaluators and administrators of social programmes have a strong interest in defining the policy-making process as rational and susceptible to reasoned argument and judgement supported by evidence, albeit in the long term. That the reality is at some considerable distance from the rhetoric is a problem for both evaluators and policy-makers alike. For both it presents problems of legitimation and the constitution of usable yet credible knowledge. Of course what can be said and done in the name of evaluation is the result of complex political adjustments — some calculated and some intuitive. Yet as MacDonald has noted, writing in another context, social action is a compromise of some kind between values, interests and circumstances (and we may add characters), and the task for evaluators is not to defend or attack that compromise but to understand its precise structure.[62] The often private nature of decision-making and political adjustment, however, makes it extremely difficult both to reach this kind of understanding and for it to have any currency for policy-makers who need to attend more to the presentational aspects than to the pilot nature of national innovations like the TVEI. Moreover, the contractual control of evaluative inquiry is increasingly being used to prevent evaluation studies from constributing to the wider critical debate about the quality and effects of public policy.

Notes

1. Hooper, R (1977) *National Development Programme in Computer Assisted Learning: Final Report of the Director*, London: Council for Educational Technology, p 15.
2. See: MacDonald, B & Jenkins, D (1979) *Understanding Computer Assisted Learning. The Final Report of the Educational Evaluation of the National Development Programme in Computer Assisted Learning*, Norwich: Centre for Applied Research in Education, University of East Anglia. Copies should also be available from the Department of Education and Science.
3. For an account of the financial evaluation see: Fielden, J & Pearson, PK (1978) *The Costs of Learning with Computers: Final Report of the Financial Evaluation*, London: Council for Educational Technology.

4. In its early stages MacDonald worked on the evaluation with Professor Robert Stake from the University of Illinois. Later David Jenkins, David Tawney and Stephen Kemmis joined the UNCAL team.

5. See: Hooper, R (1975) *Two Years On: The National Development Programme in Computer Assisted Learning*, London: Council for Educational Technology, p 45.

6. Quoted in a report prepared by Barry MacDonald for the Programme Committee following disagreements about the first report of the UNCAL evaluation [CALC(74) 11] The report was entitled: 'Educational evaluation of the National Development Programme in Computer Assisted Learning: an introduction to the work of the Independent Programme Evaluation based at the University of East Anglia' and was referred to in the nomenclature of the programme as CALC(74) 23.

7. MacDonald, B, Jenkins, D, Kemmis, S & Tawney, D (1975) *The Programme at Two*, Norwich: Centre for Applied Research in Education, University of East Englia.

8. Hooper, R (1975) op. cit. p 53.

9. Professor Annett and Mr Morris (HMI) presented this paper, 'Evaluation of the National CAL Programme' [CALC(74) 28] in September 1974. Their paper was prompted by the first report of the UNCAL team which was an issues report in dialogue form that focused on the programme rather than the projects.

10. Annett, J & Morris, J [CALC(74) 28] op. cit.

11. 'Educational evaluation of the National Development Programme in Computer Assisted Learning', a response to the Annett/Morris paper by Barry MacDonald [CALC(74) 29].

12. A copy of the evaluation proposal was included as an appendix to MacDonald, B et al. (1975) *The Programme at Two*, Norwich: Centre for Applied Research in Education, pp 74–9.

13. See: Jenkins, D, Kemmis, S & Atkin, R (1977) 'An Insider's Critique'. In Norris, N (ed.) *SAFARI Theory in Practice*, Norwich, Centre for Applied Research in Education, University of East Anglia, pp 79–105.

14. MacDonald, B et al. (1975) op. cit. p 77.

15. See: MacDonald, B & Stake, R (1974) *Confidentiality: procedure and principles of the UNCAL evaluation with respect to information about projects in the National Development Programme in Computer Assisted Learning*, Norwich: Centre for Applied Research in Education, University of East Anglia, Mimeo.

16. Judge, H (1984) *A Generation of Schooling*, Oxford University Press, p 153.

17. LAPP was announced by the Secretary of State in an address to the Council for Local Authorities Conference on 16 July 1982. An indication of the criteria were given in a DES press notice (169/82, 16.7.82). The Secretary of State hoped to see: (a) proposals for investigations of new forms of co-operation between schools and further education; (b) an expansion of work experience schemes; (c) activities built around practical projects in the community with full participation by local employers; (d) an investment in the in-service training of teachers; (e) the stimulation of new thinking in initial teacher training; (f) curriculum development; and (g) the assessment and recording of pupil achievements.

18. DES (1986) *Lower Attaining Pupils Programme Issues for Discussion*, London: Department of Education and Science.

19. NFER (1984) *14–16 Network DES Lower Attaining Pupils Programme*, Autumn, Slough: NFER.

20. Weston, P (1984) 'A quest for understanding, or understanding the questions',

paper presented at the LAPP Evaluators Conference, James Gracie Centre, Birmingham, 25/26 October 1984.

21. NFER (1985) *14–16 Network DES Lower Attaining Pupils Programme*, Spring, Slough: NFER.

22. Two of the LAPP projects were designated as part of the English contribution to the second phase of the European Community's pilot programme on the transition from school to working life, hence the Community's interest in LAPP. For an account of the HMI view of LAPP see: Report of HMI Inspectors (1986) *A Survey of the Lower Attaining Pupils Programme: The First Two Years*, DES Publications Despatch Centre, Stanmore, Middlesex.

23. A view expressed privately by the project manager of the NFER Evaluation, and alluded to in Weston, P (1984) op. cit. According to Weston the problem of planning the national evaluation of LAPP was further complicated by changes in personnel at the Department of Education and Science.

24. See: Report by HM Inspectors (1986) op. cit. p 4.

25. NFER (1986) *14–16 Network DES Lower Attaining Pupils Programme*, Summer, Slough: NFER, p 7.

26. See: Turberfield, AF (1986) 'LAPP — an interim assessment' paper presented to the Lower Attaining Pupils Programme open day held at the University of Warwick, 1 July 1986.

27. See Owen, J (1984) TVEI: future control. In Dancy, J (ed.) *TVEI Perspectives 14*, School of Education, University of Exeter, pp 7–17.

28. Ibid. p 11.

29. Plans for a Youth Training Scheme (YTS) were announced in a 1981 White Paper from the Department of Employment. YTS superseded the Youth Opportunities Programme as the major provision for unemployed school leavers. This Scheme came into effect in September 1983 and was administered by the MSC. For an account of the origins of YTS see: Fiddy, R (ed.) *Youth, Unemployment and Training a Collection of National Perspectives*, London: Falmer Press, pp 27–38.

30. McCulloch, G (1986) Policy, politics and education: the Technical and Vocational Education Initiative, *Journal of Education Policy*, 1, 1, pp 35–52.

31. *MSC Annual Report 1983/84*, Sheffield: MSC.

32. *Working Together — Education and Training*, London: HMSO, para 3.6.

33. Ibid. para 1.9.

34. *DES News* 284/86, 5 November 1986.

35. The TVEI Unit of the MSC was responsible for managing the evaluation and monitoring programme. The Unit comprised about 100 staff including regional TVEI advisers. Section A4 of the Unit, under the direction of Dr Gaynor Cohen with about ten staff, had responsibility for national and local evaluation as well as commissioning special studies. In an undated publication entitled *TVEI Evaluation Bulletin* the Unit described itself as responsible for: (a) ensuring a high level of professionalism is attained, (b) ensuring that evaluation studies address questions identified by the National Steering Group of the MSC; (c) ensuring compatability in methodological approaches; (d) avoiding duplication in studies; (e) facilitating collaboration between different strands of the programme; and (f) disseminating information to various audiences about monitoring and evaluation.

36. See, TVEI Unit (undated) *TVEI Evaluation Bulletin*, 236 Grays Inn Rd, London.

37. Ibid.

38. See Stoney, SM, Pole, CJ & Sims, D (1986) *The Management of TVEI: A Set of*

Interim Papers on the Themes of Management Issues, Slough: National Foundation For Educational Research, pp 1–2.

39. NFER (1985) *Educational Research News,* No 42, Spring, p 1.
40. Ibid.
41. Tenne, R (1985) How will TVEI be evaluated, *Education,* 9 August, p 131.
42. Leeds TVEI Evaluation (undated) 'Interim Report 1: Evaluation Procedures and Methodology' (draft), University of Leeds, p 10.
43. Leeds TVEI Evaluation, op. cit. p 11
44. Tenne, R (1985) op. cit.
45. See: *TVEI Evaluation Bulletin,* TVEI Unit, Grays Inn Rd, London.
46. Ibid. p 15.
47. For an account of the Lancaster consortium evaluation see: Saunders, M (1985) Developing a large scale 'local' evaluation of TVEI: aspects of the Lancaster experience. In Hopkins, D (ed.) *Evaluating TVEI: Some Methodological Issues,* Cambridge Institute of Education, pp 41–51.
48. Ibid.
49. *TVEI Finance Feasibility Study* (undated) TVEI Unit, Grays Inn Rd, London.
50. The specification stated that the evaluators were to: (a) appraise the financial data available and the ways in which it is suitable for analysis about the delivery of TVEI; (b) test methods of analysing the data which would lead to models which could be utilized when making decisions, both locally and nationally, about further developing the initiative or elements within it; (c) make recommendations as to the most appropriate ways of continuing to collect financial data; (d) advise on the feasibility of carrying out a full study on the resource implications of the introduction of TVEI as a whole and elements within it; and, (e) suggest possible methodologies for carrying out a full financial evaluation if this is deemed to be practical. See: *TVEI Finance Feasibility Study,* op. cit. p 12.
51. *TVEI Finance Feasibility Study,* op. cit. p 19.
52. Ibid. p 10.
53. Ibid. p 201.
54. Department of Employment/Department of Education and Science (1986). *Working Together — Education and Training,* London: HMSO, see paragraph 3.10.
55. Campbell, DT (1983) Reforms as experiments. In Struening, EL & Brewer, MB (eds) *Handbook of Evaluation Research,* Beverly Hills, Cal: Sage, pp 107–37.
56. See for example TVEI Unit (1986) *TVEI Evaluation,* London: TVEI Unit.
57. Wragg, T (1984) Evaluating TVEI programmes. In Dancy, J (ed.) *TVEI Perspectives 14,* University of Exeter.
58. In an overview of educational research, William Taylor noted that over 90 per cent of the NFER's sponsored research income is from central government. See: Taylor, W (1985) The Organization and funding of educational research in England and Wales. In Nisbet, J (ed.) *World Yearbook of Education 1985: Research, Policy and Practice,* London: Kogan Page, pp 42–67.
59. See, House, E (1980) *Evaluating With Validity,* Beverly Hills, Cal: Sage.
60. Fiddy, R (1987) *TVEI: Selling the Chameleon Curriculum,* Norwich: Centre For Applied Research in Education, University of East Anglia, Mimeo.
61. See: TVEI Unit *TVEI Evaluation.* The brochure contains 13 evaluation information sheets.
62. MacDonald, B (1981) Interviewing in case study evaluation, *Phi Delta Kappa CEDR Quarterly,* **14**, 4.

Chapter 5
Evaluation and the New Cult of Social Efficiency

The year after Stenhouse published his influential book on curriculum research and development, a confidential DES memorandum presented to the Secretary of State for Education, argued that central government should have a greater say in the design of the school curriculum. The memorandum was also criticial of the Schools Council and its overall performance regarding both curriculum and examinations.[1] Colin Lacey, in his reassessment of the work of the Council, suggests that this view was shared by a powerful group within the DES and HMI and that, contrary to Bell and Prescott's (1975) earlier assessment, the educational establishment was far from united on the principle of a teacher-controlled curriculum body.[2] By the mid-1970s the uneasy political accommodation of a partnership for the control of education — inherent in the Education Act of 1944, embodied in the constitution of agencies like the Schools Council and established in administrative procedure and practice — was showing signs of serious strain if not breakdown.

In 1976 James Callaghan took the unusual step for a British Prime Minister of making a major and critical statement on education. He was to launch a 'Great Debate' to be managed through a series of regional conferences concentrating on the relationship of education to industry and employment, as well as curriculum, teaching methods, assessment and standards. The politics of the 'Great Debate' were dominated by economic crisis. By late 1975 unemployment had risen above one million for the first time in over 30 years, overall living standards were declining and a sterling catastrophe prompted a series of tied loans from the International Monetary Fund conditional on a deflationary fiscal policy. Callaghan's speech at Ruskin College in October 1976, has assumed considerable symbolic importance for it marked a change in attitudes towards education and signalled a prolonged period of limitation and contraction.

The initiative most closely associated with Callaghan's call for greater accountability from an education service costing some £6 billion per year, was the creation of the Assessment of Performance Unit (APU) within the Schools 111 branch of the DES.[3] It is customary to see the accountability movement as a response to, or a product of, the economic contraction of the 1970s. However, MacDonald has argued that:

managerial concern for accountability was an effect of educational expansion and the growth of local government in the sixties, a consequence of the need for more sophisticated thinking about increasingly complex administrations. That a transformation of rationale for accountability took place in the seventies is undeniable, and hardly surprising in view of the pressures for cost-effectiveness and the competition for scarce resources that stringency generated. But accountability as a concept was already prominent in the plans and experiments of local as well as national governments before the Treasury axe fell.[4]

Clearly in a situation of fiscal constraint, accountability and its associated procedures for evaluation assume more significance than in conditions where resource allocations are not so contested. From the perspective of the DES, MacDonald suggests, the APU came to be seen as a potent mechanism for providing the Secretary of State with quantitative performance indicators to support bids for resources in Cabinet and defend the Department against a powerful Treasury looking for cuts.

The path, by which the APU came into existence underlines MacDonald's argument about the origins of the accountability movement. In fact, the APU had its origins in a number of monitoring initiatives during the late 1960s and early 1970s and, in part at least, represented concerns about curriculum control and the effectiveness of resource allocation. In 1970, for example, a working group on the measurement of educational attainment was set up by the DES. The working group consisted of two HMIs, two members of the planning branch of the DES, the Director of Research at the Schools Council, Jack Wrigley; the Director of Research for the Inner London Education Authority, Alan Little; a research advisor for the DES, Bill Taylor; and the Deputy Director of the National Foundation for Educational Research, Douglas Pidgeon.[5] This group reported at the end of 1971, concluding that regular measurements of educational attainment was desirable, feasible and should be carried out by sampling the main educational stages and school subjects.[6] Arising from this a feasibility project was commissioned at the National Foundation for Educational Research to develop tests of attainment in mathematics, and their interim report indicated that large-scale monitoring was feasible and could be undertaken by the Foundation.[7] Finally, in 1975 when the Bullock Committee reported, its monitoring sub-committee recommended a national system of monitoring using light sampling, matrix sampling, and item banking techniques.[8]

The measurement of educational performance

The APU was quietly announced as part of an initiative on disadvantage and under-achievement and was to work in conjunction with the Educational Disadvantage and the Eduational Needs of Immigrants.[9] The APU's original terms of reference were to 'promote the development of methods of assessing and monitoring the development of children at school, and seek to identify the incidence of under-achievement'. The focus on under-achievement and disadvantage was, however, soon discarded. Instead, the APU directed its attention towards test development and surveys to provide information about educational standards, national trends in performance, organizational and curriculum change, and the effectiveness of schooling.[10]

The development of the APU to some extent mirrors American experience. Indeed the Head of the APU, Brian Kay, and the Deputy Director of the NFER, Clare Burstall, visited the American National Assessment of Educational Progress (NAEP) to see what could be learnt from federal attempts to measure national educational performance. Efforts in this direction began in 1965 at the instigation of John Gardner, Secretary of Health Education and Welfare (1965–68), and with the support of the Carnegie Corporation. In 1967 William Gorham, then also at Health Education and Welfare, gave an indication of the perceived federal need for a programme of national assessment. In a lunchtime address to an invitational conference organized by the Educational Testing Service, he spoke of the general lack of 'information about the relationship between student performance and the resources that go into education'.[11] He went on to suggest that federal policy-makers needed some indication of the relationships between resource inputs, the use of resources and the performance of students.

NAEP was set up to provide evidence about the direct outcomes of education in a variety of subject areas through a national sample of four age groups. The aim of such a programme was to improve the policy-making of both state and federal agencies by providing information which could be used to judge the relationship between inputs and outputs, in an analogous way to measurements of industrial productivity. As MacDonald has noted and Burstall and Kay discovered, American experience of national monitoring on this scale was not at all promising.[12] There are obviously some arresting methodological and technical problems with attempts to measure national trends in educational performance, not least of which is the provision of a sound educational justification for test construction, survey design, sampling and calibration. By the time the APU was established, some technical guidelines for its work had already emerged: light sampling, item banking and Rasch calibration of the item banks.[13] It was the Rasch model and the related problem of studying trends over time that presented the APU with some of its most serious difficulties and some of its most cogent critics.[14]

The establishment and subsequent work of the APU represents a markedly different trend in evaluation to the development of curriculum under the aegis of the Schools Council. It could be argued that the concern for national monitoring and evaluation was a long-term and calculated response by the DES to a system of curriculum development over which it had little influence and no control. The fact that the APU was almost smuggled into existence suggests it was seen by the DES as part of a long-term strategy commensurate with other accountability developments in Whitehall that were politically sensitive in the public arena of education.[15] That the DES was persuaded of the technical feasibility and educational desirability of measuring national performance over time, suggests either something of the self-serving nature of the advice it received or a lack of experience to deal with the complex technical issues that such an initiative raised. In any event by 1983, when Caroline Gipps and Harvey Goldstein completed their Social Science Research Council funded evaluation of the APU, there had been little progress made on monitoring standards and measuring changes in them over a period of time.

The cult of social efficiency

Reflecting on his research into the development of modern educational administration in the United States of America, Raymond Callahan commented that what was unexpected was the extent not only of the power of business-industrial groups, but the strength of the business ideology in American culture and the extreme weakness and vulnerability of teachers, especially school administrators.[17] His study — *Education and the Cult of Efficiency* — examined the social forces and political responses that shaped the administration of public education in the early part of the twentieth century. Callahan's account begins with the intense public criticism of the school system, criticism that was stimulated and bolstered by the profits to be gained from muckraking journalism. Popular and vociferous criticism of education turned on the charges of low standards, economic irrelevance and above all inefficiency. The American pattern of local support and control of education meant that the school administrator was especially vulnerable to public pressure and opinion.[18] These conditions provided a strong motive and clear opportunity for reforms that exploited and popularized the emerging technologies of educational measurement and scientific management.

What has characterized the educational debates of the 1980s, are issues that are remarkably similar in tone and substance to those identified by Callahan: public criticism of the effectiveness of schooling; questions of economic relevance and the importance of basic skills; accountability, choice and the rights and roles of parents; teacher competency and teacher appraisal; standards, the promotion of excellence, testing and monitoring; and, of course, the efficient use of resources. Callahan's work indicates how public disquiet about schooling and political pressures for social efficiency had a powerful and tragic effect on American society, strengthening an anti-intellectual climate and fostering a mechanical view of education. From 1910 onwards, argues Callahan, American schooling was treated like industrial production; it was subject to the same values and process of valuing as business. Cost analysis and basic accounting procedures were increasingly used to evaluate the effectiveness of schools, administrators, teachers and instruction.

Over a relatively short period of time the techniques and ideology of a spurious science of management gained widespread support and were applied to education in efforts to increase its productivity. A new breed of consultant/administrator emerged at the centre of the management stage: the educational engineer and the efficiency expert.[19] School administrators, almost as a matter of self-preservation, readily saw themselves as business executives rather than educationalists or scholars.

During the 1980s, schooling was the focus of considerable public criticism. At the same time questions of productivity and control, as well as the role of government and the individual, have come to dominate the agenda of social policy. One interpretation of this new social efficiency movement is that central governments are gradually drawing back from the political goals of social policy in an attempt to limit their initiatives to more narrowly defined fiscal and economic objectives. Whether this diagnosis is correct or not, economic considerations have again come to dominate educational policy. From consumer choice to competition the political language of education has a profoundly economic ring. Recession, unemployment and large-scale structural changes in Western economies have altered the political circumstances and goals for education, but so too has the accompanying disillusion and ideological climate.

In the USA and Britain the rise of the New Right and the appeal of neo-conservative political economy is having a significant impact on policy-making. In the USA the 'Great Society' programmes of the Johnson years are now being adjudged a failure. Charles Murray's book *Losing Ground*, for example, presents a vivid attack on US social policy and has had a great influence on the tone and content of social policy debates.[20] The Murray thesis is simple, powerful and to a British audience no doubt familiar: the social (ie socialist) 'programs and policies of the past 25 years have actually caused a decline in the well-being of the poor'. Social policy has been positively harmful to the people it was trying to help.[21] In spite of the populist and libertarian appeal of New Right ideology, in Britain there are evident complicating, some might say contradictory, trends towards central control and authoritarianism. Whereas in the USA the Reagan and Bush administrations have been trying to curtail and reshape the federal role in education and return the initiative for innovation to state governments, in Britain the Thatcher admistration has been pursuing policies aimed at reducing the power and discretion of local elected governments and representative bodies. The extent of these changes and their effect on the theory and practice of evaluation is obviously difficult to gauge, but clearly the political context of policy-making and programme evaluation is changing.

Effective schooling

In the USA the long-term trend towards centralization represents a shift away from local and parental arrangements for schooling and towards greater state involvement in financial, curricular and staffing policies.[22] While the 1960s and 70s saw the rapid increase in programme evaluation associated with federal policies aimed at promoting social justice, the evaluation issues of the 1980s appear more concerned with state measures aimed at increasing social efficiency. In his review of the effective schools movement, Larry Cuban described it as a mission 'targeted like a rifle-shot on lifting test scores'.[23] Cuban argues that the initial impulse behind the study of 'effective schools' was to improve the academic performance of low income minority groups.[24] It was also a reaction to the 1966 Coleman Report which was widely interpreted as demonstrating that teachers and administrators had little effect on student achievement.[25] However, effective schooling is also associated with other concerns.

In 1983, the federal government published a report by the National Commission on Excellence in Education entitled: *A Nation at Risk: The Imperative for Educational Reform*. The report warned of a rising tide of mediocrity and claimed that unless educational standards were raised the country would be overtaken by its competitors.[26] One response to this apparent crisis was the 1983 Californian Hughes-Hart Educational Reform Act, which released funds for improving public education through raising graduation standards; providing incentives for student, teacher, and school achievement; improving student discipline: and increasing instructional time.[27] In parallel with the Act, the Department of Education instituted an accountability programme based on indicators of educational progress and school performance.[28] California's response was by no means an isolated one. As the cost of education to state governments increases so too will the demands for centralized systems of accountability based on performance indicators.

Britain too has seen an increase in evaluation research aimed at isolating the key features of 'successful' schools.[29] Effective schools research has provided some Local Education Authorities with evidence that could be used to identify the apparent characteristics of unsatisfactory schools and poor teaching. The Inner London Education Authority (ILEA) Junior School Project developed by the Research and Statistics Branch is an interesting recent example.[30] This four-year longitudinal survey was conducted between 1980 and 1984, and involved nearly 2,000 pupils from 50 'randomly' selected primary schools. The project tried to establish whether and why some schools were more effective than others. The study focused on three kinds of measures: measures of the pupils' background characteristics, measures of the pupils' progress and development, and measures of the classroom learning environments and what were called school processes. Whatever else might be claimed for the study, it was an attempt to isolate — in the statistical sense — those variables associated with effective junior schooling. For instance, the study suggested that a 'a work-centred environment, consistency among teachers, limited focus within sessions and positive climate' had beneficial effects on the measurable outcomes of schooling.[31] Like many American studies, the ILEA Junior School Project relied on measurements of pupil progress as the main index of effectiveness. While disclaiming any attempts to produce a 'blueprint for success', the researchers felt able to identify 12 key factors that were consistently related to effective junior schooling, thus providing the Authority and others with an apparently scientific model of the characteristics of good schools.[32]

Professional insulation

By the mid-1970s the experience of British curriculum developers and evaluators alike suggested that 'centrally defined programmes should give way to local initiatives within a framework of facilitative suport'.[33] Localism has found expression in other more general developments: teacher-as-researcher, the Classroom Action Research Network, and school-based in-service training and curriculum development. We could see such developments as both organizational and political, embodying preferences for 'grass-roots', 'bottom-up' curriculum research and reform. For all the apparent centralist implications of categorical funding, programmes like TVEI and LAPP are still largely teacher-based developments. It is the teachers who design the content of the innovation, albeit within a framework of national criteria and local authority administration. The importance of the role of the teacher has provided a certain continuity across the twists and turns of changing innovation strategies during the last 25 years.

The values of localism have also found expression in evaluation through such developments as self-evaluation, school self-evaluation, institutional self-evaluation, and the apparent growth of formative evaluation activities. A typical pattern for evaluation in the 1980s is a mix of local project-based formative evaluation and national summative programme evaluation. Those who write about their work from the local perspective tend to do so in terms of teacher professional development and self-evaluation. Peter Holly refers to this kind of formative feedback as 'professional evaluation' — evaluation by the profession for the profession.[34] It is evaluation in support of professional development and judgement which tends to focus on issues of implementation rather than value. Such a view of self-evaluation for formative purposes is related to certain conceptions of educational improvement and is calculated to appeal to a profession that feels itself vulnerable to criticism. Whether it could or should provide a credible alternative to external programme evaluation is highly questionable; it is an insular approach to evaluation in a politically charged and contentious public service that has a multiplicity of clients and interests. In effect, 'professional evaluation' is an approach for a consensual social system with clear agreement about goals, values and criteria for success, and where professionals are entrusted to pursue the common good. Under such 'ideal' circumstances the need for external independent evaluation is significantly reduced, but ideal circumstances hardly describe the case of contemporary education and professional insularity is not a politically viable strategy for educational evaluators or evaluation.

The privatization of public knowledge

As Kushner and MacDonald (1987) observe, evaluators who attempt to pursue their tasks in a more critical, democratic and public fashion are now facing serious threats to their independence. There has been a significant change in the way both national and local administrators define their relationship to educational innovation; administrators have become managers rather than programme facilitators. This change in role and attitude has increased their need for evaluation while at the same time heightening their sensitivity to bad news about programme success. The result has been growing attempts to control both the agenda and reporting of evaluative inquiry. Indeed, it could be argued that one of the main reasons for the popularity of formative evaluation (as Michael Scriven argued some 20 years ago) is that it is less threatening and more easily controlled.

In their synopsis of the current climate for innovation, Kushner and MacDonald offer a pessimistic political diagnosis of the state of educational evaluation in Britain. Their analysis could be summarized in the following way:

1. there has been a collapse of mediating agencies characteristic of the collaborative partnership in the post-war management of education;
2. local administrators are now being defined as branch agents of the central executive, creating a bureaucratic monolith ready to enact governing political convictions in curriculum matters;
3. although there is more funded programme evaluation and much of it is officially independent, evaluators are largely co-opted into a conspiracy of pretence that programmes are by definition educationally and economically sound;
4. evaluators and their institutions are more than ever dependent upon the patronage of administrators, particularly at the local level where responsibility for programme impression management is greatest;
5. the provision of useful knowledge in the public sphere is not consistent with the requirements of the programme managers who dominate evaluation sponsorship;
6. the space for dissent at all levels of involvement has closed down and tolerance of independent criticism is low;
7. trends in the management of curriculum development have coalesced into patterns of control which are authoritarian and anti-democratic;
8. evaluation, in so far as it embodies a promise of impartial and useable knowledge for those who are not party to government action, is in danger of becoming a descreditable activity.[35]

This is an especially pessimistic analysis and some might argue rather overstated. However, there is mounting evidence of both local and central government taking steps to control the dissemination of evaluative information and strictly limit the purview of programme evaluation to administratively defined short-term needs. As the analysis of the contractual conditions for evaluative inquiry in Chapter 6 indicates, government departments are increasingly behaving as if they were private purchasers of a commodity which they own and can control to suit the political purposes of the moment. The relationship between programme evaluators and those agencies responsible for commissioning and sponsoring evaluation has always been marked by issues of access and control to favour the systematic privatization of knowledge about public policy. The prospects of central government acting like a private corporation, defining their domestic interests in much the same way as IBM might define its commercial interests, is more than a little alarming. Access to knowledge about the conduct and effects of social policy is part of the process of checks and balances necessary for the maintance of democratic accountability and control. In Britain, at least, there is good reason to believe that the already tenuous public access to information is being yet further eroded.

Notes

1. *Times Educational Supplement*, 15/10/76 No 3202: 'DES report to Prime Minister sparks off angry protests.'
2. See: Lacey, C (1984) The Schools Council: an evaluation from a research perspective. In Skilbeck, M (ed.) *Evaluating the Curriculum in the Eighties*, London: Hodder & Stoughton, pp 157–64; and Bell, R & Prestcott, W (1975) *The Schools Council: A Second Look*, London: Ward Lock Educational, p 1.
3. The Unit had a staff of 11, four of whom were part-time. It had two heads: an HMI who was the professional head and an Assistant Secretary who was the administrative head. The Unit had two bodies, the Consultative Committee and the Statistics Advisory Group, to advise on research and survey matters. In its widest sense the APU also included monitoring teams at the NFER, Chelsea College and Leeds University. For a fuller account of the structure of the APU see: Dawson, J (1984) The work of the Assessment of Performance Unit. In Skilbeck, M (ed.) *Evaluating the Curriculum in the Eighties*, London: Hodder and Stoughton, pp 124–32.
4. MacDonald, B (1979) Hard times: educational accountability in England, *Educational Analysis*, **1**, 1, Summer, pp 23–43.
5. Gipps, C & Goldstein, H (1983) *Monitoring Children: An Evaluation of the Assessment of Performance Unit*, London: Heinemann Educational Books, p 174.
6. Ibid. p 6.
7. Ibid. p 7.
8. Gipps, C & Goldstein, H (1983) op. cit.
9. DES (1974) *Educational Disadvantage and the Educational Needs of Immigrants* (Cmnd 5720), London: HMSO.
10. See Gipps, C & Goldstein, H (1983) op. cit., especially Chapter 7.
11. See: Gorham, W (1967) Testing and public policy. In *Educational Testing Service Invitational Conference on Testing Problems*, Princeton, NJ: Educational Testing Services, pp 76–82.
12. MacDonald, B (1978) 'Accountability, standards and the process of schooling'. A paper commissioned by the Educational Research Board of the Social Science Research Council as part of a programme of seminars on accountability. In Becher, T & Maclure, S (ed.) *Accountability in Education*, Slough: NFER Pub Co, pp 127–51.
13. Gipps, C & Goldstein, H (1983) op. cit., p 63.
14. The Rasch model is a mathematical equation which describes how the probability of a correct response to an item in a test is related to two characteristics: one is the 'difficulty' of an item and the other is the assumed ability of the person

taking the test. The model supposes that the difficulty of each item is unchanging so that for every child tested, the items have the same ordering of difficulty. It also assumes that an individual's response is determined by a single trait. The decision to apply the Rasch model created considerable debate, much of which was technical. For an account of this see: Gipps, C & Goldstein, H (1983) op. cit., especially Chapter 4. Also see: Goldstein, H (1979) Consequences of using the Rasch model for educational assessment, *British Educational Research Journal*, **5**, 2, pp 211–20; Preece, PFW (1980) On rashly rejecting Rasch: a response to Goldstein. With a rejoinder from Goldstein, *British Educational Research Journal*, **6**, 2, pp 209–12; Goldstein, H & Blinkhorn, S (1982) The Rasch model still does not fit, *British Educational Research Journal*, **8**, 2, pp 167–70.

15. For an account of these changes, especially the introduction of Programme Analysis and Review (PAR), see: Heclo, H & Wildavesky, A (1974) *The Private Government of Public Money*, London: Macmillan Press. For a more recent analysis of developments in public sector accountability and control mechanisms under the Conservative administrations of the 1980s, see Hopwood, A & Tomkins, C (1984) (eds) *Issues in Public Sector Accounting*, Deddington: Phillip Allan.

16. Gipps, C & Goldstein, H (1983) op. cit., pp 161–2.

17. Callahan, RE (1962) *Education and the Cult of Efficiency*, University of Chicago Press, pp vii–viii.

18. Ibid. p viii.

19. Ibid. p 95.

20. For an analysis of Charles Murray's *Losing Ground*, New York: Basic Books (1985), see House, E & Madura, W (1987) *Race, Gender and Jobs — Losing Ground on Employment*, Laboratory for Policy Studies, School of Education, University of Colorado at Boulder.

21. House, E & Maduar, W (1987) op. cit., p 7.

22. For account of the long-term trends towards centralization see: Kaestle, CF & Smith, MS (1982) The federal role in elementary and secondary education, 1940–1980, *Harvard Educational Review*, **52**, 4, pp 384–408.

23. Cuban, L (1984) Transforming the frog into a prince: effective schools research, policy, and practice at the district level, *Harvard Educational Review*, **54**, 2, p 133.

24. Ibid. p 130.

25. Ibid.

26. Quoted in: Prakash, MS & Waks, LJ (1985) Four conceptions of excellence, *Teachers College Record*, **87**, 1, pp 79–101. See also: National Commission on Excellence in Education (1983) *A Nation at Risk: The Imperative for Educational Reform*, Washington DC: Government Printing Office.

27. See: Fetler, M (1986) Accountability in California public schools, *Educational Evaluation and Policy Analysis*, **8**, 1, pp 31–44.

28. Ibid.

29. For an account of effective schools research and efforts at school improvement in Britain see: Reid, K, Hopkins, D & Holly, P (1987) *Towards the Effective School*, Oxford: Basil Blackwell.

30. For an account of the Junior Schools Project see: ILEA Research and Statistics Branch *The Junior School Project: A Summary of the Main Project* (undated).

31. Ibid. pp. 33–8.

32. Ibid.

33. Kushner, S & MacDonald, B (1987) The limitations of programme evaluation. In Murphy, R & Torrance, H (eds) *Evaluating Education: Issues and Methods*, Harper & Row.

34. For various accounts of this kind of development in the theory of formative evaluation see: *Cambridge Journal of Education*, **16**, 2, summer term; a special edition entitled *Symbolism or Synergism? Curriculum Evaluation in the 1980s*. In particular see: Holly, P (1986) Developing a professional evaluation, pp 68–83.
35. Kushner, S & MacDonald, B (1987) op. cit.

Chapter 6
The Control of Evaluative Inquiry

Ten years ago it might have been presumed that all evaluations in accordance with the conventions and canons of responsible impartial reporting in research were independent in the conduct of their inquiry and dissemination of their products. Now there seems to be a need to establish the case.[1]

Independent evaluation

Helen Simons argued that in the context of programme evaluation independence means two things. First, it means that the evaluator should be free to report events and different value perspectives fairly, accurately and impartially. Second, it means that the evaluator should be free to make results assessible to all groups who have a right to knowledge about the programme.[2] In summary, Simons says that 'independence means being able to conduct an evaluation without fear or favour, not subscribing to any one vested interest or allowing oneself to be predisposed to the view of any one group.'[3] Of course not all conceptions of evaluation rest on the need for independence and not every situation demands a fully independent evaluation, but the evaluation of educational policies and programmes, however, belongs in the public domain as part of the process of democratic accountability. If programme evaluation is to provide a credible source of information to a range of audiences, then it needs to be conceived and conducted as an independent service for those who have a right to know.

In a recent review of the activities of the US General Accounting Office, its Deputy Director of Programme Evaluation and Methodology, Ray Rist, noted that any material produced by the Office that was not classified for reasons of national security was available free to the public. The role of the General Accounting Office is both that of a Congressional support agency and a centre for the independent evaluation of all aspects of the federal government. Its brief is to ensure that the activities of government are conducted in an efficient and effective manner, and it regularly conducts evaluations of federal policies, programmes and agencies.[4] Britain has no real parallel to the US General Accounting Office and even if it had, citizens would not necessarily have the right of access to its reports. Freedom of Information legislation is a significant political difference between the USA and Britain. As Walter Williams has observed in a short article comparing British and American policy analysis, a key element in the USA has been a bias against secrecy and towards supporting a process that both legitimized openness and facilitated the development of institutions necessary for its support.[5] Based on his experience of studying the organization and staffing of the Central Policy Review Staff, Williams concluded that the British concern for secrecy has limited the development of policy analysis and research both within and outside the government.[6] The separation of powers between the judiciary, executive and legislature that characterizes the American political system, provides a supportive environment for independent evaluation. By contrast, the relatively unified system of government, the lack of constitutional checks and balances, and the culture of administrative secrecy in Britain, seriously limit the possibilities for independent evaluation. At the risk of some oversimplification, independence is taken for granted in the USA whereas in Britain it is regarded as highly problematic.

Over the last 20 years there had been a shift in the control of educational inquiry away from the universities and nearer to centres of political power.[7] Helen Simons has argued that the severe financial pruning of higher education in the 1980s, threatens the conditions necessary for independent evaluation. In particular, she notes that academics desperately in need of funding are in a relatively weak position when it comes to negotiating their independence.[8] More recently, MacDonald has made a number of observations about changes in the political climate for independent inquiry: first, that the sponsorship of independently conceived research has largely been replaced by the commissioning of research along customer-contract lines, with the customer specifying the definition of the problem, claiming ownership of the data and discretion with regard to its utilization; second, academics now compete with private firms for research contracts; and third, success in the marketplace is beginning to replace publication as the currency of career advancement in higher education, and thus docility to stipulative constraints carries fewer penalties for the research community. What we have been witnessing is a shift from an independent to a consultancy relationship with government which is changing research services from a public to a private activity, and restricting research to questions of immediate practical utility and questions of concern to the powerful.[9]

Contractual control

The largest proportion of investment in externally funded social and educational inquiry is accounted for by government departments or agencies, and much of this research is policy-oriented rather than *curiosity-driven*.[10] It is hard to judge the extent of a tightening of control over the conception and dissemination of government-funded research, yet the general trend and experience suggests that it is becoming more difficult to secure adequate contractual arrangements for independent inquiry.

In 1980 Peter Willmott noted that over ten years of work with the Department of Environment, the conditions governing the publication of research findings had substantially changed from a position in 1972, where results were to be published 'freely in accordance with academic practice', to a position in 1980, where the Department had to approve drafts before publication 'although such approval would not be unreasonably withheld'.[11] Mirroring these developments within the Department of Environment, the conditions governing the publication of the results of Departments of Health and Social Security funded research have recently changed. Prior to 1987, DHSS research contracts stated that 'papers and reports should be submitted to DHSS for comment at least 28 days before the intended date for submission to a journal', but the contract also stated that the researcher 'shall nevertheless be free to allow publication to go forward as he thinks fit'. The revised conditions for Department of Health funded research now include a clause stating that: 'any publication or research material or results of research . . . or of matters from arising such material or results is subject to the prior consent of the Secretary of State, which consent shall not be unreasonably withheld', although it may be conditional.[12] The Society for Social Medicine, in seeking clarification from the DHSS on the need for such changes, were informed by the Department that they were necessary because of the Secretary of State's responsibilities for Crown Copyright and because previous contractual conditions 'left him with little or no control over the use and publication of research work . . . commissioned and paid for on his behalf'.[13]

A recent contract between the Department of Trade and Industry and a university for an independent evaluation of a research and development programme in educational technology, provided another example of similar contractual conditions regulating the dissemination of research. The contract specified that:

> The [university] may retain copies of the information produced or collected pursuant to the investigation but shall not publish such information and shall not exploit any such information commercially without the consent of the Secretary of State given in writing to such publication or exploitation, which consent may be conditional but not unreasonably withheld.[14]

The contract also gave the Secretary of State wide-ranging powers to terminate payment of the grant to make the grant repayable if he considered progress to be unsatisfactory.[15] An example of the conditions governing publications arising from research funded by the Department of Employment can be seen from a contract letter (1988) covering a small grant from the DE to a university Department of Education:

> The results of any research are the property of the Department. It is not expected that any publications will arise directly from the results of the research but any publication by research workers of or arising from these results is subject to the agreement of the Department, which will not be unreasonably withheld.[16]

In this instance the contract also specified that it was 'not intended to restrict the freedom of the research workers to publish material directly emanating from the research or drawing on this material, in accordance with academic practice'.[17]

A typical MSC (now the Training Agency) contract for educational research included various statements to the effect that material produced from the research is Crown copyright. The Commission's research contracts also included clauses restricting the dissemination of research products without prior consultation with and the written permission of the Commission. The Commission does say that it will not unreasonably withhold permission, but in one contract with a university it indicated that such permission would be subject to further agreement with HMSO.[18] The MSC seemed to use standard conditions which were amended to fit the circumstances of particular projects. A recent contract between the Commission and a higher education institution included a clause allowing the inclusion of material arising from the research project in a thesis prepared by any team member. The contract also stated that copies deposited in the library could be made available to readers only with the permission of the Director of the institution and then only after consultation with the Commission. These restrictions were to last for one year after the thesis had been deposited in the library.[19]

The Health Education Authority's Rules Governing the Payment of Grants (April 1987) provide some of the stringent conditions covering the dissemination of research. The rules state that:

> No information concerning work undertaken by the grant-holders at the Authority's expense my be published or released to the press in any form without the prior agreement of the HEA project officers. The term 'published' is defined as 'the communication of such information to anyone other than the staff of the grant-holding institution or of the HEA, or to recognized workers in the same field of inquiry, who shall in their turn be required to observe confidentiality as a condition of receipt of such information'.
>
> The grant-holder will therefore not release any information to the press or to broadcasters without first consulting the Authority, through the HEA project officer. Where the academic institution concerned has a Press and Public Relations Officer, the latter must be informed of this rule as soon as the contract is signed.[20]

The Authority also reserves the right to determine whether any patents should be taken out on work arising from their grants and claims copyright.

The Home Office's Standard Provisions Governing Research Agreements have in the past been rather different in tone from other government departments. While ensuring that the results of Home Office sponsored research are the 'property of the Secretary of State', it is acknowledged that the results of work 'should be published in accordance with academic practice', but before any publication the Research Body is required to consult with the Secretary of State.[21] Those undertaking research for the Home Office, however, may well be required to sign the Official Secrets Act.

An examination of changes to the standard terms and conditions for Department of Education and Science funded research provide particular cause for concern. In 1978, for example, the DES Standard Agreement (Form P2) made no mention of any conditions or restrictions governing the dissemination of research reports.[22] By 1985, the DES *Form P2 Standard Contract* had been revised to include the following conditions:

[1] Copyright and rights in the nature of copyright in the materials produced in the performance and during the currency of this contract shall vest in the Crown.

[2] The said materials shall not be reproduced or disseminated . . . without prior consultation with the Secretary of State and the written permission of the Secretary of State and the Controller of Her Majesty's Stationery Office. Nor shall the said materials be used for the purpose of developing any further materials or for any other purpose whatsoever without prior consultation with and the written permission of the Secretary of State and the Controller of Her Majesty's Stationery Office.

[3] The Secretary of State shall be consulted before any written statement paper or press notice is published, or press or other conference held, in connection with the project or the said materials. A draft of any such written statement, paper or press notice shall be sent to the Secretary of State in sufficient time to allow him a reasonable opportunity to comment on it before the proposed date of publication, any such statement shall be subject to his approval.[23]

What is noticeable about new DES contracts is that they do not even include a statement to the effect that permission for publication 'will not be unreasonably withheld'. Moreover, current DES contracts also state that the research body shall furnish the Secretary of State with 'such material or data prepared, or information collected, for the purposes of the project as he may describe or specify',[24] thus establishing not only the Department's control over publication but also over access to data.

By contrast with these trends in England and Wales, the Scottish Education Department's (SED, April 1987) standard conditions for research currently provided for much less government control over dissemination and publication. Although the Department reserves the right to claim Crown copyright on research reports or materials, it formally states that it 'envisages such cases will be few in number' and that in all other cases copyright would be held by the grant-holding institution.[25] It is also revealing to contrast the Economic and Social Research Council's standard conditions governing research awards with other national funding agencies. The ESRC clearly state that grant holders should 'give priority to publicizing and disseminating the findings of ESRC-funded research'. The ESRC also emphasizes the importance of dissemination to potential users and non-academic audiences, as well as other researchers.[26]

As is evident from these examples of research contracts, a recurrent theme is the responsibility of government departments to protect the copyright and commercial interests of Her Majesty's Stationery Office. The SED and Home Office Standard Conditions reveal that this can be achieved without recourse to the inclusion of powers additional to those implied by Crown copyright and in ways that do not unduly restrict public access to research. Yet even these two departments are likely to bring their contractual conditions for funded research and evaluation into line with the majority of governmental departments. Given the frequent use of conditions requiring researchers to obtain the Secretary of State's permission to publish or communicate findings, it is difficult not to conclude that such powers have been introduced to provide some explicit measure of control over the dissemination of research. It ought to be noted, however, that in some cases what appears to be new powers may well be old powers that are only now being given emphasis.

The political control of public knowledge

There is nothing new about specific attempts to control the publication of reports and restrict public access to information about policy. What is surprising is that political control should be embodied in general contractual terms and conditions. There are, no doubt, those who would argue that when a contract includes a clause to the effect that permission to publish will not be unreasonably withheld, the notion of reasonableness offers a sufficient guarantee of independence. Much depends upon whether the onus is on the researcher to prove unreasonableness or on the government department to demonstrate good cause for withholding consent. It is noticeable that DES, the major funder of educational research and evaluation, does not include any clauses offering even minimal assurances about publication in accordance with academic practice.

Naturally, the assumption is that government departments will use their powers only in exceptional cases, and even if they were tempted to use them more often would be dissuaded from doing so by the potential for drawing attention to the issue. The contractual power to withhold consent for publication does not have to be used in order to have an effect, however. In an academic climate where individual promotion and prestige, as well as departmental ratings on performance measures, depend on recognized publications and research contracts, there are obvious pressures towards self-censorship. In the current competitive climate of the 1990s, researchers need to weigh carefully the possible reactions of sponsors to the scope of the inquiry and to unfavourable or inexpedient reports. The consequences of loss of patronage can extend well beyond the loss of prestige, status and research opportunities. Research contracts generate non-tenured employment, which in turn generates social and moral obligations towards the individuals concerned. The point is that power does not have to be used to be a constraint on the independence of researchers to report openly on the effects of public programmes and policies.

Notes

1. Simons, H (1984) Negotiating conditions for independent evaluations. In Adelman, C (ed.) *The Politics and Ethics of Evaluation,* London: Croom Helm, p 56.
2. Ibid. p 57.
3. Ibid. p 58.
4. Rist, RC (1987) Social science analysis and Congressional uses: the case of the United States General Accounting Office. In Bulmer, M (ed.) *Social Science Research and Government: Comparative essays on Britain and the United States,* Cambridge University Press, pp 303–17.
5. Williams, W (1983) British policy analysis: some preliminary observations from the US. In Gray, A & Jenkins, B (ed.) *Policy Analysis and Evaluation in British Government,* London: Royal Institute of Public Administration, pp 17–24.
6. Ibid. p 22.
7. MacDonald, B (1982) *Educational Evaluation in the Contemporary World.* Invited presentation to the Symposium Internacional De Didactica Generla y Didacticas Especiales, La Manga del Mar Menor, Spain, 27 September–2 October 1982. Mimeo, Norwich: Centre for Applied Research in Education, University of East Anglia.
8. Simons, H (1987) *Getting to Know Schools in a Democracy: The Politics and Process of Evaluation,* London: Falmer Press, p 252.
9. MacDonald, B (1987) 'Research and action in the context of policing'. A paper commissioned by the Police Foundation. Norwich: Centre for Applied Research in Education, University of East Anglia.
10. Taylor, W (1985) The organization and funding of educational research in England and Wales. In Nisbet, J (ed.) *World Yearbook of Education 1985: Research, Policy and Practice,* London: Kogan Page, pp 42–67.
11. Willmott, P (1980) A view from an independent research institute. In Cross, M (ed.) *Social Research and Public Policy: Three Perspectives,* London: Social Research Association.
12. An account of these changes are detailed in: Boddy, A (1988) 'DHSS Research Contracts'. Internal briefing document for the Society for Social Medicine.
13. Ibid.
14. Department of Trade and Industry letter of contract, 1987. The letter appears to be based on a standard terms and conditions used for DTI commercial contracts.
15. The contract states that: 'The Secretary of State shall be under no obligation to pay the grant, and any grant already paid may become repayable, in whole or in part, at his discretion, if: – [i] he considers that the future of the investigation is in jeopardy; [ii] in his opinion, progress towards completion of the investigation is unsatisfactory of if the investigation is not completed by 30 September 1988; [iii] there is a change in the nature or scale of the investigation which in the opinion of the Secretary of State is substantial; [iv] the University . . . does not comply with, or observe, the condition of this letter.'
16. Department of Employment letter of contract, 1988.
17. Ibid.
18. Agreement between the Manpower Services Commission and a university 1987. The contract states that : 'Copyright and rights in the nature of copyright in the materials produced in the performance and during the currency of this Agreement by using the funds provided by the Commission shall vest in the Crown. The said materials shall not be reproduced or disseminated in the United Kingdom

or elsewhere without prior consultation with and the written permission of the Commission. Nor shall the said material be used either for the purpose of developing any further materials or for any purpose whatsoever without prior consultation with and the written permission of the Commission. The Commission will not unreasonably withhold permission although this will be subject to a further agreement between the MSC, HMSO and the researchers. Permission may however involve the payment of fees/royalties.'

19. Agreement between the Manpower Service Commission and an institution of higher education, 1986.
20. The Health Education Authority (1987) *Rules Governing the Payment of Grants*, April, pp 4–5, clauses 30 and 31.
21. Home Office, *Standard Provisions Governing Research Agreements Between the Secretary of State for the Home Department and Research Bodies*. While these provisions provide a more reasonable framework for the dissemination of research, some Home Office contracts also specify that the Research Body ensures that persons engaged on the work sign a declaration (Form E 74) that they understand that the Official Secrets Act applies to them and will continue to apply after completition or termination of the Agreement.
22. Department of Education and Science (1978) *Form P2 Standard Agreement*, August.
23. Department of Education and Science (1985) *Form P2 (Revised) Standard Contract (FP)*, January.
24. Ibid. p 4, clause 10.
25. Scottish Education Department (1987) *Standard Conditions Governing the Award of Major Education Research and Development Grants* (Form RES2 Revised April 1987).
26. Economic and Social Research Council (1988) *ESRC Research Funding*. See: Part 4, para 132, p 12.

Part 3
The Way We Think About Evaluation

Chapter 7
Theories of Evaluation

Evaluation and research

It is generally assumed that evaluation is the application of research methods to elucidate a problem of action. Looked at in this way evaluation is not strikingly different from research. For those theorists and practitioners who see evaluation as a separate undertaking to research, there is clearly a problem in providing an adequate account of the difference between them. One reason why it might be important to pursue the distinction between research and evaluation is that our general perceptions of their similarities and differences will influence the way we conceive of the definition, design, conduct and reporting of empirical enquiry in education.

There are those who would see the difference between evaluation and research as one of purpose and degree. From this perspective evaluation is an extension of research, sharing its methods and methodology and demanding similar skills and qualities from its practitioners. The continuity thesis probably remains the most pervasive and persuasive view among educational researchers and evaluators alike, finding concrete expression in the term 'evaluation research'. Why should evaluation be considered as in essence different from research? After all, evaluators are called upon to assess the effectiveness of social and educational programmes precisely because of the social authority of research. Marilyn Brewer describes the position rather well when she writes:

> The original proponents of evaluation research clearly recognized that the purposes of such research were different from those of basic science. Yet the basic concept of the field was that of extending the scientific model into the domain of policy-making, and adherence to the traditions of scientific methodology was the hall mark of evaluation research, distinguishing it from other forms of political fact-finding.[1]

If evaluation is an extension of the logic of research and an application of its methods to practical problems, what follows is that the domain of inquiry — the particular programme or policy — has to be conceived in ways that make it amenable to methodology. So, for example, in much evaluation research a programme is construed an an experiment, its aims are operationally specified, its work described with reference to observable and measurable characteristics, questions about its effectiveness are seen in terms of causal hypothesis testing, and the evaluation is judged good or bad on the validity of its conclusions. In an important sense, the programme or policy is defined by the methodology of research. While acknowledging the political and administrative difficulties involved in treating social policies as experiments, there are many who regard such difficulties as largely technical problems of design — how best to apply existing methods to the uncontrolled variation that is typical of programmes. Donald Campbell, for example, recommends that if reforms must be introduced across the board then interrupted time-series designs are available; while Lee J Cronbach, taking issues with the conventional view of the primacy of eliminating threats to internal validity, has devoted much of his recent work to specifying an algebra for designing evaluations that pay more attention to need for external inference.[2]

Not everyone, of course, shares the continuity thesis. Gene Glass and Blaine Worthen, for example, have argued that while educational research and evaluation have much in common, the practice of evaluation is not well served by treating it as a subset of research. In an attempt to provide the basis for an adequate theory of evaluation, they outlined the following 11 characteristics of inquiry that distinguish evaluation from research:

1. *the motivation of the inquirer* — research is pursued largely to satisfy curiosity, evaluation is undertaken to contribute to the solution of a problem;
2. *the objectives of the search* — research and evaluation seek different ends. Research seeks conclusions, evaluation leads to decisions;
3. *laws versus description* — research is the quest for laws (nomothetic), evaluation merely seeks to describe a particular thing (idiographic);
4. *the role of explanation* — proper and useful evaluation can be conducted without producing an explanation of why the product or project is good or bad or of how it operates to produce its effects;
5. *the autonomy of the inquiry* — evaluation is undertaken at the behest of a client, while researchers set their own problems;
6. *properties of the phenomena that are assessed* — evaluation seeks to assess social utility directly, research may yield evidence of social utility but often only indirectly;
7. *universality of the phenomena studied* — researchers work with constructs having a currency and scope of application that make the objects of evaluation seem parochial by comparison;
8. *salience of the value question* — in evaluation value questions are central and usually determine what information is sought;
9. *investigative techniques* — while there may be legitimate differences between research and evaluation methods, there are far more similarities than differences with regard to techniques and procedures for judging validity;

10. *criteria for assessing the activity* — the two most important criteria for judging the adequacy of research are internal and external validity, for evaluation they are utility and credibility;
11. *disciplinary base* — the researcher can afford to pursue inquiry within one discipline and the evaluator cannot.[3]

Glass and Worthen's analysis starts from a conceptual reconstruction of scientific research. They take as their definition of research: 'the activity aimed at obtaining generalizable knowledge by contriving and testing claims about relationships among variables or describing generalizable phenomena', and much follows from their discussion of the motivation for inquiry and the role of explanation.[4] While fairly typical of efforts to distinguish evaluation from research, their analysis is based on a misleading account of science and a rather arcane view of educational research confined to a textbook version of methodology. Their account of the process of explanation, for example, is derived solely from the natural sciences and provides a very restricted view of educational research, taking no account of the role of theory or contributory disciplines other than experimental psychology. Their argument that researchers work with universal constructs while evaluators focus on particular objects, rather obscures the fact that evaluators also employ and develop constructs — such as, intelligence, motivation, readiness, reinforcement, social class — when examining the effects of educational programmes. However, the crucial inadequacy of their analysis is that it ignores the social context of educational inquiry, the hierarchic nature of research communities, the reward structure of universities, the role of central governments in supporting certain projects and not others, and the long-established relationships between social research and reform. It is, in short, an asocial and ahistorical account.

Another evaluation theorist who has cautioned against subscribing too readily to the continuity thesis is Barry MacDonald. He argues that the position of the evaluator is quite distinct and much more complex than the position of the researcher.[5] For MacDonald a crucial difference is that the researcher 'is free to select his questions, and to seek answers to them'. The research will 'naturally select questions which are susceptible to the problem-solving techniques of his craft — in a sense he uses his instruments to define his problems'.[6] Conversely, the evaluator, according to MacDonald:

> must never fall into the error of answering questions which no one but he is asking. He must first identify the significant questions, and only then address the technological questions which they raise. To limit his inquiries to those which satisfy the critical canons of conventional research is to run a serious risk of failing to match the 'vocabulary of action' of the decision-maker . . . The danger, therefore of conceptualizing evaluation as a branch of research is that evaluators become trapped in the restrictive tentacles of research respectability.[7]

MacDonald's distinction between evaluation and research is based on his analysis of the political role of evaluation — in particular the need to feed the judgements of a range of non-specialist audiences in forms that reflect their ways of knowing. In his view it could be much more productive 'to define research as a branch of evaluation — a branch whose task it is to solve the technological problems encountered by the evaluator'.[8]

While it may be the case that evaluators can become trapped by conventional research, nonetheless both the evaluation and research community tend to appeal to the cultural superiority of science and instrumental values as sources of legitimation. Evaluators appeal to notions of truth and validity to no lesser extent than researchers, not least for reasons of political expediency. Equally researchers appeal to instrumental values for reasons of survival and conscience. The public purse, especially of late, is not easily prised open by purely aesthetic interests in truth, no more than evaluators are immune from public and professional criticisms of their methodology and methods.

Providing a satisfactory and convincing account of the difference between research and evaluation is a difficult task. Clearly, educational research and educational evaluation have much in common; by and large, for example, we are not speaking of separate communities of researchers and evaluators. Evaluation is not isolated from general developments in educational research nor is it necessarily the case that the interests of evaluation are different from those of research. Educational research is often described as a form of applied research aimed at improving practice; or as Stenhouse, hopefully, conceived it: 'educational research has as its overriding aim the support of educational acts'.[9] If this is or should be so, then distinctions between educational research and evaluation based on the abstract ideals of pure research are unlikely to prove instructive.

In trying to distinguish evaluation from research an important question is whether to begin from an idealist (prescriptive) or realist (descriptive) account of the activities. One serious problem is that we lack closely observed descriptive studies of the conduct of either educational research or educational evaluation. Instead we have sanitized accounts of the research process or introductory texts and primers offering rational reconstructions of what are seen as the necessary steps and processes of scientific inquiry. The problem is that we rarely get beyond those idealized representations to accounts of the process of educational research, let alone to an adequate theory that integrates the prescriptive and descriptive elements of methodology. The task of developing an adequate theory of evaluation will not be well served by mythologizing the practice of research and mistaking rational reconstruction for reality. Clearly, we need to take care that when attempting to locate the differences and similarities between educational research and evaluation, we are not simply comparing recipes or textbooks. In the absence of a descriptive theory or theories of educational research, discussions about differences and similarities need to proceed with some caution.

When speaking of 'educational' research and evaluation, we are in fact referring to a diverse range of practices that have been influenced greatly by methodological customs and traditions outside education — most notably from biology, psychology, anthropology and sociology. In any event, in so far as educational research is aimed ultimately at improving practice, it is difficult to see how this aim does not imply some kind of evaluation.

Increasingly, resources for educational research are directed towards questions and tasks that are determined not by the curiosity of researchers or the needs of teachers and students, but by the demands of governments for solutions to centrally defined problems. Under the present conditions there can be little doubt that government will continue to provide most of the total budget for educational research. The political agenda may change, but the demand for problem-oriented policy-related research and information is unlikely to diminish. In this and other respects there may be significant similarities between contemporary research and evaluation, suggesting that educational research is becoming more evaluative in character.

Evaluation and decision-making

One commonplace way of thinking about evaluation is with reference to its objects. In education we talk, for example, of curriculum evaluation, course evaluation, teacher evaluation, and of project and programme evaluation, where the noun/adjective refers to the class of objects to be evaluated. This system of classification suggests a relationship between the nature of the object and the form its evaluation should take. Different kinds of object demand different kinds of evaluation, or to express the relationship more formally we could say that the object of evaluation stands in a determinant relationship to the methodology of evaluation. Many evaluation theorists would agree that the form of an evaluation should reflect the nature and circumstances of the project or programme to be evaluated. For example, Michael Patton suggests that good evaluations are characterized by 'situational responsiveness'; and Lee J Cronbach has argued that designing an evaluation is an art and that each new design 'must be chosen afresh in each new undertaking'.[10]

Most definitions of evaluation suggest that its purpose is to conceive, obtain and provide information which decision-makers in their many forms (voters, opinion-leaders, stakeholders, policy-makers, social planners or administrators) can use to make decisions about the future of specificied programmes or policies. The everyday rhetoric of evaluation is utilitarian, consensual and ameliorative. Carol Weiss, for example, writing about the American tradition of evaluation research has argued that a basic assumption for evaluators is that 'careful and unbiased data on the consequences of programs should improve decision-making', and 'by providing "the facts", evaluation assists decision-makers to make wise choices among future courses of action.'[11] Keith Cooper, writing about the different definitions and boundaries of project evaluation, suggested that a useful formulation for a curriculum evaluation was: 'the collection and provision of evidence, on the basis of which decisions can be taken about the feasibility, effectiveness and educational value of curricula'.[12] David Tawney, considering the evaluations of Schools Council projects, argued that the task of providing decision-makers with information 'is made harder because we lack understanding of the decision-making process'.[13] Yet he still emphasized that the primary task of the evaluator was to 'help decision-making be as rational and as open as possible', and to do this evaluators should 'provide information and help the decision-makers explore both their own value positions and the options open to them'.[14] From a similar stable of Schools Council project evaluators, Barry MacDonald, when designing the evaluation of a development programme in computer-assisted learning, defined evaluation as: 'the process of conceiving, obtaining, and communicating information for the guidance of educational decision-making with regard to a specified programme'.[15] Other evaluation practitioners and theorists, for example, Stufflebeam et al. (1971); Anderson, Ball, Murphy and Associates (1973); Parlett and Hamilton (1977); Patton (1978); Alkin, Daillak and White (1979); Edwards, Guttentag, and Snapper (1983); Alkin and Associates (1985), to name but a few, have all emphasized some form of relationship between evaluation and decision-making. Whether formative or summative evaluation is being considered, it is generally assumed that evaluation should ascertain and provide useful information for judging decision alternatives; or that an evaluation study is one that is designed to assist an audience or audiences to judge and improve the worth of some educational object and can be used by significant actors to improve policies and programmes.

Models, approaches and philosophical orientations

Another way of classifying evaluation is by conceptual approach and orientation. Many kinds of models of evaluation have been adumbrated by different reviewers of the field. Worthen and Sanders (1973), for example, present eight models of evaluation labelling them by their authors or advocates; Stake (1976) lists nine separate approaches; while House (1980), making extensive use of earlier classifications, presents an eight-category taxonomy of major evaluation approaches (systems analysis, behavioural objectives, decision-making, goal-free, art criticism, professional review, quasi-legal and case study) which he describes and differentiates in terms of the audiences to which the evaluation is addressed, the issues upon which they assume there is consensus, methodological assumptions, intended outcomes and the typical questions they try and answer.

It has become common to think about approaches to evaluation in terms of a set of methodological or epistemological differences — interpretive versus technical, qualitative versus quantitative, idiographic versus nomothetic, agricultural-botany pradigm versus the social anthropological paradigm, cases versus samples, naturalistic versus scientific — that divide practitioners and theorists into philosophical camps of different intellectual traditions and apparent world-views. William Filstead, for instance, contrasts what he calls the qualitative and quantitative paradigms, claiming that at the heart of the distinction between them 'lies the classic argument in philosophy between the schools of realism and idealism'.[16] Donald Campbell also writes of the controversy between quantitative and qualitative modes of knowing, contrasting humanistic with scientific approaches to evaluation.[17] Egon Guba and Yvonna Lincoln make a similar distinction when they contrast what they call the scientific and naturalistic paradigms.[18]

A different kind of paradigmatic analysis, this one based on the social epistemology of Jurgen Habermas, is offered by Walter Werner.[19] He begins from the premise that evaluation is a sense-making activity and that the kind of sense that is made of a programme or setting depends upon the interpretive schema (the paradigm) that the evaluator brings to the case. Werner draws from Habermas' analysis of the connections between knowledge and human interests in deriving three major paradigms that provide different sense-making activities in evaluation: ends-means, situational, and critical forms of sense-making, each of which is roughly synonomous with Habermas' three forms of knowledge-constitutive interests.[20]

The 'ends-means paradigm' corresponds to the empirical analytic constitutive interests articulated by Habermas. According to Habermas, such an interest discloses reality from the perspective of possible technical control over the objectified processes of nature. From this perspective evaluation activities focus on the means (ie, teaching methods or materials) to the ends (ie, objectives or intended outcomes). The ends-means paradigm can be described as technical or technological in orientation and the consequent system of evaluation is based on the values of control, certainty, efficiency, precision, cost-effectiveness, predictability, standardization and speed.[21] Within this paradigm problems are defined in terms of the gap between the ideal and the actual. Data for problem analysis is defined as that which increases control within the system and only data that can be manipulated are deemed relevant. For Werner each paradigm makes assumptions about the nature of programmes and appropriate criteria of worth. Within the ends-means paradigm an educational project or programme is defined as a statement of intended outcomes together with the methods and techniques for their achievement, and judgements about worth are based on measures of goal attainment. Also for Werner, any evaluation activity will have an implied view of social relationships which he defines as the relationship between the evaluator and the evaluated. Within the means-ends paradigm the nature of the relationship, he claims, is determined by the evaluator's differential access to specialized knowledge. The evaluator is the sole producer of knowledge, the evaluated are the consumers or objects of knowledge.

The 'situational paradigm' corresponds to the interpretive (hermeneutic) constitutive interests discussed by Habermas. According to Habermas, such an interest discloses reality from the perspective of the understanding of meaning. The evaluator working from this purview is concerned to uncover the meanings of an educational programme and the activity of evaluation can be viewed as the situational interpretation of educational action. The situational paradigm sees programmes as interpreted differently by different people or groups. The programme has no unequivocal definition and worth is judged on the basis of its relevance and meaningfulness to the various participants. According to Werner, from the perspective of the situational paradigm 'there is no one program as defined by the master curriculum plan but as many programs as there are groups interpreting and experiencing something they refer to as a "program" in different situations.'[22] Relationships between the evaluator and the evaluated are characterized by Werner as a form of balanced reciprocity where each bring their own, equally valuable, expertise and knowledge to the evaluation.

The 'critical paradigm' corresponds to the critical-theoretic constitutive interests outlined by Habermas, and goes beyond the goals of description, interpretive understanding and nomological knowledge to determine:

> when theoretical statements grasp invariant regularities of social action as such and when they express ideologically frozen relations of dependence that can in principle be transformed.[23]

The methodological framework for this paradigm is critical self-reflection. According to Werner, the evaluator working within this paradigm tries to uncover the foundations of the programme and makes problematic that which is taken for granted.[24] The primary aim of the critical sense-making paradigm is that educators be self-reflective and aware of the beliefs that inform everyday practice. This paradigm suggests that programmes are a set of assumptions, beliefs and values which unfold and are latent in the activities of educators or programme personnel. The implied view of worth that Werner uses to delineate the other two paradigms does not feature in the critical paradigm. The implied view of social relations Werner describes as mutual self-reflection and he likens the role of the evaluator to that of a 'therapist' or 'psycho-analyst'.[25]

Evaluation as political action

The analysis of social inquiry in terms of the connection between knowledge and interests, highlights the importance of political as well as methodological values to our understanding of educational evaluation. Few theorists who have thought in these terms have tried to make explicit the political implications of different paradigms, preferring instead to concentrate on the match between paradigm, methodology and constructions of social reality. Both Ernest House and Barry MacDonald, however, have, with some consistency, pursued a political analysis of evaluation — an analysis which at times touches on the debate about the relationships between interests, paradigms and methodology.

MacDonald has provided us with a political classification of evaluation in terms of the selection of roles, goals, audiences, issues and techniques.[26] He describes three types of evaluation — bureaucratic, autocratic and democratic — each of which have a distinctive political orientation. The tripod of bureaucratic, autocratic and democratic evaluation is set out as ideal types against which we can compare intended or actual evaluative studies. The typology has proved to be both heuristically and theoretically useful. It indicates, for example, the elements in evaluation studies that give clues to the political interests represented in the choice and form of approach. MacDonald classifies evaluations according to the way in which they define their 'service role, value orientations, techniques, criteria of evaluation success, and their forms of independence and justification'. Empirically evaluation studies can be classified in terms of the degree to which they approximate one of these ideal types. The very choice of labels and indicators, however, makes explicit the type we should be working towards in a democratic society. The typology attempts to provide a political conception of evaluation and outline the principles for its moral justification. It is thus a system of classification with a moral imperative but it also provides a political language with which to describe evaluation.

Like House, MacDonald is concerned not only with articulating a role and procedure for evaluation that maximizes democratic values and empowers citizens as well as the managers of social programmes, he is also explicitly concerned about the fairness and distributive consequences of educational policies and policy-making. It is this concern that has led him to claim that there is no policy evaluation since:

> what we have by and large is evaluation of the effects of policy upon those
> who are declared to be its intended beneficiaries. We evaluate the instruments
> of policy, the programs of social action that emanate from agency offices . . .
> We evaluate the managed, not the managers; the objects of policy and not
> the originators; the 'have nots', not the 'haves'.[27]

For MacDonald, if evaluation is concerned with choices between alternatives then it should concern choices between policies and choices between policy-making processes — that is, political evaluation.[28]

Ernest House begins from a somewhat different position and, to a certain extent, his analysis is more thorough. Like MacDonald, he is sceptical of the faith that the evaluation community and social managers place in abstract notions of science. House sees the presentation of evaluative evidence as acts of persuasion. His reasons for this are twofold. First, he argues that science produces more or less credible arguments not certainty, and if this is so for the physical sciences it is even more the case for educational evaluation.[29] Second, he argues that if evaluation was confined to producing knowledge by the application of textbook scientific methodology relying strictly on inductive and deductive reasoning, then evaluators would have to abandon a great deal of the reasoning power people ordinarily use in the conduct of their lives.[30] According to House, 'such a limitation results from confusing rationality with logic' and 'in place of compelling propositions derived from rigorous logic, one may substitute the non-compelling arguments of persuasion'.[31] House is particularly concerned with the moral consequences of this epistemological position. He argues that if evaluative information is not compelling then audiences are free to choose their own degrees of commitment; the rational decision belongs to them and not the evaluator, and there are considerations other than just objectivity that should govern the design and conduct of evaluation.

At the heart of House's political analysis lie the concepts of interests and power, and here he relies to a large measure on the work of the social theorist Steven Lukes.[32] House is critical of liberal 'pluralist' approaches — democratic and responsive evaluation — because, he claims, they discriminate against certain kinds of issues, assume that interests are subjective wants to be understood as actual policy preferences, and face serious difficulties in identifying the common good. By contrast, a 'reformist' view of power and interests, while still conceiving of interests as observable subjective wants, would emphasize the differential opportunities that groups have to place their values and interests on the political agenda. Furthermore, a 'radical' view of power would emphasize the structural biases inherent in social arrangements that constrain the articulation of real as opposed to subjective interests — a view of power based on notions of false consciousness or the absence of genuine consensus. It is this last view of power and interests that informs House's political analysis and his reformulation of democratic approaches to evaluation. In a hopeful resolution of the problem of determining real interests, House says:

> The position I have taken is that 'real' interests may be discovered through a particular form of participation, one which gives the individual choice under conditions of autonomy . . . This moves towards defining 'real' interests or what the individual would define autonomously, the radical position, but retains individual choice itself. The individual can discover his real interests through participating with others in deciding the evaluation.[33]

In summary, House proposes the following four basic values that should serve as the moral basis of evaluation:

1. moral equality — that all people are to be taken as members of the same reference group and are consequently to be treated equally;
2. moral autonomy — that no one should impose his will on others by force or coercion or by other illegitimate means;
3. impartiality — conflicts of wants and interests are to be settled impartially, that is, by having all interests represented and none favoured by whatever decision procedure is employed;
4. reciprocity — that there should be no priviledged positions among people; treating others as one would be treated.[34]

He is primarily concerned with articulating the basis for valid and just evaluations that represent the relevant interests, and that anticipate (and are symmetrical with) rational, participatory and democratic forms of policy-making based on unfettered and informed discourse. Although sharing a primary interest in fairness, MacDonald appears more concerned with the realisation of democratic values, with revealing the process of policy-making and evaluating its adequacy for the purposes and intents of a democratic society. His is a focus on access to policy-making and decision-making in a political and administrative culture that is representative, paternalistic and above all secret.

The extent of the global village makes it all too easy to forget how much of our thinking about evaluation is conditioned by the practical and political circumstances in which both practitioners and theorists live and work. There are significant differences between American and British evaluation theorists, reflecting different political cultures and constitutional arrangements, different political relationships between the university and the polity, and different attitudes and commitments to planned social change. Just as educational programmes are context-bound, occurring in particular circumstances and times, so too are theories of educational evaluation. In this respect theories of evaluation — especially political theories — may be less transferable and more prone to decay than we customarily recognize.

Notes

1. Brewer, MB (1983) Evaluation: past and present. In Struening, EL & Brewer, MB (eds) *The University Edition of the Handbook of Evaluation Research*, Beverly Hills, Cal: Sage, p 16.
2. See: Cronbach, LJ (1983) *Designing Evaluations of Educational and Social Programmes*, San Francisco: Jossey-Bass Pub. Also see: Campbell, DT (1983) Reforms as experiments. In Struening, EL & Brewer, MB (eds) *The University Edition of the Handbook of Evaluation Research*, Beverly Hills, Cal: Sage, pp 107–37.
3. Glass, GV & Worthen, BR (1971) Evaluation and research: similarities and differences. In *Curriculum Theory Network*, Fall, pp 149–65. Also see Worthen, BR & Sanders, JR (1973) *Educational Evaluation: Theory and Practice*, Belmont, Cal: Wadsworth Pub Co, especially Chapter 2 — 'Evaluation as Disciplined Inquiry', pp 10–40.
4. Glass, GV & Worthen, BR (1971) op. cit., p 150.
5. MacDonald, B (1976) Evaluation and the control of education. In Tawney, D (ed.) *Curriculum Evaluation Today: Trends and Implications*, London: Macmillan Educational, pp 125–36.
6. Ibid. p 130.
7. Ibid. pp 131–2.
8. Ibid.
9. Stenhouse, LS (1980) The study of samples and the study of cases, *British Educational Research Journal*, **6**, 1, pp 1–6.
10. See: Patton, QM (1981) *Creative Evaluation*, Beverly Hills, Cal: Sage, p 277. And, Cronbach, LJ (1982) *Designing Evaluations of Educational and Social Programs*, San Francsico: Jossey-Bass, p 1.
11. Weiss, CH (1983) Evaluation research in the political context. In Struening, EL & Brewer, MB (eds) *Handbook of Evaluation Research*, Beverly Hills, Cal: Sage, pp 31–45.
12. Cooper, K (1976) Curriculum evaluation — definition and boundaries. In Tawney, D (ed.) *Curriculum Evaluation Today: Trends and Implications*, London: Macmillan Educational, pp 1–10.

13. Tawney, D (1976) Evaluation — information for decision-makers. In Tawney, D (ed.) *Curriculum Evaluation Today: Trends and Implications*, London: Macmillan Educational, pp 11–28.

14. Ibid. p 14.

15. See: MacDonald, B et al. (1975) *The Programme at Two*, Norwich: Centre for Applied Research in Education, University of East Anglia, p 5.

16. Filstead, WJ (1979) Qualitative methods: a needed perspective in evaluation research. In Cook, TD & Reichardt, CS *Qualitative and Quantitative Methods in Evaluation Research*, Beverly Hills, Cal: Sage, pp 33–48.

17. Campbell, DT (1979) Degrees of freedom and case study. In Cook, TD & Reichardt, CS *Qualitative and Quantitative Methods in Evaluation Research*, Beverly Hills, Cal: Sage, pp 49–67.

18. Guba, EG & Lincoln, YS (1982) *Effective Evaluation*, San Francisco; Jossey-Bass Pub, pp 56–8. For a full account of the distinguishing features of the 'naturalistic paradigm' see Chapter 4, pp 53–84. In a later article Guba and Lincoln refer to the scientific paradigm as the rationalistic paradigm. They give two reasons for the change in terminology. First they say that readers have tended to view the naturalistic paradigm as less scientific and therefore less valid. Second, they say that several critics have accused them of setting up a straw man. Nonetheless, they claim that the scientific paradigm as they have outlined it still characterizes the work and thinking of the large majority of scientists. See: Guba, EG & Lincoln, SL (1983) Epistemological and methodological bases of naturalistic inquiry. In Madaus, GF, Stufflebeam, DL and Scriven, MS (eds) *Evaluation Models: Viewpoints on Educational and Human Services Evaluation*, Boston, Mass: Kluwer-Nijhoff, pp 311–33.

19. Werner, W (1978) Evaluation: sense-making of school programs. In Aoki, T (ed.) *Curriculum Evaluation in a New Key*. Monograph series No 1, Vancouver, Centre for the Study of Curriculum and Instruction, Faculty of Education, University of British Columbia.

20. Habermas refers to these as (i) empirical analytic, (ii) historical-hermeneutic and (iii) the critical/self-reflective. See: Habermas, J (1978) *Knowledge and Human Interests* (2nd edn) London: Heinemann Educational Books. In particular the Appendix — 'Knowledge and Human Interests: A General Perspective,' pp 301–17. Habermas's conception of interests underlying the different forms of inquiry have also been referred to as (i) technical interests, (ii) practical interests and (iii) emancipatory interests. For an account of Habermas' theory of knowledge constitutive interests see: Held, D (1980) *Introduction to Critical Theory*, London: Hutchinson & Co.

21. Werner, W (1978) op. cit. p 7.

22. Ibid. p 13.

23. Habermas, J (1978) op. cit. p 310.

24. Werner, W (1978) op. cit. p 16.

25. Ibid. p 18.

26. MacDonald, B (1976) Evaluation and the control of education. In Tawney, D (ed.) *Curriculum Evaluation Today: Trends and Implications*, London: Macmillan Educational, pp 125–36.

27. See: MacDonald, B and Norris, N (1981) Twin political horizons in evaluation fieldwork. In Popkewitz, TS & Tabachnick, BR (eds) *The Study of Schooling: Field Based Methodologies in Educational Research and Evaluation*, New York: Praeger, pp 276–90.

28. Ibid. p 282.

29. House, ER (1980) *Evaluating with Validity*, Beverly Hills, Cal: Sage, p 71.
30. Ibid p 72.
31. Ibid.
32. See Lukes, S (1974) *Power: A Radical View*, London: Macmillan.
33. House, ER (1980) op. cit. p 180.
34. Ibid. pp 189–191.

Chapter 8
Models, Metaphors and Paradigms in Evaluation

Models and metaphors

The concept of model is normally used loosely to refer to a conception of, approach to, or sometimes methods for evaluation.[1] But what is a model of evaluation? What is its function? What is the role of a model in the development of a theory of evaluation. An adequate definition of model is notoriously difficult to find. W G Runciman, commenting on the concept of model in social theory, remarks that it is used by different authors in a wide variety of different senses and the same is true of its use by evaluation theorists.[2] So, for example, we have models as frameworks for planning and conducting evaluation studies; models as exemplars, idealizations or ideal-types; models as theories of knowledge or significance; models as paradigms or prototypes; models as key beliefs about evaluation; and models as idealized problem-solving strategies. Most authors who write about evaluation models use the concept interchangeably with the term 'approach', so that this too is subject to the same variety of meaning.

In everday language the word model is used in a number of senses and contexts. A model is often a representation of structure on a smaller scale. We call something a model when it accurately represents or resembles another entity. We also speak of a model as an object of imitation or as a pattern of excellence, like W S Gilbert's model of a modern major general. In economics, models are often used to represent a theoretical system of relationships which try and capture the essential elements of a real-world situation; as such models are meant to have explanatory power. In social theory the concept of ideal-type has been closely associated with that of model, an ideal-type being an abstraction of the outstanding aspects from some historical complex or a rational ideal for social action in specified circumstances. The most important point about a model, its principal defining characteristic, is that it preserves or captures the most significant features of the reality or idea we are trying to represent or explain. But the selection of properties in a model repsupposes some theory of the nature of the reality being represented. Models have a didactic as well as a mimetic quality. Looked at in this way a model is rather different from a metaphor.

Metaphors are arbitrary assertions of similarity, an association of two entities or qualities which ordinarily belong to quite different contexts. In order for a model adequately to represent or explain something, its relationship to the thing itself must not be purely arbitrary. Yet models can contain metaphors and may well operate like metaphors in the way we think about evaluation.

House argues that evaluation concepts 'are often derived from fundamental, generative, and deep-seated metaphors that remain hidden', but 'substantially define the reality of the evaluator's world'.[3] He identifies a number of metaphors that are characteristic of much evaluative thinking: the delivery of social services as industrial production, social programmes as machines, delivery systems as conduits, social problems as targets, programme activities as goal-directed movements. House says that industrial production and sporting contests are often used as metaphors in evaluation because they are pervasive experiences in American society, 'and production and competition are primary values'.[4] Taking the Technical and Vocational Education Initiative (TVEI) as an example, it is not difficult to discern some of the key metaphors that House regards as indicative of much American thinking about evaluation: programmes are bridges — spanning different sectors of the economy; programmes are assembly lines producing certain kinds of products — marketable skills and qualifications; programmes are experiments or trials — development and marketing exercises.[5]

When Oscar Wilde observed that life imitates art, he had in mind that we compose reality through languages that are cultural rather than natural in origin. It is possible that some of the metaphors that shape our everyday thinking about evaluation are constructions that no longer have the characteristic of arbitrariness associated with metaphor. House suggests that the evaluative metaphors of industrial production and sport or warfare somehow have their origins in the central value systems of the USA or more generally capitalist societies. It is a persuasive argument. But such metaphors, if that is what they are, are not simply reflective, they are also constitutive.

Models of evaluation contain much that is metaphoric and are, in certain ways, like metaphors. The CIPP model, for example, employs metaphors derived from several other disciplines — like *homeostasis* and *metamorphism* from biology, *environment* from evolutionary theory and social ecology, *diagnosis* from medicine, and *input* and *product* from industrial production. The root metaphor for the CIPP model, however, appears to be society as organism. Other models, for example the judicial or legal model and the connoisseurship or art criticism approach, are built on an explicit metaphor with all it entails or implies: adjudication, case building, testimony, defenders and prosecutors; the cultivation of taste and sensibility.[6]

Just as the paraphernalia of experimental design has come to stand for science, some models or approaches have come to stand for evaluation. The objectives model and the discrepancy approach are prime candidates, but only for certain communities at certain times. The folklore of the British innovation community of the 1980s, requires that evaluations are primarily formative. It could be argued that the idea of formative evaluation with its connotations of constructive feedback, shared goals, common problems and the integration of development and evaluation, is rooted in or appeals to the metaphor of social programmes as organisms containing interdependent and related parts. Indeed, one of the meanings ascribed to the term 'formative', circa 1877, was: 'producing or attended with the production of new tissue'.[7] But other explanations are both possible and probable — for one thing, formative evaluation is less threatening and more politically docile. One explanation may not, of course, preclude the other. The point is, however, that the social function and origins of metaphor is not at all clear either in general or with respect to particular cases.

If models are paradigms, prototypes or theories of knowledge, then they can function much like metaphors or archetypes providing the basis for established patterns of thought. For evaluators, models provide a language through which to describe evaluation; they also, as House would suggest, provide a compelling theoretical language for the characterization of social programmes. Yet what kind of analysis or argument is this? The idea that much of our thinking about evaluation is controlled by deep-seated metaphors is based on a structuralist analysis of theories of innovation and evaluation. It is a kind of social anthropology of knowledge described through the lenses of structural linguistics and it represents a theory of culture and communication, albeit a rather underdeveloped one. It is also, if I understand it correctly, very deterministic. When House writes of metaphors being 'deep-seated' and 'generative', two things come to mind. First, that we are dealing with patterns of thought embedded deep in the culture; second, that over time these patterns of thought, these metaphors, are added to and generate others through successive historical transformations. If this is so, then the project of recovering the meaning of evaluative metaphors cannot be confined to the here and now or to the extant text, and the point at which one stops is likely to be arbitrary.

Most models of evaluation provide a sequential framework of steps and principles for solving problems and guiding action. They are heuristic devices for planning and organizing evaluation and abstract formulations for the analysis of evaluation. They are also theories of significance indicating what is important to attend to in the evaluation of innovation and how an innovation should be construed for the purposes of inquiry.

Ernest House has been a consistent critic of the influence of technological thinking on educational innovation, and his analysis of the metaphors that guide much evalutive activity forms part of this project. Before the eighteenth century, science and technology were only related tangentially.[8] Since then, and throughout the twentieth century, science has become bound up with technology, each being dependent on the other. However, technology like science is not static and technocratic metaphors are being developed and transformed. The metaphors of industrial production may not be as deep-seated as they now appear. Other, probably equally pernicious, metaphors will eventually take their place. Information processing not industrial production is likely to provide the generative metaphors for the new technology of educational innovation. Some of its features are already apparent: the privatized learner on line and on screen to the 'open tech' or school, brains as computers, thinking as information processing, artificial intelligence as learning, and intelligence as information skills, are all aspects of the new technocratic metaphor. Part of the power of technology comes from its association with science and it would be surprising, therefore, if part of the generative power of technocratic metaphors was not associated with the social authority of science. If House is right and the metaphors which influence and structure our thinking about evaluation reflect core social values, then we would expect to find scientific as well as technological metaphors in the language of innovation and, of course, we do. Social programmes as experiments, pilot projects and field tests made up of dependent and independent variables and evaluators as social scientists, methodologists or even epidemiologists, are examples. If life imitates art it also imitates science as well.

Paradigmatic tendencies

It has become fashionable to talk in paradigms; to describe major theoretical and methodological debates in terms of world-views, overarching metaphors, orthodoxy, revolution, and intellectual struggles for hearts, minds, legitimation and funding. Guba and Lincoln (1982), like Parlett and Hamilton (1977), invoke Thomas Kuhn's 1962 work on *The Structure of Scientific Revolutions* as justification for their own analysis of paradigms in the social and psychological sciences. Walter Werner (1978), in many ways following a similar analytical path, takes sustenance from a different but no less important tradition, namely critical theory. And Michael Patton (1980) has written about a paradigm of choices, suggesting a pragmatic approach to the selection of evaluation methods and methodologies. In any event, the vocabulary of the history and philosophy of science has percolated into discussions about evaluation in a largely uncritical and unexamined way.

The use of the term paradigm to clarify methodological choices or articulate alternative epistemologies for evaluation has created certain difficulties. First, there is a general lack of clarity and agreement as to what is meant by the term paradigm. Margaret Masterman, for example, has listed not less than 21 senses in which Kuhn uses the term.[9] Second, within the philosophy of science paradigms are usually thought of as incommensurate; there is no common ground between competing paradigms since there is no logic, just a psychology of scientific discovery. Third, perceived paradigm shifts in the methodology of the social sciences do not appear to alter significantly the problem structure of educational evaluation. As such, the notion of paradigm may have only limited application and import. Finally, explaining methodological choices and alternative epistemologies in terms of paradigm shifts presents us with a problem regarding the relationship between paradigms and practice.

In the detailed textual analysis of *The Structure of Scientific Revolutions,*

Margaret Masterman has delineated three kinds of Kuhnian paradigm: *metaphysical paradigms* or *metaparadigms* in the sense of world-view, set of beliefs, new way of seeing, or an organizing principle governing perception; *sociological paradigms* in the sense of an institution, set of scientific habits for successful problem-solving, or a universally recognized or concrete scientific achievement; and *artefact paradigms* or *construct paradigms* referring to textbooks and classic works, tools, methods and instrumentation, or grammars and analogies.[10] Most philosophers of science and most evaluation theorists who have considered the matter, have concerned themselves with the first kind of paradigm — the metaphysical. Parlett and Hamilton (1977), for example, suggest that a paradigm 'is an overarching concept similar in meaning to world-view, philosophy, or intellectual orthodoxy'; Patton (1978) says that it 'is a world view, a general perspective, a way of breaking down the complexity of the real world', while in their analysis of scientific and naturalistic paradigms, Guba and Lincoln (1982) begin by contrasting one with the other in terms of basic philosophical assumptions.

An immediate problem with a metaphysical view of paradigms is that it tends to be based on idealist textbook accounts of science. It is slightly ironic to find advocates of the development and use of naturalistic methods, like Guba and Lincoln, relying almost exclusively on generalization and caricature — writing of science as if it was a convergent phenomenon. There is something especially convenient and compelling about bipolar and oppositional forms of thought, but like idealist accounts of research such descriptions of 'scientific' and 'naturalistic' evaluation might well do more to reify and obscure the significance of different forms of inquiry, than they do to reveal their distinct characteristics. Certainly it would be wrong to minimize the significance of different and competing epistemologies, for practical purposes, however, the differences between naturalistic and scientific theory or between experimentalism and ethnography can be overdrawn to an extent that is misleading and confusing.

If we take Guba and Lincoln's analysis for instance, it is clear that they are uncertain about the strength of the epistemological claims they want to make. At times they insist that the choice between paradigms in any inquiry ought to be made on the basis of a best fit between the assumptions and postures of a paradigm and the phenomenon being studied.[11] On other occasions they suggest that it is neither desirable nor possible to integrate the scientific and naturalistic paradigms at the epistemological level, and for the field of the behavioural sciences the naturalistic paradigm should be chosen.[12] In the Preface, the authors write of the 'social science model' as doomed and agree with Michael Scriven that the social scientific establishment will 'rot away before they give way', adding:

if we cannot help to persuade the establishment of the inadequacy of that view, we can at least aspire to contribute to the enhancement of the state of rot.[13]

And, in their conclusion to a section on the basic assumptions of the paradigms, we find that:

> It is not the intent of the authors to demolish the scientific paradigm as unworkable. What we have tried to say so far is that [. . .] there is no guaranteed path to ascertaining truth. There are instead a number of competing paradigms that describe different methods for determining 'truth', and that no one of these is, on its face, intrinsically superior to any other. There is no way to prove that one is superior to others.[14]

Apart from the question of internal consistency, there are problems with each of these claims. The argument that the choice of paradigm should be made on the basis of the best fit with the phenomenon, at first glance appears pragmatic and sensible. However, it likens the selection of an epistemology to the problem of choosing ingredients for a Sunday lunch — merely a matter of deciding what one is trying to cook. It assumes that we can stand outside a metaphysical paradigm to discern independently the true nature of phenomena. Yet according to this account of paradigms, they are precisely world-views or organizing principles governing perception. Parlett and Hamilton appear to be taking a weaker but similar position when they state that illuminative evaluation aims to be eclectic and the problems define the methods used, not vice versa.[15] This suggests that problems can be defined independently of a particular epistemological perspective and that eclecticism is an attainable goal.

I will return to the problem of the irreconcilability of paradigms at a later stage. For the present, two observations will suffice. First, from the perspective of the eclectic, paradigms in principle need to be commensurable and Kuhn argues that they are not. Second, the issue of commensurability — one implication of which is that paradigms cannot be logically integrated — could well reflect the analytic rationality of historians of science and their methodological disciples rather than contradictions in the practice of science. It may simply be an instrument effect.

Another difficulty with Guba and Lincoln's epistemological claims concerns the warrant they have for making them and the coherence of their analysis. If, as they suggest, the naturalistic inquirer assumes that there are multiple and divergent realities where none can be considered more true than any other, or more accurately, none can be considered wrong or false, then why should epistemology, paradigms, methodology and the philosophy of science not be viewed in a similar fashion? Clearly, Guba and Lincoln wish to commend, with good reasons, the epistemological virtue and practical superiority of naturalistic inquiry. But in a world of multiple realities, conflicting and irreconcilable truths, cultural and cognitive relativity, there is no reason for accepting their argument over and above any others, save that of psychological preference or political advantage. We could conclude here by suggesting that either their account of epistemology is wrong or its consequences profoundly embarrassing. However, it is worth while adding that in our everyday experience, in our profane and natural lives both as citizens and as social inquiriers, we do in fact operate as if things were true and false, right and wrong, good and bad. Whatever the epistemological hazards involved, we do proceed in practice by assuming an external reality independent of its descriptions.

Guba and Lincoln's account of the epistemology of social inquiry is not strictly an abstract and logical account, it partly rests on empirical claims about the logic and procedures of science and the beliefs of scientists. It does then seem reasonable to question the extent to which their account and other similar accounts correspond to the practice of social science research. While there is little doubt that their account broadly corresponds to those found in some textbooks, these may bear only passing resemblance to actual research accomplishments and the beliefs which sustain them.

Let us now return to the problem of incommensurability. Describing Kuhn's position of the growth of science, Imre Lakatos wrote:

> in Kuhn's conception, anomalies, inconsistencies always abound in science, but in 'normal' periods the dominant paradigm secures a pattern of growth which is eventually overthrown by a 'crisis'. There is no particular rational cause for the appearance of a Kuhnian 'crisis'. 'Crisis' is a psychological concept; it is a contagious panic. Then a new 'paradigm' emerges, incommensurable with its predecessor. There are no rational standards for their comparison. Each paradigm contains its own standards . . . The new paradigm brings a totally new rationality. There are no super-paradigmatic standards. The change is a bandwagon effect. Thus in Kuhn's view scientific revolution is irrational, a matter for mob psychology.[16]

Kuhn himself has rejected such a radical interpretation of paradigm incommensurability, but he has also re-emphasized that we have no neutral means to describe and reconcile competing paradigms.[17] Thus, according to Kuhn, scientific communities operating with different paradigms always face the problem of translation when trying to understand each other.[18]

Given that some evaluation theorists would want to see a more eclectic approach to programme evaluation, combining the strengths of different methodological traditions and applying different paradigms to different situations, the problem of incommensurability is of some importance. The implications of the incommensurability thesis for the practice of evaluation are hard to predict. One thing the thesis suggests is that efforts to mount programme evaluations that integrate experimental/scientific with ethnographic/naturalistic methodologies are likely to flounder at the stage of data analysis and interpretation, assuming, that is, that the different practitioners could agree on an integrated design. Theoretically, the implications are more significant, however, In as much as the incommensurability thesis is taken seriously, it suggests that:

1. it will not prove possible to render an adequate account of an eclectic methodology of evaluation;
2. long-term theoretical development in evaluation will not be well served by attempts to combine different methodologies; and

3. the promise of interdisciplinary approaches to the study of innovation will remain unfulfilled.

In concluding this brief discussion of incommensurability, it is important to note that it is a problem which arises as a consequence of adopting an analysis of different approaches to evaluation based on a metaphysical notion of paradigms. From this perspective the choice of strategy and methods is irrevocably linked to the paradigmatic prison within which one works. Adopting a metaphysical notion of paradigm makes it very difficult to account for change either in the theory or practice of evaluation.

New ways of thinking about and doing evaluation have emerged partly as a response to the perceived failure of traditional approaches to inform and improve policy-making. Since the 1970s, a growing number of evaluation theorists have advocated the development of alternative approaches that can be broadly grouped together as naturalistic. Whether this trend should be described as an emergent paradigm or a paradigm shift is a matter of debate. As Helen Simons has indicated, naturalistic inquiry is not new.[19] Moreover, the social sciences in general consist of a bewildering variety of theoretical systems, theories, models, methodologies, concepts, grammars, methods and research communities. There is not one social science model but many — only some of which are adaptations of a received view of natural science. Likewise it is doubtful whether it is accurate or useful to think of a naturalistic model of inquiry as a satisfactory unifying construct. There is then a problem concerning the connection between theories of research and the practice of research, and we will return to this issue again. If, however, we for the moment subscribe to the two-paradigm account of educational evaluation — the scientific and the naturalistic — it seems clear that the particular problem structure of evaluation is not altered significantly by paradigm shifts from one to the other. Both the scentific and naturalistic models of inquiry have to address political, moral, theoretical and methodological issues in the circumstances of programme evaluation. They may deal with these recurrent issues in different ways and arrive at different solutions, but both the naturalistic and scientific evaluator faces practical and moral questions of utility, justice, politics, ethics, role relationships and social responsibility. Evaluators from either side of the methodological trench have to make the inevitable compromises between the demands of validity and the need for social utility and justice that are the hallmarks of programme evaluation.

It could, of course, be argued that each paradigm defines these recurrent issues and problems in very different ways and reaches different compromises. This may or may not be the case — it is, in fact, a matter for empirical investigation. Nonetheless, there seems to be nothing inherent in either model of inquiry that precludes the possibility of similar practical resolutions and similar political roles being reached by both. There is nothing about the naturalistic paradigm that prevents it from being used as a bureaucratic service or being presented in an autocratic way. Similarly naturalistic inquiriers, especially in the context of programme evaluation, should be as much concerned with questions of sampling, reliability, internal and external validity, and generalization as their scentific counterparts. And, we may add in parenthesis, that naturalistic judgement plays a crucial role in the design of scientific inquiries and the interpretation of the evidence they yield.

We shall consider a central issue relating to the concept of paradigm. Are accounts of paradigms methodological descriptions or prescriptions? What is the connection between paradigms and actual practice, between the theories of research and the realities of research? Parlett and Hamilton's account of the agricultural-botany and social-anthropological paradigms is so brief that it could not aspire to any kind of empirical adequacy; it is a caricature to advance an argument. While Parlett and Hamilton define the concept of paradigm in a metaphysical way, when they account for the two paradigms they do so in the *construct* sense of its meaning. Guba and Lincoln's account is much more extensive and thorough but they admit to its basic inadequacy.[20] Like Parlett and Hamilton, they too shift from an metaphysical to a construct account of the differences between naturalistic and scientific inquiry. What these authors actually mean by the concept of paradigm is somewhat confused.

Employed in its sociological sense to mean a set of methodological habits that have become institutionalized, a paradigm should describe practice. In this sense it represents an empirical claim about the processes of doing and accounting for evaluation within a certain community. Used in its metaphysical sense to mean an organizing principle governing perception or as shared presuppositions, a paradigm should tell us how particular communities look at and know the world. In this sense it represents an empirical claim about the philosophical beliefs of evaluators within a certain community. Used in its construct or artefactual sense to mean an institutionalized analogy or methods, a paradigm is a technology or metaphor employed by a community in the course of problem-solving. In this sense it represents an empirical claim about the methodological resources that define a certain evaluation community. In each case of usage, however, it is possible to ask about the empirical adequacy of an account of a paradigm. Part of the problem with the concept of paradigm is the inevitable simplification that is involved when it is applied to the endeavours of research communities. When we use the concept we assume a great deal, much is held constant, internal differences are obscured while external differences are magnified. What is needed, if the notion of paradigm is to prove sociologically useful, is research on the beliefs and practices of particular evaluation communities. What is needed, if the notion of paradigm is to prove methodologically instrustive, is research into concepts, methods and techniques in use. To put it another way, before accepting accounts of evaluation based on paradigmatic tendencies we need naturalistic descriptions of how evaluations are accomplished.

Thinking about evaluation in terms of metaphysical paradigms polarizes methodological choice and suggests that it is principally an epistemological rather than a practical and political problem. Clearly, methodological choices have epistemological consequences, but very few choices in evaluation are made on the basis of a coherent epistemology. Although methodological choices are determined largely by training and custom there is, nonetheless, also a considerable element of situational problem-solving involved in any programme evaluation.

Naturalistic and scientific paradigms, in as far as people use or accept the labels, are social flags of convenience; by this is meant that they circumscribe certain groups who apparently share, in a rough-and-ready way, norms and values which affect the practice of evaluation. Thus we might think of evaluation paradigms as indicative of the methodological specialities and languages shared by a community — a paradigm as a social institution. This is to strip the concept of paradigm of its metaphysical significance except inasmuch as it describes the epistemological beliefs shared by a community of practitioners.

The idea of evaluation paradigms has highlighted the way in which scientific dogma has infected our understanding of innovation and routinized the assessment of its impact. However, while the scientific paradigm has been described as orthodox institutionalized practices, the naturalistic paradigm tends not to be considered in this light. The one purports to be a description of practice the other a prescription for practice. As more evaluation theorists turn their attention to elaborating a technology for naturalistic inquiry and proving training programmes based on the mastery of technique, we can envisage the institutionalization of a naturalistic methodology and the consequent creation of another orthodox model of inquiry.

Notes

1. Scriven, M S (1981) *Evaluation Thesaurus*, (3rd edn) Inverness, Cal: Edgepress, pp 97–8.
2. Runciman, WG (1983) *A Treatise on Social Theory. Volume 1: The Methodology of Social Theory*, Cambridge University Press, p 186.
3. House, ER (1983) How we think about evaluation. In House, ER (ed.) *Philosophy of Evaluation*, San Francisco: Jossey-Bass, pp 5–25.
4. Ibid. p 19.
5. For example: (i) the remit for both the national evaluations of TVEI emphasized operating issues and resource implications; (ii) a major aim of the financial evaluation was to indicate ways of appraising cost-effectiveness and good practice; and (iii) at the outset the TVEI Unit of the MSC specified the questions to be asked in evaluating the Initiative including: (a) the measurable characteristics of young people included in the scheme; (b) the average unit costs of educating young people under the scheme compared with the average unit costs of educating 14–18 year olds in the pilot authorities; (c) the proportion of unit costs due to the experimental nature of the scheme; (d) the skills and qualifications that young people on the scheme achieve at 16, at 17 and at 18; the time spent on work experience; (e) the topics introduced for young people on the scheme and how much they spend on these; (f) how available the specialized

equipment/staff resources required under the scheme have been made to pupils; (g) how the Initiative has strengthened co-operation between employers and schools, betwen schools, and between schools and colleges. See: TVEI Unit *Technical & Vocational Education Initiative Evaluation*, Grays Inn Rd, London. Especially 'Questions to be asked in evaluating TVEI' — EIL/5.

6. See, for example: Stufflebeam, DL et al. (1971) *Educational Evaluation and Decision Making*, Bloomington, Ind: PDK National Study Committee on Education; Wolf, RL (1983) The use of judicial evaluation methods in the formulation of educational policy. In Madaus, GF, Stufflebeam, DL & Scriven, MS (eds) *Evaluation Models: Viewpoints on Educational and Human Services Evaluation*, Boston, Mass: Kluwer-Nijhoff, pp 189–203; and, Eisner, EW (1983) Educational connoisseurship and criticism: their form and functions in edcucational evaluation. In Madaus, GF, Stufflebeam, DL & Scriven, MS (eds) ibid.

7. *Shorter Oxford English Dictionary* (1983 edn).

8. Braudel, F (1981) *Civilization and Capitalism 15th — 18th Century: The Structures of Everyday Life*, Vol 1, London: William Collins & Co, p 431.

9. Masterman, M (1970) The nature of paradigm. In Lakatos, I & Musgrave, A (eds) *Criticism and the Growth of Knowledge*, Cambridge University Press, pp 59–89.

10. Ibid. p 65.

11. Guba, EG & Lincoln, YS (1982) *Effective Evaluation*, San Francisco: Jossey-Bass, p 56.

12. Ibid. p 77.

13. Ibid. p xii.

14. Ibid. p 62.

15. Parlett, M & Hamilton, D (1977) Evaluation as illumination: a new approach to the study of innovatory programmes. In Hamilton, D et al. (eds) *Beyond the Numbers Game*, London: Macmillan, p 13.

16. Lakatos, I (1978) *The Methodology of Scientific Research Programmes* (Philosophical Papers Vol 1, edited by Worrall, J & Currie, G) Cambridge University Press, pp 90–91.

17. See: Kuhn, TS (1970a) *The Structure of Scientific Revolution* (2nd edn), University of Chicago Press. Especially the Postscript. Also: Kuhn, TS (1970b) Reflections on my critics. In Lakatos, I & Musgrave, A (eds) *Criticism and the Growth of Knowledge*, Cambridge University Press, pp 231–77.

18. Kuhn, TS (1970b) op. cit. pp 266–9.

19. See: Simons H (1980) (ed.) *Towards a Science of the Singular*, Norwich: Centre for Applied Research in Education, University of East Anglia, p 1.

20. Guba, EG & Lincoln, YS (1982) op. cit. p 56.

Chapter 9

Evaluation, Science, Methodology and Society

The legacy of positivism

Educational research and evaluation, like other forms of social inquiry, was cast in the image of the natural sciences. It is commonplace although not very helpful to call this conception of social inquiry 'positivist'. Positivist has, in fact, become an indecisive word of abuse devoid of any particular meaning.[1] When Auguste Comte first coined the term positivism he did so as part of a general theory of historical development. For Comte positive thought — positivism — was the final stage in the evolution of consciousness and society. One of the most significant aspects of Comte's conception of positivism was the mutual necessity of order and progress.[2] Positivism provided the methodology for orderly social progress, giving particular importance to observation, experiment and comparison: it was a non-revolutionary theory of social change.[3] It is this emphasis on systematic empirical inquiry providing the basis for orderly social progress that is one of the most important remaining legacies of nineteenth century positivism.[4]

The problem of the right relationship between social inquiry and public policy has been with us for some time. Historically the social sciences have been associated with social improvement and stability: stability founded on a better understanding of social trends and forces and a more accurate description of social circumstances and practices than common sense and contemporary wisdom provide; improvement founded upon the application of the findings and methodology of science to social problems. This chapter is about different conceptions of evaluative inquiry and the social philosophy of planned social change.

The experimenting society and the authority of science

One tradition of evaluation calls for an experimenting society, a society in which social progress is judged on the basis of carefully conducted experiments. In their survey of experimental and quasi-experimental designs for research, Donald Campbell and Julian Stanley stated their commitment to the experiment as the only means for settling disputes regarding educational practice, as the only way of verifying educational improvements, and as the only way of establishing a cumulative tradition in which improvements can be introduced without the danger of a faddish discard of old wisdom in favour of inferior novelties.[5]

They note that experimentation is hazardous, slow and full of disappointment, but insist that it is the only available route to cumulative progress. Theirs is an evolutionary perspective on useful knowledge where experimentation sharpens the selection of good practice. Following Campbell and Stanley, Saxe and Fine argue that experimentation provides a methodology for planned change in which social planners collaborate with evaluation researchers in order to design and analyse innovations.[6] Scientific logic — the means to produce valid, accurate and generalizable knowledge — is at the heart of social experimentation.[7] Saxe and Fine regard the procedures by which concepts are translated into concrete entities that can be tested, controlled observation of human behaviour where the experimenter actively varies the treatment, and procedures for randomizing the assignment of participants to treatment and non-treatment groups as key methods for improving the validity of comparisons and judgements about programme effects.[8]

'The experimenting society', says Campbell, 'would be a scientific society' in which the 'scientific values of honesty, open criticism, experimentation, willingness to change once-advocated theories in the face of experimental and other evidence would be exemplified'.[9] The experimenting society attempts innovations as solutions to problems. It promotes ameliorative programmes without excess commitment and is able to test the results and accept the diagnosis. It is a society that is prepared to treat social arrangements as provisional and place its trust in science and technology to improve them. It has a social philosophy that denies the necessity of immanent historical forces and Utopian attempts at remodelling the whole of society, and instead values what Karl Popper has called piecemeal social engineering.[10] Although the precise specification for the experimenting society has changed over the years (for example, there is now less emphasis on large-scale social experiments and a greater emphasis on many more small-scale natural experiments under local control), the basic idea that governments should test social interventions to see what arrangements are worth adopting on a large scale is at the core of the political economy of experimental evaluation research. As Cronbach has observed, experimentalists echo the Deweyan faith that ingenuity can improve social institutions and are committed to the hardheaded testing of new ideas.[11]

Under the experimental mission, evaluation becomes a problem of testing hypotheses through application of procedural rules and the control of conditions so as to reduce uncertainty over the long run. It is a project that attempts deliberately to fashion or refashion social institutions and arrangements, replace or at least chasten the process of political judgement, relieve the burden of administrative choice, control corruption and support honesty, and redress the imbalance between the advocacy of solutions and the serious consideration of social problems. The experimental mission provides for a system of evaluation based on organized scepticism.

Experimentalism is a form of applied science. Rossi, Freeman and Wright (1979) for example, say that 'systematic evaluations are those which employ the basic approaches to gathering [   ] valid and reliable evidence that have been developed in the social sciences.' They go on to state that programme evaluation ideally has the following characteristics: observations can be duplicated by observers using the same instruments, evidence on results is subject to test regarding whether or not the findings could have occurred without the intervention, and information is presented on whether or not programme funds were used efficiently.[12] According to Rossi, Freeman and Wright, a systematic evaluation should contribute to every stage of the planning, design and implementation of a social programme. Innovation is also applied science.

Experimentalism has come under attack from several quarters close to home. Donald Campbell, for example, has listed a number of problems with traditional conceptions of evaluation as applied science: the greater equivocality of causal inference and greater likelihood of bias in policy research; the mistaken belief that quantitative measures replace qualitative knowing; the specifying of programme goals as fallible measures open to bureaucratic manipulation; and overemphasis on external evaluation, on immediate evaluation and on single national once-and-for-all evaluations; a gross overvaluing and financial investment in external validity; and the neglect of the fact that scientific truths are a collective product of a community at any given time.[13]

By virtue of the importance of measurement and control, experimentalism raises ethical questions perhaps more starkly than other conceptions of evaluation. As Alice Rivlin and Michael Timpane have observed, social scientists who are involved in the design and execution of experiments tend to emphasize the good that can come from increased understanding.[14] What is at issue, say Rivlin and Timpane, is balancing the benefits of experimentation against the harm that might be done.[15] While the experimentalist project might not go as far as the Benthamite recipe, the greatest happiness of the greatest number, nonetheless ethical questions are interpreted in a utilitarian manner. In the end, what is at issue are the kind of agreements, principles and procedures needed to safeguard participant and citizen rights: the right of informed consent, the right to withdraw or not participate, and the right to confidentiality. Such rights are, however, conceived of as matters of individual choice.

Of course most educational innovations are not designed as experiments, indeed the reverse is more often the case. Despite the rhetoric of trial and pilot programmes there is little political commitment to the putative values of an experimenting society.[16]

It is tempting to regard an applied science view of the relationship between evaluation and the management of change as undemocratic and authoritarian. Undemocratic because it suggests that decisions about social

policy should be made on the basis of scientific rather than political judgement, by evaluators who are only accountable to a community of peers of
social planners. Authoritarian because it precludes forms of knowing and
judgement other than those of science, thus presenting us at any one time
with a unitary set of values. To borrow from Michael Bakunin, we could
argue that the scientific state — the experimenting society — must be the
'most flagrant, the most cynical, and the most complete negation of humani-
ty'.[17] Until such time as the polity completely appropriates science for its
own purposes and its alone, we should resist this temptation and prefer
instead to regard the experimentalists as offering a germane corrective to
the tendency to treat intention as reality, ideology as truth and the path to
social efficiency as self-evident. Saxe and Fine, for instance, argue that in
the absence of scientific data, pragmatic responses to social problems are
not likely to be any more humanistic than those established empirically.[18]
One of the strengths of applied science and especially experimentalist
thought is that it represents a sceptical and sometimes oppositional culture
based on the values of empiricism. At its best it can provide a potent and
authoritative challenge to excessive idealism or conviction as well as to the
exercise of administrative power to manipulate information for political convenience or advantage.

Social efficiency and the technology of science

As the technology (as opposed to the methodology) of applied science is
being incorporated into administrative life, however, it is becoming a new
orthodoxy of evaluative measures subject to a variety of corrupting
influences. While there may be little commitment to the values of
experimentalism, there is in many industrial societies a strong commitment
to the pursuit of social efficiency based on the technology of applied science.
Cronbach and his Associates have noted the tension between the ideal of
efficiency in government and the ideal of democratic participation. They
regard such forms of 'rationalism as dangerously close to totalitarianism',
and it is clearly important to recognize this tendency, especially given the
re-emergence of scientific management.[19]

Continued fiscal constraint has given rise to new and more powerful
demands to improve the efficiency of the public sector. It has also prompted
increased attention to the development of new procedures for programme
monitoring and external evaluation based largely on audit. For example, the
contemporary rhetoric of 'value for money' in the provision of social services has created a need to establish routine ways of measuring value and,
as Anthony Hopwood has noted, the selective visibility which accounting
gives to organizational action plays an important role in shaping what is
seen as significant and in the end valuable.[20] Recently, the pursuit of efficiency — minimizing programme inputs in relation to outputs — has acquired
a prominence as a political value and administrative virtue beyond the capacity of either central or local government to produce the information such a

goal requires. As applied science becomes more institutionalized, especially through the application of information technology, and incorporated into governmental procedures for programme planning and review', we can expect the routine evaluation of public policy to be confined to a limited range of input/output measures and performance indicators. At the heart of this process is the translation of social goods and goals into measurable objectives.

The precise specification of objectives and the measurement of their attainment has proved to be a powerful technology in evaluation, a technology of considerable longevity. Used by a classroom teacher as a tool for curriculum planning and instructional decision-making, it has its limitations but also has its place. However, undue reliance on measuring the discrepancy between stated objectives and actual outcomes has serious consequences for the ways in which institutions and temporary change agencies account for their work. Leaving aside for one moment the problems associated with goal consensus, objectives-based evaluation can all too easily lead to an overvaluing of measurable tasks and excessive attention to impression management. Holding people to account for the attainment of objectives that they themselves have had little say in shaping is likely to breed cynicism and systematic deceit, especially in organizations with a strong occupational culture and high degree of social solidarity. Exactly the same problems occur with the specification of performance indicators as objective measures of success or effectiveness.

Objectives-based approaches to evaluation presuppose that it is possible and desirable to reach consensus about ends and means, or simply assume that a consensus exists. To put it another way, the objectives approach rests on an assumption that values are relatively unimportant in the process of evaluation. While it is obvious that in certain circumstances it is possible to reach fair agreement about desirable ends and effective ways of achieving them, in pluralist societies consensus has to be demonstrated rather than assumed.

Applied science, pluralism and political accommodation

Cronbach and his colleagues have taken issue with the assumption of goal consensus and the orthodoxy of experimentalism, claiming that most evaluation theorists 'seem convinced that there is just one best way to evaluate, and most of them advocate a summative, hypothesis-testing style'.[21] They advance a view of evaluation as applied science that is at once more pragmatic, more realistic, more political and more pluralist than the classical experimentalist position. They offer a reassessment of the social function of evaluation and its methodological preoccupations. A theory of evaluation, they say, 'must be as much a theory of political interaction as it is a theory of how to determine facts'.[22] Cronbach's work is, however, an attempt to preserve the values while improving the performance and utility of the applied science model.[23]

Cronbach begins from the position that the planning of evaluation is as much concerned with substance and politics as with methodological procedures. According to Cronbach, what is required of an evaluation is information that supports political negotiation rather than information calculated to indicate the correct decision.[24] While many evaluation theorists would concur, it is Cronbach who has come closest to a *rapprochement* of applied science and pluralist political assumptions. At the core of this *rapprochement* is a reaction against methodological dogmatism and a reformulation of the concepts of validity and utility.[25] It is to Cronbach's reformulation of the social philosophy and methodology of applied science that we now turn.

According to Cronbach, at its best evaluation assists in a smooth accommodation of social activities and structures to changing conditions and ideals.[26] As Cronbach notes, evaluation thus conceived is both meliorist and conservative; it is committed to a project of orderly and organized change. The concept of accommodation is crucial to Cronbach's analysis of the politics of social programmes and evaluation. He sees power and influence as widely distributed as opposed to concentrated. He sees American social policy-making as shaped by a pluralist community of interests — a policy shaping community — and characterized by 'muddling through' based on negotiation and compromise, resulting in decisions emerging rather than being made. This kind of political system that Cronbach has in mind when he writes that evaluation should contribute to the process of political accommodation. For these reasons and others Cronbach describes the role of evaluator as that of 'public scientists' serving the public interest to the limit that terms of employment will allow.[27] Here the public interest is best understood as those values and concerns articulated by a policy-shaping community, and the evaluator has the responsibility to consider all sectors of this community in a non-partisan and disinterested fashion. It seems that the ideal of public scientist is also crucial to Cronbach's political analysis. It is crucial because the role of the disinterested scientific inquirer helps foster credibility and places pressure on others to act reasonably.[28] It is crucial too because Cronbach wishes to preserve the ideal that the application of scientific methodology, albeit reformulated, is the best path to orderly progress.

The procedures of experimental design are generally intended to increase the internal validity of a study — or more accurately, the conclusions drawn from a study. For experimentalists internal validity is the *sine qua non* of good evaluation and judgements about the external validity of a study or its conclusions are entirely dependent on it. We can think of this as the scientific warrant an interpreter has for making causal inferences about an experimental treatment and its effects. Cook and Campbell's original definition of internal validity refers to questions about whether the experimental treatment actually caused a difference in the specific experimental instance.[29]

Cronbach has been concerned to redefine the process of making inferences from evaluative data and judging their validity. In so doing he distinguishes between the domain of investigation and the domain of application. The domain of investigation consists of the population or sites about which a conclusion is sought, the plan for the programme or treatment, the plan for observations and data collection, and the programme setting. The domain of application is the possible populations or sites to which the programme might apply. In effect, it refers to the places and circumstances to which a programme might be transferred to a local policy-shaping community who might wish to adapt the programme for their own ends.[30] In Cronbach's reformulation, internal validity (the reproducibility of inference) concerns conclusions made from within the domain of investigation and external validity (extrapolations beyond the data) concerns conclusions made from within the domain of application.[31]

Cronbach argues that the balance between internal and external validity is a matter of degree, and, more importantly, that external validity does not depend directly on internal validity.[32] His definition of internal validity refers to the ability of a statement about a programme or treatment to withstand a challenge. He is primarily concerned with credibility and policy relevance and therefore it is inferences that go beyond the data — the validity of extrapolations — that are the crux. For Cronbach, increasing internal validity by elegant design often serves to reduce the relevance of policy findings.

Like the experimentalists, Cronbach wants to reduce uncertainty through scientific empirical inquiry and for this reason he does not rule out the methodology of experimental design. However, his position contrasts sharply with the experimentalists in a number of respects. First, while many experimentalists would argue that summative evaluations should employ strong experimental designs, Cronbach disagrees. Instead he argues that there is a single best plan for an evaluation and that is is often sensible to adopt some of the procedures of experimentalism without others.[33] Second, experimentalists emphasize the importance of operational definitions and the measurement of change. Cronbach recommends against formulating evaluative questions in terms of change.[34] Third, experimentalists regard random experiments as the ideal and a potent counter to most threats to validity. Cronbach, conversely, regards the reach of random samplings as limited, especially when one is concerned with the transferability of a treatment. He argues that random assignment reduces some uncertainty, but that estimates of outcomes in a population not strictly sampled remain suspect. What he objects to is 'the unsophisticated conception of random assignment as a magic bullet that kills off all threats to validity'.[35] While acknowledging that random sampling has its place, he regards other sampling techniques as offering distinct advantages to the evaluator.[36] Fourth, Cronbach argues that strong control over the assignment of cases to treatments and/or programmes is most advantageous only when the following four severe conditions are met:

1. treatments have been refined to the point where revision is unlikely to be necessary;
2. there is a defined population to which the winning treatment is to be applied;
3. experimental mortality is unlikely to be a serious problem;
4. it is appropriate to judge treatments on the same outcome measures.[37]

Fifth, most experimentalists advise that it is necessary to standardize the treatment so that the researcher will know the variable he is drawing a conclusion about. Cronbach argues that such advice has been overvalued and that looking at a diversity of naturally occurring expressions of the treatment is likely to do more to inform judgements about future dissemination.[38] Sixth, the experimentalists regard internal validity — the validity of inference from and confined to an experiment — as a necessary but not sufficient condition for establishing the generalizability of a cause and effect relationship. Without eliminating threats to internal validity (rival hypotheses that could explain away the results) Campbell and Stanley argue that an experiment is uninterpretable.[39] Thus external validity — to what populations, settings and treatment variables the experimental effect can be generalized — depends on demonstrating internal validity.

Cronbach takes a different view of the relative importance of internal and external validity. He also defines them differently, from say, Campbell and Stanley. Cronbach associates internal validity with the concept of reproducibility. He defines reproducibility as hypothetical replication; a a thought experiment which tries to anticipate sources of unwanted variation.[40] In his definition of internal validity he is not that far from Campbell and Stanley. Where he differs is in his assessment of the warrant that is attached to valid internal inferences. For Cronbach it is not helpful to speak of a conclusion as true or false, but only as justified or plausible.[41]

The logic of experimentalism suggests that is is the responsibility of the evaluator to decide under what conditions, to which settings, circumstances, and populations a treatment of programme might generalize. Part of the answer to the question of whether the experimental treatment will work in the same way in other situations depends upon the representative nature of the samples chosen for the experiment. Cronbach's position on generalization and external validity is quite different and is derived as much from a political as it is from a methodological analysis. Cronbach argues that it is the responsibility of a policy-maker to decide how the conclusions from an experimental study apply to her setting. Moreover, programmes are not replicated but instead a new programme put in place which may or may not resemble the experimental programme, depending on the context and the judgement of relevant decision-makers. Hence external validity refers to the validity of extrapolations from the original experiment and study. The evaluator may anticipate the way in which potential policy-makers may wish to extrapolate but they cannot with certitude make predictions about the success of the programme in non-experimental settings, not least because the new programme will not be the same as the experimental programme.[42]

Validity, justice, fairness and social purpose in evaluation

Cronbach's reformulation of the methodology and social philosophy of applied science owes much to the work of Ernest House and especially to his book *Evaluating With Validity*. House is primarily concerned with a set of related issues: validity, justice, fairness and social purpose in evaluation.

As such, he provides something of a bridge between those theorists working within the tradition of applied science and those theorists who are equivocal about its social efficacy or who reject its political and epistemological assumptions.

House's criticisms of contemporary evaluation are far-reaching and are not just limited to the applied science model. All the major approaches to evaluation, according to House, assume freedom of choice, an individualistic methodology with a strong empirical orientation, and a free marketplace of ideas in which consumers will buy the best.[43] In describing evaluation as a liberal institution, he argues that it discriminates against certain kinds of issues and interests, tends to favour strong individuals over weak, is prone to a naive 'referee' view of governments and operates with an individualistic definition of interests and pluralist assumptions about the distribution of power that ignore the biases inherent in administrative organizations, social and political structures, customs and tradition.[44]

Like other evaluation theorists, House stresses the political nature of evaluation. He argues that evaluation properly understood is an act of persuasion that is part of a complex of social or moral decision procedures.[45] Evaluation can provide the 'credible, the plausible, and the probable', says House, but not certainty.[46] Like Cronbach he sees validity as 'always concerned with purpose and utility for someone'. According to House, scientific objectivity and disinterest do not fully address the problem of bias.[47] Rejecting the primacy of operational definitions of validity, House thinks of the validity of an evaluation as dependent on whether it is true, credible and normatively correct and he has extended the concept of validity so that it includes considerations of audience and ethics. For House there is an important relationship between validity and fairness, and much of his recent work is about exploring the connections between them, and elaborating the conditions for fair agreements and conduct between the relevant and affected parties in an evaluation.

House is critical of the utilitarian ethics of most evaluation theory and practice. His principal objections are that utilitarian ethics serve the status quo and embody existing inequalities, and are thus infair. In its place he proposes a pluralist/intuitionist theory of justice — which can be called naturalistic — where evaluators and others involved in an evaluation must take account of certain key values, namely: moral equality, moral autonomy, impartiality and reciprocity. It is these values or principles that House believes should provide the foundation for fair agreement and conduct in an evaluation. No one principle is given primacy and instead House argues that they constitute a family of values that can only be given priority in specific circumstances.[48]

House outlines 12 conditions that must obtain for an evaluation agreement to be considered fair:

1. non-coercion — in the effort to reach agreement parties must not be coerced;
2. rationality — the parties to an agreement should be rational;

3. acceptance of terms — parties must accept the operating rules for reaching agreements;
4. joint agreement — the result of agreements must be considered to be an object of commitment and mutually binding;
5. disinterestedness — in arriving at agreements participants should not pay excessive attention to their own interests;
6. universality — parties should attempt to arrive at agreements that affect everyone equally, or if an agreement requires that people be treated differently, then the parties should be willing to occupy any of the positions relative to the application of the agreement;
7. community self-interestedness — in their efforts to reach agreement parties must select a policy that is best for themselves as members of the group to whom the policy is to apply;
8. equal and full information — parties should be informed of the relevant facts and they should be equally informed;
9. non-riskiness — one of the purposes of an evaluation agreement is to diminish the risks of the evaluation for those being evaluated;
10. possibility — it should be practical and possible to implement the agreement;
11. count all votes — for an agreement to be fair the parties to it must have an opportunity to register whatever they wish to register in the final step of the process;
12. participation — all parties should be allowed to participate.[49]

Ignoring the question of whether these conditions could in practice be satisfied, they are indicative of the form of social relationships necessary for an ideal fair agreement. Moreover, they are not that far removed from the values that Campbell outlines for an experimenting society: social relations marked by a lack of dogma and a high degree of honesty; mutual accountability; a willingness to change; and a respect for due process. What we need to observe is that the methodology of evaluation presumes certain forms of social relationships and anticipates certain kinds of political life. The methodology of evaluation — the underlying thinking behind problem definition, design, sampling, the selection justification of methods and forms of reporting — is redolent of nascent social theories.

The marked feature of House's perspective on evaluation is the importance he gives to fairness and his expansion of the conception of bias to include not just technical considerations but social and political structures. While House would agree with Cronbach that a theory of evaluation must be as much a theory of political interaction as it is a theory of how to determine facts, he goes further than this. House suggests that any theory of how to determine facts must take account of political interactions — that is, validity cannot be divorced from social and political circumstances and considerations. Cronbach's theory of political interaction is liberal, pluralist and pragmatic. House, on the other hand, while liberal in tone and pluralist in aspiration is less optimistic about the realities of liberal democracy, less certain about its pluralist political assumptions and less inclined to a pragmatic approach to the politics of evaluation. Curiously, neither House nor Cronbach offer the evaluator a theory of political action.

Few, if any, of the major approaches to evaluation are as explicitly political as democratic evaluation.[50] Barry MacDonald, who coined the term, has been its major theoretical and practical proponent. Much of MacDonald's work has been directed towards exploring non-partisan yet radical and justifiable political roles for evaluation. He has consistently argued that evaluation should be seen as a significant form of political action but that the options facing the evaluator are 'not limited to a choice between strengthening or subverting existing power relationships'.[51] At the heart of democratic evaluation theory lies the problem of articulating the ethical and political conditions for the practice of independent evaluation in pursuit of democratic values.

Another advocate of democratic evaluation, Helen Simons, describes it as a strategy for using the negotiable rhetoric of liberal democracy 'as a means of equalizing the power relationships in which programmes are embedded'.[52] As Simons also notes, democratic evaluation represents an attack on the political authority of science and the right of researchers to make definitive judgements about the social world. The ideal of making both reports and methods accessible to non-specialist audiences is an aspiration to democratize access to the process as well as the products of evaluation.

Evaluation, case study and naturalistic inquiry

Democratic evaluation is closely associated with case study and there are, I think, at least two reasons for this. The first reason is that case study appears to provide a medium for reporting to a wide range of audiences — some close to the programme others not so. The second reason has something to do with the emphasis on the particular characteristics of programmes and the institutions in which they work. Implicit in case study is a respect for, or at least an interest in, cultural and educational diversity. The emphasis on the singular characteristics of programmes is not only an empirical judgement about the heterogeneity of the educational world, it is also a stance that values diversity — a value that is also clearly evident in MacDonald's conception of democratic evaluation.

Thinking about evaluation as case study has a certain persuasive logic to it. Programmes are more often than not temporary change systems set up to address certain problems, exploit certain opportunities or develop and test particular ideas, techniques or materials. They are unique events. If programmes are to be judged fairly and if judgements about their value are to have some claim to validity, then they must be adequately and accurately represented.

Case study has been described as the study of an instance drawn from a class or as the study of a bounded system.[53] Adelman, Jenkins and Kemmis claim that case studies are 'strong in reality, down-to-earth and attention-holding, in harmony with the reader's own experience, and thus provide a natural basis for generalization'.[54] Stake makes similar claims for case study when he says that they may be epistemologically in harmony with the reader's experience.[55] He writes about case studies providing naturalistic generalizations on the part of the reader. Stake claimed that these naturalistic generalizations are arrived at by recognizing the 'similarities of objects and issues in and out of context and by sensing the natural covariations of happenings'. According to Stake:

> Naturalistic generalizations develop within a person as a result of experience. They form the tacit knowledge of how things are, why they are, how people feel about them, and how these things are likely to be later or in other places with which this person is familiar. They seldom take the form of predictions but lead regularly to expectations.[56]

In this account of naturalistic generalization, Polanyi's distinction between tacit and propositional knowledge is clearly important. Stake equates propositional knowledge with all interpersonally shareable statements. Tacit knowledge, by contrast, he defines as all that is remembered somehow, minus that which is remembered in the form of words, symbols or other rhetorical forms.[57] Stake says that explanation belongs more to propositional knowledge, understanding more to tacit.[58] Like Stake, most of those who write about naturalistic generalization also mention the work of Michael Polanyi and his distinction between tacit and propositional knowledge. Adelman, Kemmis and Jenkins (1976), for instance, claim that case study research offers a 'surrogate experience and invites the reader to underwrite the account, by appealing to his tacit knowledge of human situations'.[59] For them the truths contained in a case study are 'like those in literature "guaranteed" by "the shock of recognition" '.[60] Kemmis (1980) sees case study as offering the possibility that tacit knowledge may be communicated through the use of rich description.[61] Guba and Lincoln (1982) make similar claims about the importance of tacit knowledge in naturalistic inquiry. For them naturalistic inquiry

> permits and encourages connotative or tacit knowledge to come into play, for the sake of both contributing to the formation of grounded theory and improving communication back to information sources in their own terms'.[62]

The idea of naturalistic generalization is an attractive one for several reasons. Naturalistic generalization suggests a realignment of the responsibility to generalize and evaluate away from the evaluator and towards the reader. We could regard such a view of generalization as empowering or democratizing, or at least as limiting the cultural authority of science. Naturalistic generalization might better represent the cognitive process of generalization and what actually happens when an evaluation study — of whatever kind — is used. However, the idea of naturalistic generalization is, to say the least, rather obscure — the more so since it has become associated with notions of tacit and propositional forms of knowledge. In what ways does a case study more than any other form of inquiry appeal to the tacit knowledge of a reader? What does it mean to say that a reader is invited to underwrite the account? In what way is truth guaranteed by the shock of recognition? And, why the shock? Why does naturalistic inquiry, more than other forms of inquiry, permit tacit knowledge to come into play and how does this contribute to the formation of grounded theory?

For Polanyi all knowledge falls into one of two classes — 'it is either tacit or rooted in tacit knowledge'.[63] Put like this, the distinction between tacit and propositional knowledge can easily be overstated. Formal, propositional, scientific, publicly accessible knowledge is rooted in tacit knowledge not just for its inventor or discoverer but also for its many readers. Polanyi says that when we look at knowledge as personal knowing — an activity or process of knowing — we depart from the scientific ideal of a strictly justifiable knowledge in two related respects: we recognize that it is possible to acquire knowledge even though we cannot fully specify the grounds for knowing, and we recognize that 'knowing is exercised within an accidentally given framework that is largely unspecifiable'.[64] Yet such personal knowing is not divorced from some external reality. In fact, Polanyi suggests that we can account for this capacity of ours to know more than we can tell only if we believe in the presence of an external reality with which we can establish contact.[65]

If naturalistic generalization is the act of perceiving commonalities among empirically different (but conceptually equivalent) human experiences, then it seems appropriate to question the empirical adequacy of both sides of the author-reader equation. If we consider our decision-maker trying to decide whether or how 'x' will work in his or her particular setting, then the quality of his or her judgement is likely to depend not just on the adequacy and richness of an evaluation report, but also on the adequacy and richness of his or her own understanding of the situation in which he or she wishes to adopt the innovation. However, in some instances, it is precisely a lack of understanding about circumstances that prompted evaluation in the first place. It can be argued that in the context of programme evaluation policy-makers rarely have a sufficient understanding of the context of application to permit naturalistic generalization.

Much of what is written about case study and naturalistic generalization is unhelpful for programme evaluators looking to justify a case study approach and articulate the problem of generalization. I am not sure that naturalistic generalization is a theory of generalization at all, rather it seems like the beginnings of a theory of interpretation. The problem of generalization might better be looked at as a problem of the social utility of evaluation. As such, it will clearly involve questions of validity but not independently from questions of fairness and social purpose.

When thinking about programme evaluation it is important to discriminate between two types of generalization: those about a programme and those from the experiences of a programme. Generalizations about the programme concern judgements of its nature, processes and effects. Generalizations from the programme concern judgements about the transferability or usefulness

of its experience and ideas for others. Programme evaluators need to collect and make both kinds of generalizations. When describing a programme,
an evaluator is making generalizations about the programme. In making
generalizations from the programme, an evaluator is looking for those things
that might help guide or inform future action. The status of generalizations
about the programme seem quite clear. Their validity rests on the following
three factors:

1. coherence and reasonableness — including the fairness of judgement;
2. empirical adequacy of accounts including the meaning of judgements for
   those who are involved in the programme; and
3. the social utility of accounts in providing a basis for understanding and
   judgement.

It is with generalizations from the programme that we usually run into difficulties. Few if any programmes are organized in such a way as to permit
sound interference from case to class or from an experimental population
to other populations. Generalizations from the programme are therefore,
more often than not, theories requiring further elaboration and test. Like
Stenhouse's view of curriculum they are provisional specifications or
theories that need to be tried out anew. This, of course, suggests that innovation and evaluation should be seen as cumulative processes rather than
one-off events. The problem of generalization in programme evaluation is
a problem of creating and sustaining the conditions for the accumulation
of understanding across particular instances of innovation and change. Looked at like this, generalization is just as much a political problem as a
methodological one.

The significance of case study is that it provides a way of judging action
in context; a way of understanding a programme as well as representing
its work. Yet while the advocates of case study make claims about its accessibility and its capacity to support a broad range of generalizations, it
is a form of inquiry and medium of presentation that remains politically un-
convincing. Those who sponsor evaluation and those who have immediate
needs for its products do not appear to accept readily the advantages of case
study.

Democratic evaluation has also been closely associated with naturalistic
inquiry. In spite of attempts at its definition and methodological specification, naturalistic inquiry remains an umbrella term that covers a variety of
loosely connected approaches to evaluation and applied research — for example, illuminative, responsive, democratic, transactional, ethnographic and
case study. Any attempt at a thorough specification is likely to under-
represent the diversity of interpretation and be over-prescriptive. Any
distillation of essential elements is bound to leave some of its advocates feel-
ing uncomfortable. Nonetheless, there appear to be certain values, a certain social philosophy, which inform these various interpretations of
naturalistic inquiry. Naturalistic inquiry tends to be populist. One of its
features is an emphasis on informing the public as opposed to some select

group. A basic value of those who support or advocate naturalistic inquiry seems to be participatory democracy. As a movement, participatory democracy tends to be progressive although some might argue that the emphasis on description as opposed to analysis is highly conservative. None the less, like others engaged in social research, advocates of naturalistic inquiry believe that the quality of human action and reform can be improved through or by research; thus another basic value of naturalistic inquiry is informed decision-making leading to social improvement. The attention to the individual and respect for individual perspectives and rights that are so characteristic of naturalistic inquiry, suggest a liberal political orientation. A third basic value of naturalistic inquiry then is value pluralism. Naturalistic inquirers also tend to eschew the deliberate construction and artificial control of social circumstances for the purposes of researching new ideas. In this respect naturalistic inquiry appears to stand in sharp contrast to the social philosophy of experimentalism as writers like Guba and Lincoln would have us believe.

In making a distinction between pure and applied sociology, the American social theorist Lester Ward argued that applied sociology was essentially practical; it had to do with social ideals, with ethical considerations, with what ought to be, with objects, and with purposes.[66] For Ward, the subject-matter of applied sociology was the artificial phenomena consciously and intentionally directed by society for the purpose of social improvement. Ward's book on applied sociology was first published in 1906 — a time when state intervention in social or economic affairs was still regarded as in some ways unnatural. Indeed, Ward contrasts artificial forms of life with natural forms of life, suggesting that applied sociology proceeds on the assumption of the superiority of the artificial to the natural. Ward and some few of his contemporaries, like the Professor of Jurisprudence Roscoe Pound, took exception to the prevailing views that social progress was automatic, that social inequalities were a natural result of individual abilities and that there were such things as natural law and order. For them, progress was about the conscious application of sociology to the design and implementation of programmes of social improvement. In stark contrast to the *laissez-faire* political economy of the times, men like Ward and Pound thought it both possible and desirable to modify social phenomena by artificial means so as to render them more useful or less harmful. In a sense, that debate is still going on today, presenting at least some evaluation theorists with new and rather curious contradictions. To what extent, for example, can social and educational policy be viewed as a form of experimentalism — as an artificial intervention into the operation of market economies? The problem with ideas about naturalness, as Ward clearly understood, is that they are all too easily associated with that which is god-given, or given by nature, and unalterable.

Notes

1. For an account of the development of positivism see: Giddens, A (1977) *Studies in Social and Political Theory*, London: Hutchinson & Co. Especially Chapter 1: 'Postitivism and its Critics', pp 29–89.
2. Ibid. p 35.
3. Ibid.
4. Nineteenth century positivism as distinct from the logical positivism of the Vienna Circle.
5. Campbell, DT & Stanley, JC (1966) *Experimental and Quasi-Experimental Design for Research*, Chicago: Rand McNally College Pub Co, p 2.
6. Saxe, L & Fine, M (1981) *Social Experiments: Methods for Design and Evaluation*, Beverly Hills, Cal: Sage, p 29.
7. Ibid p 44.
8. Ibid. p 46–55.
9. See Campbell's introduction to Saxe, L & Fine, M (1981) op. cit. p 14.
10. Popper, KR (1957) *The Poverty of Historicism*, London: Routledge & Kegan Paul, p 64.
11. Cronbach, LJ & Assoc (1981) *Toward Reform of Program Evaluation*, San Francisco: Jossey-Bass, p 274.
12. Rossi, PH, Freeman, HE & Wright, SR (1979) *Evaluation: A Systematic Approach*, Beverly Hills, Cal: Sage, p 31–2.
13. Campbell, DT (1984) Can we be scientific in applied social science? In Corner and Assoc (eds) *Evaluation Studies Review Annual*, Vol 9, Beverly Hills, Cal: Sage, p 26–48.
14. Rivlin, AM & Timpane, PM (eds) (1975) *Ethical and Legal Issues of Social Experimentation*, Washington DC: Brookings Institution. See: Introduction and Summary, pp 1–17.
15. Ibid. pp 4–7.
16. However, Larry Orr points out that since the mid-1970s, experimental methods have been incorporated into a variety of programme evaluations in employment, welfare health and long-term care policy. See: Orr, LL (1985) Using experimental methods to evaluate demonstration projects. In Aiken, LH & Kehrer, BH (eds) *Evaluation Studies Review Annual*, Vol 10, Beverly Hills, Cal: Sage, pp 577–89.
17. Quoted in Chomsky, N (1973) *For Reasons of State*, London: Fontana/Collins, p 7.
18. Saxe, L & Fine, M (1981) op. cit. p 44.
19. Cronbach, LJ & Associates (1981) op. cit. p 4.
20. Hopwood, A (1984) The pursuit of efficiency. In Hopwood, A & Tomkins, C (eds) *Issues in Public Sector Accounting*, Oxford: Philip Allan, p 178.
21. Cronbach, LJ & Assoc (1981) op. cit. p 215.
22. Ibid. p 3.
23. This is clearly evidenced in Cronbach, LJ (1983) *Designing Evaluations of Education and Social Programs*, San Francisco: Jossey-Bass.
24. Cronbach, LJ & Assoc (1981) op. cit. p 4.
25. This is the central project of much of Cronbach's work on validity and evaluation.
26. Cronbach & Assoc (1981) op. cit. pp 156–7.
27. Ibid. pp 207.
28. Ibid. p 183.
29. Campbell, DT & Stanley, JC (1986) op. cit.
30. Cronbach develops special notation to describe the elements in an evaluation design: Units, Treatments, Operations and Settings [UTOS], and their sub-sets

[sub-UTOS, utoS, *UTOS]. It is this notation he uses to elaborate his theory of validity and utility. For reasons of economy and clarity I have not used Cronbach's notation here.

31. For a very useful account of Cronbach's position on validity also see: House, ER, Mathison, S & McTaggart, R (1985) Validity and its Advocates. Unpublished paper, University of Illinois, Urbana-Champaign.
32. Cronbach, LJ (1983) op. cit. p 107.
33. Ibid. pp 321–2.
34. Ibid. p 190.
35. Cronbach, LJ (1981) op. cit. p 304.
36. Ibid. pp 295–304.
37. Cronbach, LJ (1983) op. cit. p 331.
38. Cronbach, LJ & Assoc (1981) op. cit. p 276.
39. Campbell, DT & Stanley, JC (1966) op. cit. p 5.
40. Cronbach, LJ (1983) op. cit. p 120.
41. Ibid. 109.
42. This analysis of Cronbach's theory of validity and utility owes much to discussions with Ernest House, and to his paper: House, ER, Mathison, S & McTaggart, R (1985) op. cit.
43. House, ER (1980) *Evaluating With Validity*, Beverly Hills, Cal: Sage, p 141.
44. Ibid. pp 175–96.
45. Ibid. p 155.
46. Ibid. p 73.
47. Ibid. pp 92–3.
48. Ibid. pp 162–70.
49. House's account of the conditions for a fair evaluation agreement is based on the work of Care, NS (1978) Participation and policy. In *Ethics*, **88**, July pp 316–37. According to House, Care's original analysis concerned the conditions under which policy agreements are morally acceptable.
50. MacDonald originally defined democratic evaluation as: 'an information service to the whole community about the characteristics of an educational programme. Sponsorship of the evaluation study does not in itself confer a special claim upon this service. The democratic evaluator recognizes value pluralism and seeks to represent a range of interests in his issue formulation. The basic value is an informed citizenry, and the evaluator acts as broker in exchanges of information between groups who want knowledge of each other. His techniques of data gathering and presentation must be accessible to non-specialist audiences. His main activity is the collection of definitions of, and reactions to, the programme. He offers confidentiality to informants and gives them control over his use of the information they provide. The report is non-recommendatory, and the evaluator has no concept of information misuse. He engages in periodic negotiation of his relationships with sponsors and programme participants. The criterion of success is the range of audiences served. The report aspires to "best seller" status. The key concepts of democratic evaluation are "confidentiality", "negotiation" and "accessibility". The key justificatory concept is "the right to know".' See, for example, MacDonald, B (1976) Evaluation and the control of education. In Tawney, D (ed.) *Curriculum Evaluation Today: Trends and Implications*, London: Macmillan Educational, p 134.
51. MacDonald, B & Norris, N (1981) Twin political horizons in evaluation of fieldwork. In Popkewitz, TS & Tabachnick, BR (eds) *The Study of Schooling: Field Based Methodologies in Educational Research and Evaluation*, New York: Praeger, p 282.

52. See: Simons, H (1987) *Getting to Know Schools in a Democracy*, London: Falmer Press, p 48.
53. See: Adelman, C, Jenkins, D & Kemmis, S (1980) Rethinking case study: notes from the second Cambridge conference. In Simons, H (ed.) *Towards a Science of the Singular*, Norwich: Centre for Applied Research in Education, University of East Anglia, pp 47–61.
54. Ibid.
55. Stake, RE (1980) The case study method in social inquiry. In Simons, H (ed.) *Towards a Science of the Singular*, Norwich: Centre for Applied Research in Education, Occasional Publication No 10, p 64. This paper was originally published in: *Educational Researcher*, 7, 2, 1978.
56. Ibid. p 69.
57. Ibid. p 66.
58. Ibid. p 67.
59. Adelman, C, Kemmis, S & Jenkins, D (1980) op. cit.
60. Ibid. p 52.
61. Kemmis, S (1980) The imagination of the case and the invention of the study. In Simons, H (ed.) *Towards a Science of the Singular*, Norwich: Centre for Applied Research in Education, University of East Anglia, p 127.
62. Guba, EG & Lincoln, YS (1982) *Effective Evaluation*, San Francisco: Jossey-Bass, p 70.
63. See: Grene, M (ed.) (1969) *Knowing and Being: Essays by Michael Polanyi*, London: Routledge & Kegan Paul, p 195.
64. Ibid. p 134.
65. Ibid. p 133.
66. Ward, LF (1906) *Applied Sociology: A Treatise on the Conscious Improvement of Society by Society*, Boston: New York.

Chapter 10

Utility and Social Responsibility in Evaluation

Teachers as researchers

In his original conception of evaluation, Tyler saw it as a tool for the teacher, a tool to help in planning the curriculum and making instructional decisions. Tyler and Waples were advocating the study of classroom problems by teachers and supervisors as early as 1930. They argued that the study of teaching problems occupied a halfway house between 'the teacher's off-hand solution to difficulties and the more intricate methods of research'. Systematic classroom investigations could, according to Tyler and Waples, 'bridge the gulf between arbitrary selection of teaching procedures and selection on the basis of valid criteria'.[1] Tyler and Waples made a distinction between proper educational research and the service study. They regarded research as an activity undertaken to test existing theories and formulate new ones, and it was an activity that belonged to the specialist who had the time to search for abstract truth. The service study, by contrast, was oriented towards practical problems, was larger in scope, arose out of particular settings, demanded prompt results therefore less precise methods, and had to be susceptible to investigation by the teacher on the basis of assumptions that could seldom be verified.[2]

In many ways Stenhouse took a similar view. He saw teacher research as fundamental to the improvement of education. Echoing Tyler, Stenhouse argued that there was a need to develop a unified research model that integrated development and evaluation, and that the key to integration was research-based teaching.[3] As a partial solution to the problem of relating theory to practice, values to action, in the classroom it was a simple yet potent idea. In Tyler's view the purpose of evaluation was to improve practice, and the producer and consumer of evaluative information were one in the same. Stenhouse had other, yet related, concerns. He took the view that the dominant approaches to curriculum development implied that a curriculum was a policy recommendation expressed in a framework of action. Given this, argued Stenhouse:

> the curriculum developer is seen as one who offers solutions rather than as one who explores problems. And his success depends on his finding the right

solution, his advocating the 'correct' course of action — or at least the best available course of action. Hence the need often seen for the separation of the function of developer and evaluator . . . [4]

Stenhouse went on to suggest that in order to integrate curriculum development and evaluation it was necessary to cast the developer not in the role of creator but in the role of investigator.[5] His theory of curriculum research and development gave primacy to the professional judgement of teachers. For him, a curriculum specification or an educational policy should be regarded as a 'provisional specification claiming no more than to be worth putting to the test of practice'.[6]

The importance accorded the role of teacher in theories of curriculum development and evaluation is a distinguishing feature of educational evaluation in Britain, and partly accounts for the emphasis on self-evaluation as a response to the growing pressure for accountability in the 1970s. John Elliott, for example, advocated the development of a 'democratic-professional system of classroom accountability' based on teachers monitoring their own practice.[7] For Elliott, however, self-evaluation was not just a way of addressing the demands for accountability, it was also an instrument teachers could use to improve their own performance.[8] Stenhouse took exception to the notion of a curriculum as a product or set of principles and processes recommended to teachers on the basis of evaluation. Elliott took exception to the assumption that educational accountability should resemble an external audit where the teacher is held to account for a limited range of measurable outcomes. What was at issue was not just teacher autonomy but different conceptions of professionalism and knowledge.

Both Tyler and Stenhouse thought in terms of inward-looking, self-developing professional systems. One way of expressing the change in thinking that their separate work embodied, is as a shift from evaluation for *the* teacher towards evaluation *by* the teacher. However, as the locus of curriculum decision-making shifted outside the classroom and the audience for evaluation changed, different conceptions of utility emerged and there was consequently a change of emphasis from formative to summative evaluation. It is not surprising, therefore, that most of the literature on the usefulness of evaluation has been concerned with the immediate utility of evaluations to executive decision-makers.

Theories of utilization

Research aimed at enhancing the impact of evaluation and isolating the factors which may have a bearing on the degree to which evaluative information is used, has produced recommendations of sorts — some of which are rather more obvious than others. For example:

- utilization is enhanced when the evaluator actively strives to facilitate and stimulate the use of information;
- the evaluator committed to use may enlist the support of an administrator in this endeavour;

- utilization can be enhanced by involving users in both the conduct of the evaluation and in planning the processes for its utilization;
- when the evaluator takes direct, personal responsibility for getting information to the right people, the utilization potential is enhanced;
- to enhance utilization, evaluators should adopt a more collaborative role, involving the decision-maker and the staff in decisions about the evaluation;
- utilization requires the explicit and continual action-based support of powerful administrators;
- persons with a high perceived need for evaluation information tend to be more satisfied with the evaluation and thus the potential for evaluation is increased;
- to enhance the utilization potential, the evaluator will need to gauge the existence and degree of disharmony behind users' 'espoused theories' (stated beliefs) and 'theories in use' actions.
- the evaluators who act as if their work will be used by a rational decision-maker who will make big-bang decisions should expect to be disappointed;
- a significant decision-maker's support for evaluation tends to increase utilization;
- management and evaluation functions can and should be integrated in the programme leadership role;
- utilization of evaluation information is enhanced when the decision-maker has the administrative and organizational skills necessary to get things done;
- by helping administrators identify goals, means to achieve these goals and measures to assess progress toward these goals, evaluators may encourage administrators to act as leaders and to become better information users;
- evaluators who understand that their results provide only another piece of a complicated information puzzle and who apply that understanding, are likely to produce information that has potential for utilization;
- the selection of procedures that are appropriate to project context and user expectations will help enhance the potential for utilization;
- the timing of an evaluation can by itself restrict the potential utility by not meshing with the timing of the programme planning;
- the amount of data and jargon in an evaluation report can affect the audience perception of its technicality and difficulty.[9]

What is noticeable about the research on improving the utility of evaluation is that is has concentrated on the administrative use of information. Much of the advice takes the form of getting the evaluator closer to the users — emotionally closer, politically closer, culturally closer, and closer in time and space. Of course the chances of utilization are likely to be increased the more the relationship between evaluator and user is one of intimacy, but intimacy has its price and efforts to increase the administrative use of evaluations are not without political consequences. The typical recipe for increasing the utility of evaluation reports includes: timeliness, relevance, brevity, accessibility and the specific targeting of information.

The idea that evaluation reports should be timely has considerable commonsense appeal. After all, there is not much point in furnishing decision-makers with information when the need for it has past. In certain cases some of the major policy decision points of a programme can be predicted or are schedlued in advance. In the National Development Programme for Computer Assisted Learning, for example, the principle of step-funding the projects meant that evaluation reports were timed to coincide with particular meetings of the Programme Committee.[10] The evaluation team, or their reports, were part of the decision process. In the case of a national Review of Police Probationer Training, to take another example, reporting was timed to coincide with meetings of the representative Steering Group organized by the Home Office, which in turn had to take account of the timetable for meetings of the Police Training Council.[11] With both these evaluations the demands of timeliness raised issues about the fairness of evaluations. When evaluators represent the work of others to those who have the authority to terminate such work or censure performance, then questions of fairness are obviously important. What is often at issue is whether people's work has been adequately represented in terms of the opportunities for and constraints on action — whether their performance can be seen as reasonable given the cultural and political circumstances in which they work.

The need for timeliness also raises other issues. Administrative timetables and research timetables are rarely synchronized in a neat and tidy fashion. Moreover, there is considerable pressure on evaluators to prepare reports that display a higher degree of understanding and insight then their investigations can properly support. There is pressure to generalize and even when these generalizations are hedged around with all kinds of caveats, they can be accorded a warrant they do not deserve. Like timeliness, and for much the same reasons, the need for brevity and accessibility also raises important issues. It has become something of an axiom that reports for policy-makers must be short and very much to the point. The executive summary of findings and recommendations is all that we can expect the hard-pressed policy-maker to read. Yet summary reports, by their very nature, at best under-represent the complexity and richness of innovations. Since we all deal in simplifications, this may be an acceptable price to pay for getting reports used and, of course, it is possible to provide additional and more detailed accounts as well. What is at issue, however, is fairness; summary judgement like summary justice is rarely fair.

Evaluation and public policy

From a technical perspective — one concerned with the effective and efficient use of information — the advice that evaluators should identify, collaborate with and speak directly to those individuals who are in a position to make changes is unexceptional. In order for an evaluation to be useful it must address those questions which key decision-makers are asking, and it should address them in a way and in a language that they will understand. Perhaps the best-known American attempt to link evaluation with programme decision-making was the CIPP framework articulated by Daniel Stufflebeam and colleagues as a result of their experience of evaluating Elementary and Secondary Education Act projects for the Columbus, Ohio Public Schools District during the 1960s.[12] The CIPP framework was an analytic and rational model of programme decision-making conceived of as a cycle of planning decisions, structuring decisions, implementing decisions and recycling decisions, each serviced respectively by a different form of evaluation — context, input, process and product evaluation. Stufflebeam and his colleagues thought of evaluation in terms of the types of decisions it served. Their approach was one that categorized evaluation according to its functional role with a consensual system of planned social change.[13]

Another example expressing the umbilical link between evaluation and decision-making was the 'decision theoritic approach' advocated by Edwards, Guttentag and Snapper.[14] They argued that every human decision depends on the answers to two questions: What are the odds? What is at stake? For them, evaluation existed to facilitate intelligent decision-making and the goal of decision-making was to maximize goods.[15] Like Stufflebeam, Edwards, Guttentag and Snapper saw decision-making as consisting of the following four phases:

1. the recognition of the decision problem and definition of its nature and dimensions;
2. probability evaluation — the data-gathering and diagnosis stage;
3. outcome evaluation, that is, attaching values preferably in numerical form to outcomes; and
4. choice among acts based on the values of outcomes and the probability states.[16]

While the CIPP framework was informed by systems theory, the decision theoretic approach to evaluation and decision-making was informed by the technology and values of micro-economics. Both these conceptions of evaluation were based on rational reconstructions of decision-making processes. In both cases the model of decision-making speaks more to idealized notions of what the process should be rather than to its actuality. Nonetheless, the decision-theoretic approach and the CIPP model were attempts at making evaluation directly relevant to the needs of decision-makers during the different phases and activities of a programme.

In his review of alternative methods for educational evaluation, Nick Smith observed that there is:

> general agreement . . . that the activity of evaluation has yet to fulfil its promise; that is, it has not lived up to its social role as the provider of relevant, useful timely information on the value of educational and social programs.[17]

Despite this widely observed discrepancy between the assumed purpose of programme evaluation and its actual or reported effects, both practitioners and theorists continue to conceive of the activity in terms of instrumental values. The view that programme decision-making is an event marked out in time and space persists. We know that policy-making is not a straightforward linear process and our models poorly represent it; however, we do not know it with any great enthusiasm.

Most of the literature on programme evaluation speaks of it as an attempt to serve a decision-maker.[18] That ideology has shaped much of our thinking about evaluation and it is an ideology that judges evaluation effective or not in terms of its impact on decision-making processes. In reality, the informative relationship between evaluation and decision-making has proved very difficult to effect with any measurable success. The idea that policy consists of discrete decisions which can be informed by carefully targeted information is a gross oversimplification based on a consensus model of the political process. The ideal of the key decision-maker or decision belongs to what Cronbach has called the Platonic image of concentrated power and responsibility — rational management in the context of command where the right decision can replace political agreements.[19] It would be wrong, however, to suggest that this is merely a misplaced theoretical conception, rather it is a genuine ideology that shapes and cements relationships between the executive and the academic community. For different reasons they share a common interest in imposing rational policy and management on political conflict and administrative chaos. The problem of utilization, then, is often seen as one of linkage between the administrative and research communities.

If the problem of the relationship between evaluation and decision-making is seen as one of linkage, then one solution is to develop an internal evaluation capability: to bring evaluation into the decision-making community. An example of the way in which applied social science has been incorporated into the machinery of the American federal government is the Program Evaluation and Methodology Division (PEMD) at the General Accounting Office (GOA). This Division has been responsible for producing more than 50 evaluation reports for different committees of Congress and has provided advice to many more.[20] In her 1986 plenary address to the American Evaluation Association, Eleanor Chelimsky of GOA observed that evaluations were an important adjunct of policy-making affecting Congressional decisions and setting the agenda for national debates. Contrary to popular belief, in her experience as head of PEMD, the use of evaluation findings in the legislative branch was the rule rather than the exception.[21] Britain too has a considerable number of research and policy units in central government. Michael Prince has noted that all major government departments, public corporations and many other government bodies have a policy planning or research capability.[22] Describing the organizational location of policy units in central government, Prince makes the following interesting observations:

1. In general, units are to be found at the assistant secretary or equivalent level and occasionally at the under-secretary level.

2. Units in central government departments are often located within divisions.
3. Because these research units operate within regular governmental hierarchies to survive, they have to adjust to the administrative culture with its concern for risk avoidance, the short term and the practical.

This means that planning and research is limited to immediate legislative and administrative concerns. It also means, says Prince, that units do not enjoy free access to ministers but rather report to senior officials.[23] One notable difference between Britain and the USA appears to be the extent to which internal research and evaluation units have access to the legislative branch. Throughout Prince's account of British central government research and policy units, little mention is made of their relationship to Parliament. In Britain, such units are a resource for the executive rather than the legislative and Prince concludes that the 'exigencies of organizational survival have limited policy units in providing planning and advice'.[24] If Prince is correct, then the growth of internal planning and evaluation resources is unlikely to do much to improve the quality of executive decision-making in Britain. Indeed, Prince suggests that for new advisory units in government, the goals of organizational acceptability and policy rationality are inconsistent.[25]

In contrast to the development of internal evaluation related to the needs of executive decision-makers, evaluation theorists have been tending to lessen their claims about the direct utility of evaluation while broadening their conceptions of its social function. Instead of talking about decision-makers, the concept of audiences has been used to denote the groups and individuals who might have an interest in a programme or policy. Borrowing from Robert Stake, Guba and Lincoln write about audiences as 'stakeholders', saying that by virtue of holding a stake an audience has the right to be consulted about its concerns and issues, has a right to have these honoured by the evaluator, and has the right to receive reports that respond to their information needs.[26] From this perspective evaluation is a service to the various participants in a political process of accommodation, as opposed to an administrative process of command. Accommodation is Cronbach's term for the operation of democracy based on pluralism and the diffusion of power. 'Under conditions of accommodation', says Cronbach, 'it can scarcely be said that decisions are made. Rather they emerge.'[27]

The shift from decision-maker to audience is more than a change in terminology. Cronbach argues that it more properly reflects reality since programmes are creatures of political accommodation. He also argues that the evalutor's mission is to 'facilitate a democratic, pluralist process by enlightening all the participants'.[28] Guba and Lincoln write that everyone who has a stake in a programme should also have a voice; justice and fairness require it.[29] Broadly speaking, the development of the concept of audience is part of a trend towards the democratization of evaluation, in theory at least. But like the concept of decision-maker, the concept of audience connotes a certain view of democracy and due political process.

As it is used in evaluation, the concept of decision-maker with its associated ideas of command and rational management implies that policy-making is a non-political consensual activity undertaken by public servants with the best available information and the best interests of the citizen at heart, if not always in mind. Here policy-making is a technical perhaps even scientific accomplishment aimed at maximizing utilities. The concept of audience with its associated ideas of pluralism and accommodation implies that policy-making is a cumulative affair moving forward by piecemeal adaptations.[30] Policy is arrived at through competitive deliberations. It is a compromise, a temporary and conditional statement of strategic intent. The aim is not so much to maximize utilities but to maximize agreement. Part of the problem with pluralist theories of policy-making is that they do not take account of the distribution of power and knowledge. For example, such theories tend to ignore the interests or social bias of the state, treating it rather as a referee arbitrating between the competing demands of different pressure groups and policies.

In societies like Britain where secrecy pervades the political and administrative culture, is enshrined in law, and where access to legal and political process is limited, it is doubtful whether policy-making can be described as pluralist. Whether one accepts a pluralist or power-élite view of policy-making it is clear that the polity plays a crucial role in the process of accommodation. And, as House has argued, there is no reason to suppose that the process of accommodation will be just or function in the common good.[31] Through their capacity to specify the conditions and procedures for participation; their capacity to choose the representative groups and shape the agenda; their capacity to construe the outcomes of deliberation in terms of collective goals and appeal to the rhetoric of national as opposed to sectional interests, a coterie of civil servants, ministers and advisers exercise enormous power.

In Britain central and local governments are taking a much more directive role in programme planning and implementation. As control over the agenda for innovation becomes more centralized, what is learnt from programmes is likely to become more convergent. With direct government intervention in innovation programmes we can expect both more urgency and certainty about the nature and quality of outcomes, and a corresponding reluctance on the part of those responsible for programmes to acknowledge and learn from failure. The policy analyst Aaron Wildavsky has written about the organizational pathology of public policy as a pattern of institutional deceit stemming from the frequent failure to match promise with performance and a persistent reluctance to acknowledge error.[32] In a political environment such as this, evaluators are likely to face pressures to limit both their remit and the dissemination of their reports. Innovation programmes already operate uneasily between the public domain of action and the more or less private domain of politics and administration. For those who see evaluation as a contribution to informed public and political debate, there is a need to understand better the structure of the organizational opportunities and constraints that shape executive decision-making and the design and implementation of innovatory programmes.

Back to school

Much of the discussion about policy and programme evaluation takes us a long way from the classroom and informing the practice of teachers. We began this chapter by looking at different conceptions of the relationship between educational evaluation and professionalism; at how evaluation might help the teacher and the school.

The American tradition that developed after Tyler might best be described as a technocratic ideology or rational scientific management where the teacher was seen as a worker in a productive process subject to performance evaluation and quality control. Tyler's conception of improving practice directly by encouraging teachers to evaluate their own curricular initiatives, was lost with the Eight-Year Study. Until recently, the British tradition of evaluation might have been best described as a mixture of evaluation *for* and *by* the teacher rather than *on* or *of* the teacher. But in the 1980s, power and control within the education service changed so rapidly that it is no longer safe to assume continuity of roles and expectations.

Inevitably, perhaps, as large-scale centrally funded innovation and system maintenance becomes the dominant context for educational evaluation there is a division of labour between the producers and consumers of evaluative information. When the arena for educational improvement is the single classroom, it is easy to see how the problem of the relationship between evaluation and decision-making can be addressed through research-based teaching or self-evaluation. When the arena for educational and social improvement is the system and the futures or changes envisaged are wholesale not piecemeal, then the problem of informing policy or practice no doubt looks rather different. And yet the Eight-Year Study was a large-scale innovation, and Stenhouse's conception of a teacher research model for curriculum development had its roots in a major national curriculum innovation — the Humanities Curriculum Project.

In 1977 at a Social Science Research Council seminar on accountability, Barry MacDonald commented that:

> all of a sudden, a system of planned change (the curriculum development movement) seems to have given way to a system of planned stability (the core curriculum, back to basics, the APU and the renaissance of large-scale testing).[33]

John Elliott, writing two years later, noted that the idea of school accountability was being used to transfer power from the school to other agencies.[34]

During the last decade, the clarion calls for greater school accountability have gone hand-in-hand with first the drift and then the rush towards centralization and the concentration of powers. In this context it was John Nisbet who warned against the temptation for evaluators of forming alliances with policy-makers to secure positions of power and reward.[35] Nisbet saw the action research movement as the best defence against this 'technocratic alliance of researchers and bureaucrats'.[36] Maybe he is right, but the development of self-evaluation and procedures for school-based institutional review appear to have done very little to arrest the trend towards centralization and prescription. In fact, as Helen Simons (1987) argues, although the idea of self-evaluation initially embodied the value of teacher autonomy and local opportunities for curriculum development, it 'has taken a form which reflects more powerful interests in the management of schooling'.[37] Securing the idea of teacher research-based curriculum development — a defensible integrated approach to development and evaluation — looks considerably more difficult now than it did when Stenhouse's *An Introduction to Curriculum Research and Development* was first published in 1965.

Simons notes that educational policy is now more subject to the politics conviction. At the same time she also reminds us that those who are required to represent and execute political policies are not necessarily persuaded of their merits.[38] We are, no doubt, too close to understand properly the nature and implications of these changes in the distribution of power and control in education. What is clear, is that they will have a profound impact on our thinking about the relationship between evaluation and educational decision-making.

Utility and social responsibility

Concern about the direct functional utility of evaluation arises essentially from a bureaucratic view of its roles and goals. As we have noted, much of the research on the use of evaluation has focused not on its social utility or its usefulness to teachers but on its utilization by administrators. In the rush to get evaluations used by sponsors, interests and values which fall outside the immediate administrative purview or might embarrass are easily pushed aside. Utilization theorists are apt to construe the problem of utility as one of communication and articulation between producers and users of knowledge — a question of marketing and delivery systems. When applied to or by governments, the major funders of evaluation, this market model, embodied in the idea of customer contracting, tends to reduce the role of evaluation to intelligence gathering and equates the public interest with the interests of government.

Robert Lynd once observed that the controlling factor in any science is the way it views and states its problems, adding 'that if the problem is wizened the data are but footnotes to the insignificant'.[39] The problem of utility is fundamental to evaluation. Defining it as a question of packaging and marketing knowledge is to trivialize the nature of the problem. Like research, evaluation belongs in the public domain; it is not a private commodity for public servants. The usefulness of programme evaluation lies in the contribution it can make to improving understanding and deliberations in the field of public policy. It speaks to the hope for better informed debate and political action. This is, however, a longer term aspiration than is generally recognized. The problem of utility cannot be addressed or stated without consideration of the social purpose and responsibility of programme evaluation, which in turn has to be judged in relation to the political possibilities and climate of the time.

Notes

1. Waples, D & Tyler, RW (1930) *Research Methods and Teachers' Problems*, New York: Macmillan, p viii.
2. Ibid. pp 12–16.
3. Stenhouse, L (1975) *An Introduction to Curriculum Research and Development*, London: Heinemann.
4. Stenhouse, L (1975) op. cit. p 124.
5. Ibid. p 125.
6. Stenhouse, L (1975) op. cit. p 142.
7. See: Elliott, J (1978) Classroom accountability and the self-monitoring teacher. In Harlen, W *Evaluation and the Teacher's Role*, London: Macmillan Education, pp 47–90.
8. Ibid. p 87.
9. These recommendations are based on a review of the literature on evauation use in: Alkin, MC & Assoc (1985) *A Guide for Evaluation Decision Makers*, Beverly Hills, Cal: Sage. See in particular Appendix A, pp 115–35.
10. MacDonald, B (1977) An educational evaluation of NDPCAL, in British Journal of Educational Technology, Vol 8 No 3.
11. MacDonald *et al.* (1986) *Police Probationer Training: The Final Report of the Stage II Review Team*, London: HMSO.
12. CIPP is an acronym for Context, Input, Process and Product. It refers to four kinds of evaluation serving different stages in programme decision-making. For an account of the origins of the CIPP model see: Stufflebeam, DL (1983) The CIPP model for program evaluation. In Madaus, GF, Scriven, MS & Stufflebeam, DL (eds) *Evaluation Models; Viewpoints on Educational and Human Services Evaluation*, Boston: Kluwer-Nijhoff Pub, pp 117–41.
13. For a full account of the CIPP model see: Stufflebeam, DL et al. (1971) *Educational Evaluation and Decision Making*, Itasca, Ill: Peacock.
14. Edwards, W, Guttentag, M & Snapper, K (1983) A decision-theoretic approach to evaluation research. In Struenig, EL & Brewer, MB (eds) *Handbook of Evaluation Research*, Beverley Hills, Cal: Sage, pp 139–84.
15. Ibid. pp 156–7.
16. Edwards, W, Guttentag, M & Snapper, K (1983) op. cit. p 148–51.
17. Smith, NL (1981) Creating alternative methods for educational evaluation. In Smith, NL (ed.) *Federal Efforts to Develop New Evaluation Methods*, San Francisco: Jossey-Bass, pp 77–94.
18. Cronbach, LJ (1982) *Designing Evaluations of Educational and Social Programs*, San Francisco: Jossey-Bass, p 5.
19. Cronbach, LJ (1980) *Toward Reform of Program Evaluation*, San Francisco: Jossey-Bass, pp 83–4.
20. See: Chelimsky, E (1987) What have we learned about the politics of program evaluation. In *Educational Evaluation and Policy Analysis*, 9, 3, Fall, pp 199–213.
21. Ibid. p 212.
22. Prince, MJ (1983) *Policy Advice and Organisational Survival*, Aldershot, Hampshire: Gower Pub Co.
23. Ibid. pp 115–17.

24. Ibid. p 2.
25. Ibid.
26. Guba, EG & Lincoln, YS (1981) *Effective Evaluation*, San Francisco: Jossey-Bass, pp 306–9.
27. Cronbach, LJ (1980) op. cit. p 89.
28. Cronbach, LJ (1983) Ninety-five theses for reforming program evaluation. In Madaus, GF, Scriven, MS & Stufflebeam, DL (eds) *Evaluation Models; Viewpoints on Educational and Human Services Evaluation*, Boston: Kluwer-Nijhoff, pp 405–12.
29. Guba, EG & Lincoln, YS (1981) op. cit. p 306.
30. Cronbach, LJ (1980) op. cit. p 89.
31. House, ER (1980) *Evaluating with Validity*, Beverly Hills, Cal: Sage.
32. Wildavsky, A (1979) *Speaking Truth to Power: The Art and Craft of Policy Analysis*, Boston: Little Brown & Co, p 35.
33. MacDonald, B *School Accountability — A Discussion Paper*. Paper presented to the SSRC Seminar on Accountability, Cambridge, September, 1977. Mimeo. Norwich, Centre for Applied Research in Education, University of East Anglia.
34. Elliott, J. (1979) Self-accounting schools: are they possible? *Educational Analysis*, 1, 1, Summer, pp 67–71.
35. Nisbet, J (1984) Curriculum evaluation in context. In Skilbeck, M (ed.) *Evaluating the Curriculum in the Eighties*, London: Hodder and Stoughton, pp 165–71.
36. Ibid. p 171.
37. Simons, H (1987) *Getting to Know Schools in a Democracy*, London: Falmer Press, p 231.
38. Ibid.
39. Lynd, R (1948) *Knowledge for What*, Princeton University Press, p 202.

Bibliography

Abt, C (1976) *Supply, Demand, Motives and Constraints of the Evaluation Producing Community*. Paper presented to the annual meeting of the AERA, San Francisco.

Adelman, C, Jenkins, D & Kemmis, S (1976) Re-thinking case study: notes from the second Cambridge conference, *Cambridge Journal of Education*, **6**, 3. Also published in Simons, H (1980) *Towards a Science of the Singular*, Norwich: Centre for Applied Research in Education, University of East Anglia, pp 47–61.

Aitken, WM (1942) *Adventure in American Education — The Story of the Eight Year Study* (Volume 1), New York: Harper & Brothers.

Alkin, MC & Assoc (1985) *A Guide for Evaluation Decision Makers*, Beverly Hills: Sage.

Alkin MC, Daillak, R & White, P (1979) *Using Evaluations: Does Evaluation Make a Difference*, Beverly Hills: Sage.

Anderson, SB, Bell, S, Murphy, RT and associates (1976) *Encyclopedia of Educational Evaluation*, San Francisco: Jossey-Bass.

Angoff, WH & Anderson, SB (1963) The standardization of educational and psychological tests. *Illinois Journal of Education*, February, pp 19–23. Reproduced in: Payne, DA & McMorris, RF (1967) *Educational and Psychological Measurement*, Waltham, Mass: Blaisdell Publishing Co, pp 9–14.

Atkin, JM (1963) Some evaluation problems in a course content improvement project, *Journal of Research in Teaching*, **1**, pp 129–32.

Banks, LJ (1969) Curriculum developments in Britain, 1963–68, *Journal of Curriculum Studies*, **1**, 1968–69, pp 247–59.

Baron, S et al. (1981) On the social organisation of evaluation: a case study. In Smetherham, D (ed.) *Practising Evaluation*, Driffield, Humberside: Nafferton Books, pp 89–110.

Becher, T (1984) The political and organisational context of curriculm evaluation. In Skilbeck, M (ed.) *Evaluating the Curriculum in the Eighties*, London: Hodder & Stoughton, pp 100–109.

Bell, R & Prescott, W (1975) *The Schools Council: A Second Look*, London: Ward Lock Educational.

Bhaskar, R (1979) *The Possibility of Naturalism*, Sussex: Harvester Press.

Blum, JM et al. (1981) *The National Experience: A History of the United States* (5th edn), New York: Harcourt Brace Jovanovich, Inc.

Boddy, A (1988) *DHSS Research Contracts*. Internal briefing document for the Society for Social Medicine, London.

Boruch, RF & Cecil, JS (eds) (1983) *Solutions to Ethical and Legal Problems in Social Research*, New York: Academic Press.

Bowden, B. Presidential address to the Science Masters' Association, *School Science Review*, **44**, 1962–63, pp 256–82.

Braudel, F (1981) *Civilization and Capitalism 15th — 18th Century: The Structures of Everyday Life* (Vol 1), London: William Collins & Co.

Brennan, EJT (1975) *Education for National Efficiency: The Contribution of Sidney and Beatrice Webb*, London: Athlone Press.

Brewer, MB (1983) Evaluation: past and present. In Struening, EL & Brewer, MB (eds) *The University Edition of the Handbook of Evaluation Research*, Beverly Hills: Sage, pp 15–27.

Bridges, D, Elliott, J & Klass, C (1986) Performance appraisal as naturalistic inquiry: a report of the fourth Cambridge conference on educational evaluation, *Cambridge Journal of Education*, **16**, 3.

Brodbeck, M (1963) Logic and scientific method in research on teaching. In Gage, NL (ed.) *Handbook of Research on Teaching*, Chicago: Rand McNally, pp 44–93.

Brogan, H (1985) *Longman History of the United States of America*, London: Guild Pub.

Brundage, A (1978) *The Making of the New Poor Law*, London: Hutchinson.

Bulmer, M (1978) Social science research and policy making in Britain. In Bulmer, M (ed.) *Social Policy Research*, London: Macmillan Press, pp 3–43.

Bulmer, M (ed.) (1987) *Social Science Research and Government: Comparative Essays on Britain and the United States*, Cambridge University Press.

Bulmer, M (1987) Governments and social science: patterns of mutual influence. In Bulmer, M (ed.) *Social Science Research and Government: Comparative Essays on Britain and the United States*, Cambridge University Press, pp 1–23.

Callahan, RE (1962) *Education and the Cult of Efficiency*. University of Chicago Press.

Cameron, M (1970) Modern Language Teaching. In Butcher, HJ & Pont, HB (eds) *Educational Research in Britain 2*, University of London Press, pp 82–106.

Campbell, DT (1976) *Assessing the Impact of Planned Social Change*. Evaluation Centre, College of Education, Western Michigan University, Kalamazoo. Occasional Paper No 8.

Campbell, DT (1979) Degrees of freedom and case studies. In Cook, TD & Reichardt, CS *Qualitative and Quantitative Methods in Evaluation Research*, Beverly Hills: Sage, pp 49–67.

Campbell, DT (1983) Reforms as experiments. In Struening, EL & Brewer, MB (eds) *Handbook of Evaluation Research*, Beverly Hills: Sage, pp 107–37.

Campbell, DT (1984) Can we be scientific in applied social science? In Corner and Assoc (ed.) *Evaluation Studies Review Annual*, Vol 9, Beverly Hills: Sage, pp 26–48.

Campbell, DT & Stanley, JC (1963) Experimental and quasi experimental designs for research on teaching. In Gage, NL (ed.) *Handbook of Research on Teaching*, Chicago: Rand McNally, pp 171–246.

Campbell, DT & Stanley, JC (1966) *Experimental and Quasi-experimental Designs for Research*, Chicago: Rand McNally.

Care, NS (1978) Participation and policy. In *Ethics*, **88**, July, pp 316–37.

Central Advisory Council For Education (1963) *Children and their Primary Schools*, London: HMSO. (The Plowden Report.)

Chapman, R (1973) *The Role of Commissions in Policy-Making*, London: George Allen & Unwin.

Chelimsky, E (1987) What have we learned about the politics of program evaluation, *Educational Evaluation and Policy Analysis*, **9**, 3, Fall, pp 199–213.

Childs, D (1986) *Britain Since 1945: A Political History* (2nd edn), London: Methuen.

Chomsky, N (1973) *For Reasons of State*, London: Fontana/Collins.

Cicarelli, V (1969) *The Impact of Head Start: An Evaluation of the Effects of Head Start on Children's Cognitive and Effective Development*. Ohio University Report to the Office of Economic Opportunity, Washington, DC: Clearinghouse for Federal Scientific and Technical Information (ED036321).

Clift, P (undated) *Policy on Evaluation*. Unpublished paper, London: Schools Council.

Cmnd 9230 (1917) *Machinery of Government* (the Haldane Committee), London: HMSO.

Cmnd 6824 (1946) *Scientific Manpower: Report of a Committee Appointed by the Lord President of the Council*, London: HMSO.

Cmnd 9703 (1956) *Technical Education*, London: HMSO.

Cmnd 2316 (1964) *Education in 1963*, London: HMSO.

Cmnd 2612 (1965) *Education in 1964*, London: HMSO.

Cmnd 5720 (1974) *Educational Disadvantage and the Educational Needs of Immigrants* (DES), London: HMSO.

Cohen, DK & Garet, MS (1975) Reforming educational policy with applied social research, *Harvard Educational Review*, **45**, 1, February, pp 17–43.

Coleman, J et al. (1966) *Equality of Educational Opportunity*, Washington DC: US Government Printing Office.

Cook, TD & Campbell, DT (1979) *Quasi Experimentation: Design and Analysis Issues for Field Settings*, Boston, Mass: Houghton Mifflin Co.

Cooper, K (1976) Curriculum evaluation — definition and boundaries. In Tawney, D (ed.) *Curriculum Evaluation Today: Trends and Implications*, London: Macmillan Educational, pp 1–10.

Crenson, MA (1971) *The Un-politics of Air Pollution: A Study of Non-decisionmaking in the Cities*, Baltimore, Maryland: John Hopkins Press.

Cronbach, LJ (1963) Course improvement through evaluation, *Teachers College Record*, **64**, May, pp 672–86.

Cronbach, LJ (1983a) *Designing Evaluations of Educational and Social Programs*, London: Jossey-Bass.

Cronbach, LJ (1983b) Ninety-five theses for reforming program evaluation. In Madaus, GF, Stufflebeam, DL & Scriven, MS (eds) *Evaluation Models; Viewpoints on Educational and Human Services Evaluation*, Boston, Mass: Kluwer-Nijhoff Pub, pp 405–12.

Cronbach, LJ & Assoc (1981) *Towards Reform of Program Evaluation*, San Francisco: Jossey Bass.

Cuban, L (1984) Transforming the frog into a prince: effective schools research, policy, and practice at the district level, *Harvard Educational Review*, **54**, 2, p 133.

Cutri, M (1935) *The Social Ideas of American Educators*, New York: Charles Scribner's Sons.

Datta, L (1983) A tale of two studies: the Westinghouse-Ohio Evaluation of Project Head Start and the Consortium for Longitudinal Studies Report, *Studies in Educational Evaluation*, **8**, pp 217–80.

Dawson, J (1984) The work of the Assessment of Performance Unit. In Skilbeck, M (ed.) *Evaluating the Curriculum in the Eighties*, London: Hodder and Stoughton, pp 124–32.

DES (1978) *DES, Form P2 Standard Agreement (August)*.

DES (1985) *DES, Form P2 (revised) Standard Contract FP (January)*.

DES (1986) *Lower Attaining Pupils Programme Issues for Discussion*, London: Department of Education and Science.

DES/Dept of Employment (1986) *Working Together — Education and Training*, London: HMSO.

DES (1986) *News 284/86 5th November*.

Downing, J (1967a) *Evaluating the Initial Teaching Alphabet*, London: Cassel.

Downing, J (1967b) Historical background and origins of the i.t.a. research; In *The i.t.a. Symposium*, Slough: National Foundation for Educational Research, pp 1–2.

Edwards, W, Guttentag, M & Snapper, K (1983) A decision theoretic approach to evaluation research. In Struening, EL & Brewer, MB (eds) *Handbook of Evaluation Research*, Beverly Hills: Sage, pp 139–84.

Eisner, EW (1967) Educational objectives: help or hindrance?, *School Review*, **75**, 3, pp 250–60.

Eisner, EW (1983) Educational connoisseurship and criticism: their form and functions in educational evaluation. In Madaus, GF, Scriven, MS & Stufflebeam, DL (eds) *Evaluation Models: Viewpoints on Educational and Human Services Evaluation*, Boston, Mass: Kluwer-Nijhoff Pub.

Elliott, J (1978) Classroom accountability and the self-monitoring teacher. In Harlen, W (ed.) *Evaluation and the Teacher's Role*, London: Macmillan Education.

Elliott, J (1979) Self-accounting schools: are they possible?, *Educational Analysis*, **1**, 1, Summer, pp 67–71.

Elliott, J (1984) Methodology and ethics. In Adelman, C (ed.) *The Politics and Ethics of Evaluation*, London: Croom Helm, pp 19–25.

Elmore, R (1976) Follow Through: Decision-making in a Large Scale Social Experiment. Unpublished Doctoral Dissertation, School of Education, Harvard University.

Fawcet, JES (1987) *The Application of the European Convention on Human Rights*, Oxford: Clarendon Press.

Fetler, M (1986) Accountability in California public schools, *Educational Evaluation and Policy Analysis*, **8**, 1, pp 31–44.

Fiddy, R (1985) The Emergence of the Youth Training Scheme. In Fiddy, R (ed.) *Unemployment and Training: A collection of National Perspectives*, London: Falmer Press, pp 27–38.

Fiddy, R (1987) *TVEI: Selling the Chameleon Curriculum*, Norwich: Centre For Applied Research in Education, University of East Anglia. Mimeo.

Fielden, J & Pearson, PK (1978) *The Cost of Learning with Computers: The Final Report of the Financial Evaluation*, London: Council for Educational Technology.

Filstead, WJ (1979) Qualitative methods: a needed perspective in evaluation research. In Cook, TD & Reichardt, SC. *Qualitative and Quantitative Methods in Evaluation Research*, Beverly Hills: Sage, pp 33–48.

Finch, J (1986) *Research and Policy*, Lewes, Sussex: Falmer Press.

Fiske, DW & Shweder, RA (eds) (1986) *Metatheory in Social Science*, University of Chicago Press.

Fitz-Gibbon, CT & Morris, LL (1978) *How to Design a Program Evaluation*, Beverly Hills: Sage.

Flugel, JC (1951) *A Hundred Years of Psychology*, London: Gerald Duckworth.

Fraser, BJ & Houghton, K (1982) *Annotated Bibliography of Curriculum Evaluation*, Jerusalem: Israel Curriculum Centre.

Fuller, R & Stevenson, O (1983) *Policies Programmes and Disadvantages: A Review of the Literature*, London: Heinemann Educational Books.

Galton, F (1892) *Hereditary Genius* (2nd edn), London: Macmillan.

Galton, M (1980) Curriculum evaluation and the traditional paradigm. In Galton, M (ed.) *Curriculum Change the Lessons of a Decade*, Leicester University Press, pp 51–63.

Giddens, A (1977) *Studies in Social and Political Theory*, London: Hutchinson & Co.

Gipps, C (1984) An evaluation of The Assessment of Performance Unit. In Skilbeck,

M (ed.) *Evaluating the Curriculum in the Eighties*, London: Hodder & Stoughton, pp 142–8.

Gipps, C & Goldstein, H (1983) *Monitoring Children: An Evaluation of the Assessment of Performance Unit*, London: Heinemann Educational Books.

Glaser, BG & Strauss, AL (1967) *The Discovery of Grounded Theory*, London: Weidenfeld & Nicolson.

Glass, GV & Worthen, BR (1971) Evaluation and research: similarities and differences, *Curriculum Theory Network*, Fall, pp 149–65.

Glass, GV (1974) Teacher effectiveness. In Walberg, HJ (ed.) *Evaluating Educational Performance*, Berkeley, Cal: McCutchan, pp 11–32.

Goldstein, H (1979) Consequences of using the Rasch Model for educational assessment, *British Educational Research Journal*, **5**, 2, pp 211–20.

Goldstein, H & Blinkhorn, S (1982) The Rasch Model still does not fit, *British Educational Research Journal*, **8**, 2, pp 167–70.

Gorham, W (1967) Testing and public policy. In *Educational Testing Services Invitational Conference on Testing Problems*, Princeton, NJ: ETS, pp 76–82.

Grene, M (1969) (ed.) *Knowing and Being: Essays by Michael Polanyi*, London: Routledge & Kegan Paul.

Guba, EG & Lincoln, YS (1982) *Effective Evaluation*, San Francisco: Jossey-Bass.

Guba, EG & Lincoln SL (1983) Epistemological and methodological bases of naturalistic inquiry. In Madaus, GF, Scriven, MS & Stufflebeam, DL (eds) *Evaluation models: Viewpoints on Educational and Human Services Evaluation*, Boston, Mass: Kluwer-Nijhoff Pub, pp 311–33.

Gumbert, EB & Spring JH (1974) *The Superschool and the Superstate: American Education in the Twentieth Century, 1918–1970*, New York: John Wiley & Sons.

Habermas, J (1978) *Knowledge and Human Interests* (2nd edn), London: Heinemann.

Halberstam, D (1973) *The Best and the Brightest*, New York: Fawcett World.

Halsey, AH (ed.) (1972) *Educational Priority Volume 1: Problems and Policies*, London: HMSO.

Hamilton, D (1976) *Curriculum Evaluation*, London: Open Books, p 15.

Hamilton, D (1977) Making sense of curriculum evaluation: continuities and discontinuities in an educational idea. In Shulman, LS (ed.) *Review of Research in Education, Vol 5*, Itasca, Ill: Peacock, pp 318–47.

Hamilton, D (1980) Some contrasting assumptions about case study research and survey analysis. In Simons, H (ed.) *Towards a Science of the Singular*, Norwich Centre for Applied Research in Education, University of East Anglia, pp 76–92.

Hamilton, D (1980) Educational research and the shadows of Francis Galton and Ronald Fischer. In Dockrell, WB & Hamilton, D (eds) *Rethinking Educational Research*, London: Hodder & Stoughton, pp 153–68.

Hamilton, D (1981) Generalization in the educational sciences: problems and purposes. In Popkewitz, TS & Tabachnick, BR (eds) *The Study of Schooling: Field Based Methodologies in Educational Research and Evaluation*, New York: Praeger, pp 277–41.

Hamilton, D, Jenkins, D, King, C, MacDonald, B & Parlett, M (1977) *Beyond The Numbers Game*, London: Macmillan Education.

Harlen, W (1973) Science 5–13 Project. In *Schools Council Research Studies: Evaluation in Curriculum Development: Twelve Case Studies*, London: Macmillan, pp 16–36.

Harlen, W (ed.) (1978) *Evaluation and the Teacher's Role*, London: Macmillan Education.

Health Education Authority (1987) *Rules Governing the Payment of Grants* (April).

Hearnshaw, LS (1964) *A Short History of British Psychology 1840–1940*, London: Methuen.

Heclo, H & Wildavsky, A (1974) *The Private Government of Public Money*, London Macmillan Press.

Held, D (1980) *Introduction to Critical Theory*, London: Hutchinson & Co.

Herman, J & Yeh, J (1980) Test use: a review of the issues. In Baker, EL & Quellmalz, ES *Educational Testing and Evaluation*, Beverly Hills: Sage, pp 219–28.

HMI (1986) *A Survey of the Lower Attaining Pupils Programme: The First Two Years*, DES Publications Despatch Centre, Stanmore, Middlesex.

Holly, P (1986) Developing a professional evaluation. *Cambridge Journal of Education*, **16**, 2, Summer Term; a special edition entitled 'Symbolism or Synergism? Curriculum Evaluation in the 1980s'.

Holt, M (1981) *Evaluating the Evaluators*, London: Hodder & Stoughton.

Holmes, JA (1967) Evaluation — 6. In *The i.t.a. Symposium*, Slough: National Foundation for Educational Research, pp 123–7.

Hooper, R (1977) *National Development Programme in Computer Assisted Learning: Final Report of the Director*, London: Council for Educational Technology.

Hopkins, D (1985) Evaluating TVEI: some methodological issues. In Hopkins, D (ed.) *Evaluating TVEI: Some Methodological Issues*, Cambridge Institute of Education.

Hopwood, A (1984) Accounting and the pursuit of efficiency. In Hopwood, A & Tomkins, C (1984) *Issues in Public Sector Accounting*, Deddington, Oxford: Philip Allan Publishers, pp 167–88.

Hopwood, A & Tomkins, C (1984) *Issues in Public Sector Accounting*, Deddington, Oxford: Philip Allan Publishers.

House, ER (1973) The conscience of educational evaluation. In House, ER (ed.) *School Evaluation: The Politics and Process*, Berkeley, Cal: McCutchan.

House, ER et al. (1978) No simple answer: critique of Follow Through evaluation, *Harvard Educational Review*, **48**, 2, pp 128–60.

House, ER (1979) The objectivity, fairness and justice of federal evaluation as reflected in the Follow Through evaluation. In *Educational Evaluation and Policy Analysis*, Washington DC, AERA, **1**, 1, pp 28–42.

House, ER (1980) *Evaluating with Validity*, Beverly Hills: Sage.

House, ER (1983) How we think about evaluation. In House ER (ed.) *Philosophy of Evaluation*. San Francisco: Jossey-Bass, pp 5–25.

House, ER, Mathison, S & McTaggart, R (1985) *Validity and its Advocates*, University of Illinois, Urbana-Champaign.

House, E & Madura, W (1987) *Race, Gender and Jobs — Losing Ground on Employment*, Laboratory for Policy Studies, School of Education, University of Colorado at Boulder.

Inner London Education Authority (undated) *The Junior School Project: A Summary of the Main Project*. Copies available from the Information Section, ILEA Research and Statistics Branch, Addington Street Annexe, County Hall, SE1 7UY.

James, HT (1971) The new cult of efficiency and education. In Browder, LH (ed.) *Emerging Patterns of Administrative Accountability*, Berkeley, Cal: McCutchan, pp 39–46.

Jenkins, D, Kemmis, S & Atkin, R (1977) An insiders critique. In Norris, N (ed.) *SAFARI Theory in Practice*, Norwich: Centre for Applied Research in Education, pp 79–105.

Jenkins, D, Simons, H & Walker, R (1981) Thou nature art my goodness: naturalistic inquiry in educational evaluation, *Cambridge Journal of Education*, **11**, 3.

Joint Committee on Standards for Educational Evaluation (1981) *Standards for Evaluations of Educational Programs, Projects, and Materials*, New York: McGraw-Hill.

Judge, H (1984) *A Generation of Schooling*, Oxford University Press.

Kaestle, CF & Smith MS (1982) The Federal Role in elementary and secondary education, 1940–1980, *Harvard Educational Review*, **52**, 4, pp 384–408.

Karier, CJ (1973) Testing for order and control in the corporate liberal state. In Karier, CJ, Violas, P & Spring, J (eds) *Roots of Crisis: American Education in the Twentieth Century*, Chicago: Rand McNally.

Kemmis, S (1977) Nomothetic and idiographic approaches to the evaluation of computer assisted learning. In Kemmis, S with Atkin, R & Wright, E *How Do Students Learn?* Norwich: Centre for Applied Research in Education, University of East Anglia.

Kemmis, S (1980) The imagination of the case and the invention of the study. In Simons, H (ed.) *Towards a Science of the Singular*, Norwich: Centre for Applied Research in Education, University of East Anglia, pp 93–142.

Kogan, M (1973) The Plowden Committee on Primary Education. In Chapman, RA (ed.) *The Role of Commissions in Policy Making*, London: George Allen & Unwin, pp 81–104.

Kuhn, TS (1970a) *The Structure of Scientific Revolutions* (2nd edn), University of Chicago Press.

Kuhn, TS (1970b) Reflections on my critics. In Lakatos, I & Musgrave, A (eds) *Criticism and the Growth of Knowledge*, Cambridge University Press, pp 231–77.

Kushner, S & MacDonald, B (1987) The limitations of programme evaluation. In Murphy, R & Torrance, H (eds) *Evaluating Education: Issues and Methods*. London: Paul Chapman Pub Ltd.

Lacey, C (1984) The Schools Council: an evaluation from a research perspective. In Skilbeck, M (ed.) *Evaluating the Curriculum in the Eighties*, London: Hodder & Stoughton, pp 157–64.

Lakatos, I (1978) *The Methodology of Scientific Research Programmes*, Cambridge University Press.

Leeds TVEI Evaluation Team (undated) *Interim Report 1: Evaluation Procedures and Methodology*. [draft]. University of Leeds.

Lippmann, W (1961) *Drift and Mastery*, Englewood Cliffs, NJ: Prentice-Hall. First Published by Mitchell Kennerley in 1914.

Lukes, S (1974) *Power: A Radical View*, London: Macmillan.

Lukes, S (1977) *Essays in Social Theory*, London: Macmillan Press.

Lynd, RS (1948) *Knowledge for What?* Princeton University Press.

Lynn, LE (1978) The question of relevance. In Lynn, LE (ed.) *Knowledge and Policy: The Uncertain Connection*, Washington: National Academy of Sciences.

McCulloch, G (1986) Policy, politics and education: the Technical and Vocational Education Initiative, *Journal of Educational Policy*, **1**, 1, pp 35–52.

MacDonald, B (1976) Evaluation and the control of education. In Tawney, D (ed.) *Curriculum Evaluation Today: Trends and Implications*, London: Macmillan, pp 125–36.

MacDonald, B (1977) An educational evaluation of NDPCAL, *British Journal of Educational Technology*, **8**, 3.

MacDonald, B (1978) Accountability, standards and the process of schooling. A paper commissioned by the Educational Research Board of the Social Science Research Council. In Becher, T & Maclure, S (eds) *Accountability in Education*, Slough: NFER Pub Co, pp 127–51.

MacDonald, B (1979) Hard times: educational accountability in England, *Educational Analysis*, **1**, 1, Summer, pp 23–42.

MacDonald, B (1981) Interviewing in case study evaluation, *Phi Delta Kappa CEDR Quarterly*, **14**, 4.

MacDonald, B (1982) *Educational Evaluation in the Contemporary World*. Invited presentation to the Symposium Internacional De Didactica Generla y Didacticas Especiales, La Manga del Mar Menor, Spain, 27 September–2 October 1982. Norwich: Centre for Applied Research in Education, University of East Anglia.

MacDonald, B (1987) *Research and Action in the Context of Policing*. A Paper Commissioned by the Police Foundation. Norwich: Centre for Applied Research in Education, University of East Anglia.

MacDonald, B & Jenkins, D (1979) *Understanding Computer Assisted Learning: The Final Report of the Educational Evaluation of the National Development Programme in Computer Assisted Learning*, Norwich: Centre for Applied Research in Education, University of East Anglia.

MacDonald, B, Jenkins, D, Kushner, S, Logan, T, & Norris, N (1981) *Evaluators at Work*, Koln: IFAPLAN.

MacDonald, B & Norris, N (1981) Twin political horizons in evaluation fieldwork. In Popkewitz, TS & Tabachnick, BR (eds) *The Study of Schooling: Field Based Methodologies in Educational Research and Evaluation*, New York; Praeger, pp 276–90.

MacDonald, B & Parlett, M (1973) Re-thinking evaluation: notes from the Cambridge conference, *Cambridge Journal of Education*, **3**, 2, Easter Term.

MacDonald, B & Stake, RE (1974) *Confidentiality: Procedure and Principles of the UNCAL Evaluation with Respect to Information About Projects in the National Development Programme in Computer Assisted Learning*, Norwich: Centre for Applied Research in Education, University of East Anglia.

MacDonald, B & Walker, R (eds) (1974) *SAFARI 1: Innovation, Evaluation, and the Problem of Control*, Norwich: Centre for Applied Research in Education, University of East Anglia.

MacDonald, B et al. (1975) *The Programme at Two*, Norwich: Centre for Applied Research in Education, University of East Anglia.

MacDonald, B et al. (1986) *Police Probationer Training: The Final Report of the Stage 11 Review Team*. London: HMSO.

MacKenzie, DA (1981) *Statistics in Britain 1865–1930: The Social Construction of Scientific Knowledge,* Edinburgh University Press.

Maclure, S (1968) *Curriculum Innovation in Practice*, London: Schools Council, HMSO.

McLaughlin, M (1975) *Evaluation and Reform: The Elementary and Secondary Education Act 1965/Title 1*. Cambridge, Mass: Ballinger.

Madaus, GF, Stufflebeam, DL & Scriven, MS (1983) Program evaluation: a historical overview. In Madaus, GF, Scriven, MS & Stufflebeam, DL (eds) *Evaluation Models: Viewpoints on Educational and Human Services Evaluation*, Boston, Mass: Kluwer-Nijhoff Publishing, pp 3–23.

Masterman, M (1970) The nature of paradigm. In Lakatos, I & Musgrave, A (eds) *Criticism and the Growth of Knowledge*, Cambridge University Press, pp 59–89.

MSC (1984) *Manpower Services Commission Annual Report*, 1983/84 Sheffield, MSC.

Murray, C (1985) *Losing Ground*, New York: Basic Books.

National Commission on Excellence in Education (1983) *A Nation at Risk: The Imperative for Educational Reform*, Washington: Government Printing Office.

National Executive Committee of the Labour Party (1961) *Singposts for the Sixties*.

NFER (1967) *The i.t.a. Symposium*, Slough: National Foundation for Educational Research.

NFER (1984) *14–16 Network DES Lower Attaining Pupils Programme*, Autumn, Slough: NFER.

NFER (1985) *14–16 Network DES Lower Attaining Pupils programme*, Spring, Slough: NFER.

NFER (1985) *Educational Research News*, No 42, Spring, Slough: NFER.

NFER (1986) *14–16 Network DES Lower Attaining Pupils Programme*, Summer, Slough: NFER.

Nisbet, J (1976) Contrasting structure for curriculum development: Scotland and England, *Journal of Curriculum Studies*, **8**, 2, November, pp 167–70.

Nisbet, J (1980) Educational research: the state of the art. In Dockrell, WB & Hamilton, D (eds) *Rethinking Educational Research*, London: Hodder & Stoughton.

Nisbet, J (1984) Curriculum evaluation in context. In Skilbeck, M (ed.) *Evaluating the Curriculum in the Eighties*, London: Hodder & Stoughton, pp 165–71.

Norris, N (ed.) (1977) *SAFARI: Theory in Practice*, Norwich: Centre for Applied Research in Education, University of East Anglia.

Norris, N & Sanger, J (1984) *Inside Information; Evaluating a Curriculum Innovation*, Norwich: Centre for Applied Research in Education, University of East Anglia.

Nuffield Foundation (1960–61) *Sixteenth Annual Report*.

Orr, LL (1985) Using experimental methods to evaluate demonstration projects. In Aiken, LH & Kehrer, BH (eds) *Evaluation Studies Review Annual*, **10**, Beverly Hills: Sage, pp 577–89.

Outhwaite, W (1975) *Understanding Social Life*, London: Allen and Unwin.

Owen, J (1984) TVEI: future control. In Dancy, J (ed.) *TVEI Perspectives 14*, School of Education, University of Exeter, pp 7–17.

Parlett, M (1970) *Evaluating Innovations in Teaching*. Mimeo, Research Unit on Intellectual Development, Department of Educational Sciences, University of Edinburgh.

Parlett, M & Hamilton, D (1972) *Evaluation as Illumination: A New Approach to the Study of Innovatory Programmes*. Occasional Paper 9. Centre for Research in Educational Sciences, University of Edinburgh. Also Published in: Hamilton, D et al. (eds) (1977) *Beyond the Numbers Game*, London: Macmillan.

Parsons, C. (1976) The new evaluation: a cautionary note, *Journal of Curriculum Studies*, **8**, 2, pp 125–38.

Patterson, JT (1981) *America's Struggle Against Poverty 1900–1980*, Cambridge, Mass: Harvard University Press.

Patton, MQ (1978) *Utilization Focused Evaluation*, Beverly Hills: Sage.

Patton, MQ (1980) *Qualitative Evaluation Methods*. Beverly Hills: Sage.

Patton, MQ (1981) *Creative Evaluation*. Beverly Hills: Sage.

Phillips, DC (1987) *Philosophy, Science, and Social Inquiry*, Oxford: Pergamon Press.

Polanyi, M (1959) *The Study of Man*, London: Routledge & Kegan Paul.

Popper, KR (1957) *The Poverty of Historicism*, London: Routledge & Kegan Paul.

Pound, R (1959) *Jurisprudence*, (Vol 1) St Paul, Minn: West Publishing Co.

Pound, R (1922) *An Introduction to the Philosophy of Law*, Yale University Press.

Prakash, MS & Waks, LJ (1985) Four conceptions of excellence, *Teachers College Record*, **87**, 1, pp 79–101.

Preece, PFW (1980) On rashly rejecting Rasch: a response to Goldstein. With a rejoinder from Goldstein, *British Educational Research Journal*, **6**, 2, pp 209–12.

Prince, MJ (1983) *Policy Advice and Organisational Survival*, Aldershot: Gower Pub Co.

Pring, R (1984) Confidentiality and the right to know. In Adelman, C (ed.) *The Politics and Ethics of Evaluation*, London: Croom Helm, pp 8–18.

Reid, K, Hopkins, D & Holly, P (1987) *Towards the Effective School*, Oxford: Basil Blackwell.

Riddell, P (1985) *The Thatcher Government*, Oxford: Basil Blackwell (revised edition).

Rist, RC (1987) Social science analysis and congressional uses: the case of the United States General Accounting Office. In Bulmer, M (ed.) *Social Science Research and*

Government: Comparative Essays on Britain and the United States. Cambridge University Press, pp 303–17.

Rivlin, A (1971) *Systematic Thinking for Social Action*, Washington: Brookings.

Rivlin, AM & Timpane, PM (eds) (1975) *Ethical and Legal Issues of Social Experimentation*, Washington DC: Brookings Institution.

Rossi, PH, Freeman, HE & Wright, SR (1979) *Evaluation A Systematic Approach*, Beverly Hills: Sage.

Runciman, WG (1983) *A Treatise on Social Theory Volume 1: The Methodology of Social Theory*, Cambridge University Press.

Rutman, L (1977) Planning an evaluation study. In Rutman, L (ed.) *Evaluation Research Methods*, Beverly Hills: Sage.

Sandifer, PD (1982) The South Carolina experience. In Smith, NL & Caulley, DN (eds) *The Interaction of Evaluation and Policy: Case Reports from State Education Agencies*, Portland, Oregan: NREL, pp 83–99.

Saunders, M (1985) Developing a large scale 'Local' evaluation of TVEI: aspects of the Lancaster Experience. In Hopkins, D (ed.) *Evaluating TVEI: Some Methodological Issues*, Cambridge Institute of Education, pp 41–51.

Savage, G (1953) Presidential address to the Science Masters' Association. *School Science Review*, **34**, 1952–53, pp 322–34.

Saxe, L & Fine, M (1981) *Social Experiments: Methods for Design and Evaluation*, Beverly Hills: Sage.

Scarman, Lord (1982) *The Scarman Report: The Brixton Disorders 10–12 April 1981*, Harmondsworth, Middlesex: Penguin.

Scheffler, I (1982) *Science and Subjectivity* (2nd edn), Indianapolis, Indiana: Hackett Pub Co.

Scottish Education Department (1987) *Standard Conditions Governing The Award of Major Education Research and Development Grants*. (Form RES April.)

Scriven, M (1973) The methodology of evaluation. In Worthen, BR & Sanders, JR (eds) *Educational Evaluation: Theory and Practice*, Belmont, Cal: Wadsworth Pub Co, pp 60–104.

Scriven, MS (1981) *Evaluation Thesaurus* (3rd edn), Inverness, Cal: Edgepress.

Scriven, MS (1983) The evaluation taboo. In House, ER (ed.) *Philosophy of Evaluation*, San Francisco: Jossey-Bass.

Searle, B (1985) *Evaluation in World Bank Education Projects: Lessons from Three Case Studies*, Washington DC: World Bank Education and Training Department, Report No EDT5.

Shanin, T (ed.) (1974) *The Rules of the Game: Cross Disciplinary Essays on Models in Scholarly Thought*, London: Tavistock Pub.

Sharpe, LJ (1978) The social scientist and policy-making in Britain and America: a comparison. In Bulmer, M (ed.) *Social Policy Research*, London: Macmillan Press, pp 303–12.

Shipman, M (1979) *In-School Evaluation*, London: Heinemann.

Silberman, G (1981) New methods in criminal justice evaluation. In Smith, NL (ed.) *Federal Efforts to Develop New Evaluation Methods*, San Francisco: Jossey-Bass, pp 25–40.

Simons, H (1980) (ed.) *Towards a Science of the Singular*, Norwich: Centre for Applied Research in Education, University of East Anglia.

Simons, H (1984) Negotiating conditions for independent evaluations. In Adelman, C (ed.) *The Politics and Ethics of Evaluation*, London: Croom Helm, pp 56–68.

Simons, H (1987) *Getting to Know Schools in a Democracy: The Politics and Process of Evaluation*, London: Falmer Press.

Skilbeck, M (1984) Curriculum evaluation at the national level. In Skilbeck, M (ed.) *Evaluating the Curriculum in the Eighties*, London: Hodder & Stoughton, pp 92–9.

Smetherham, D (1981) Defining evaluation: a brief encounter. In Smetherham, D (ed.) *Practising Evaluation*, Driffield, Humberside: Nafferton Books, pp 1–16.

Smith, ER & Tyler, RW (1942) *Adventure in American Education: Appraising and Recording Student Progress*, (Vol 3), New York: Harper & Row.

Smith, NL (1981) Creating alternative methods for educational evaluations. In Smith NL (ed.) *Federal Efforts to Develop New Evaluation Methods*, San Francisco: Jossey-Bass, pp 77–94.

Smith, NL (1982) The context of evaluation practice in state departments of education. In Smith, NL & Caulley, DN (eds) *The Interaction of Evaluation and Policy: Case Reports from State Education Agencies*, Portland, Oregan: Northwest Regional Educational Laboratory (NREL), pp 159–78.

St Perre, RG (1983) Congressional input to program evaluation: scope and effects, *Evaluation Review*, 7, August, pp 411–36.

Stake, RE (1967a) The countenance of educational evaluation, *Teachers College Record*, **68**, April, pp 523–40.

Stake, RE (1967b) Towards a technology for the evaluation of educational programs. In Tyler, R et al. *Perspectives on Curriculum Evaluation*, AERA Monograph Series on Curriculum Evaluation, No 1, Chicago: Rand McNally.

Stake, RE (1976) *Evaluating Educational Programmes: The Need and the Response*, Washington DC: OECD Publications Centre.

Stake, RE (1980) The case study method in social inquiry. In Simons, H (ed.) *Towards a Science of the Singular*, Norwich: Centre for Applied Research in Education, University of East Anglia, pp 64–65.

Stake, RE (1983) Program evaluation, particularly responsive evaluation. In Madaus, GF, Scriven, MS & Stufflebeam, DL (eds) *Evaluation Models: Viewpoints on Educational and Human Services Evaluation*, Boston, Mass: Kluwer-Nijhoff, pp 287–310.

Stenhouse, LS (1975) *An Introduction to Curriculum Research and Development*, London: Heinemann.

Stenhouse, LS (1979) Getting educational accountability in focus: an introductory statement, *Educational Analysis*, 1, 1, Summer.

Stenhouse, LS (1980) The study of samples and the study of cases, *British Educational Research Journal*, **6**, 1, pp 1–6.

Stenhouse, LS (1983) *Authority Education and Emancipation*, London: Heinemann.

Stoner, FE (1978) Federal auditors as regulators: the case of title 1 of ESEA. In May, JV & Wildavsky, AB (eds) *The Policy Cycle*, Beverly Hills, Cal: Sage, pp 199–214.

Stoney, SM, Pole, CJ & Sims, D (1986) *The Management of TVEI: A Set of Interim Papers on the Themes of Management Issues*, Slough: NFER.

Stufflebeam, DL (1983) The CIPP model for program evaluation. In Madaus, GF, Scriven, MS & Stufflebeam, DL (eds) *Evaluation Models: Viewpoints on Educational and Human Services Evaluation*, Boston, Mass: Kluwer-Nijhoff Pub, pp 117–41.

Stufflebeam, DL et al. (1971) *Educational Evaluation and Decision Making*, Itasca, Ill: Peacock.

Stufflebeam, DL & Webster, WJ (1983) An analysis of alternative approaches to evaluation. In Madaus, GF, Scriven, MS & Stufflebeam, DL (eds) *Evaluation Models: Viewpoints on Educational and Human Services Evaluation*, Boston, Mass: Kluwer-Nijhoff, pp 23–44.

Sutherland, G (1984) *Ability, Merit and Measurement: Mental Testing and English Education 1880–1940*, Oxford: Clarendon Press.

Taylor, FW (1911) *The Principles of Scientific Management*, New York: Harper & Bros.

Taylor, W (1985) The organisation and funding of educational research in England and Wales. In Nisbet, J (ed.) *World Yearbook of Education 1985: Research, Policy and Practice*, London: Kogan Page, pp 42–67.

Tawney, D (ed.) (1976) *Curriculum Evaluation Today: Trends and Implications*, London: Macmillan Educational.

Tawney, D (1976) Evaluation — information for decision-makers. In Tawney, D (ed.) *Curriculum Evaluation Today: Trends and Implications*, London: Macmillan Educational, pp 11–28.

Tenne, R (1985) How will TVEI be evaluated, *Education*, 9 August, p 13.

Times Educational Supplement, 15/10/76, 'DES report to Prime Minister sparks off angry protests.'

Times Educational Supplement, 13/2/87 'Appraisal will gradually be linked to results — Rumbold?'

Todd, A (1957) The scientist — supply and demand. Presidential address to the Science Masters' Association, reported in: *School Science Review*, **38**, 1956–57, pp 106–7.

Torrance, H (1986) *Assessment and Examinations: Social Context and Educational Practice*. Unpublished PhD Thesis, University of East Anglia.

Tuberfield, AF (1986) 'LAPP — an Interim Assessment.' Paper presented to the Lower Attaining Pupils Programme open day held at the University of Warwick, 1 July 1986.

TVEI Unit (1986) *TVEI Evaluation*, London: TVEI Unit, Grays Inn Rd, London.

TVEI Unit (undated) *TVEI EVALUATION*, London: TVEI Unit, 236 Grays Inn Rd, London.

TVEI Unit (undated) *TVEI Evaluation Bulletin*, TVEI Unit, 236 Grays Inn Rd, London.

TVEI Unit (undated) *Technical & Vocational Education Initiative Evaluation*, TVEI Unit, Grays Inn Rd, London.

TVEI Unit (undated) *TVEI Finance Feasibility Study*, TVEI Unit, Grays Inn Rd, London.

Tyack, DB (1974) *The One Best System*, Cambridge, Mass: Harvard University Press.

Tyack, DB & Hansot, E (1982) *Managers of Virtue*, New York: Basic Books.

Tyler, R (1949) *Basic Principles of Curriculum and Instruction*, University of Chicago Press.

Tyler, R (1983) A rationale for program evaluation. In Madaus, GF, Scriven MS, & Stufflebeam, DL (eds) *Evaluation Models:Viewpoints on Educational and Human Services Evaluation*, Boston, Mass: Kluwer-Nijhoff Publishing, pp 67–78.

US Commission on Civil Rights (1967) *Racial Isolation in Public Schools*, Washington DC: US Government Printing Office.

Van der Eyken (1977) *The Pre-school Years*, Harmondsworth: Penguin.

Waples, D & Tyler, R (1930) *Research Methods and Teachers' Problems a Manual for Systematic Studies of Classroom Procedure*, New York: The Macmillan Co.

Warburton, FW & Southgate, V (1969) *i.t.a. An Independent Evaluation*, London: John Murray and W & R Chambers.

Ward, LF (1906) *Applied Sociology: A Treatise on the Conscious Improvement of Society*, Boston: New York.

Waring, M (1979) *Social Pressures and Curriculum Innovation*, London: Methuen.

Weiss, CH (1978) Improving the linkage between social research and public policy. In Lynn, LE (ed.) *Knowledge and Policy: The Uncertain Connection*, Washington DC: National Academy of Sciences, pp 23–81.

Weiss, CH & Bucuvalas, MJ (1980) *Social Science Research and Decision Making*, Columbia University Press.

Weiss, CH (1983) Evaluation research in the political context. In Struening, EL &

Brewer, MB (eds) *Handbook of Evaluation Research*, Beverly Hills: Sage, pp 31–45.

Werner, W (1978) Evaluation: sense-making of school programmes. In Aoki, T (ed.) *Curriculum Evaluation in a New Key*. Monograph series No 1, Vancouver Centre for the Study of Curriculum and Instruction, Faculty of Education, University of British Columbia.

Weston, P (1984) A quest for understanding, or understanding the questions. Paper presented at the LAPP Evaluators Conference, James Gracie Centre, Brimingham, October 25/26 1984.

Whyte, WF (1984) *Learning from the Field: a Guide from Experience*, Beverly Hills: Sage.

Wildavsky, A (1979) *Speaking the Truth to Power: The Art and Craft of Policy Analysis*, Boston: Little, Brown and Co.

Wilford, M (1942) 'Foreword' to Smith, ER & Tyler, RW *Adventure in American Education: Appraising and Recording Student Progress* (Volume 3), New York: Harper & Row, pp xvii–xix.

Williams, W (1983) British policy analysis: some preliminary observations from the US. In Gray, A & Jenkins, B (eds) *Policy Analysis and Evaluation in British Government*, London: Royal Institute of Public Administration, pp 17–24.

Willmott, P (1980) A view from an independent research institute. In Cross, M (ed.) *Social Research and Public Policy: Three Perspectives*, London: Social Research Association.

Wiseman, S (ed.) (1967) *Intelligence and Ability*, Harmondsworth, Middlesex: Penguin Books.

Wiseman, S & Pidgeon, D (1972) *Curriculum Evaluation*, Windsor: NFER.

Wolf, RL (1983) The use of judicial evaluation methods in the formulation of educational policy. In Madaus, GF, Scriven, MS & Stufflebeam, DL (eds) *Evaluation Models: Viewpoints on Educational and Human Services Evaluation*, Boston, Mass: Kluwer-Nijhoff, pp 189–203.

Worthen, BR & Saunders, JR (1973) *Educational Evaluation: Theory and Practice*, Belmont, Cal: Wadsworth Pub Co.

Wragg, T (1984) Evaluating TVEI programmes. In Dancy, J (ed.) *TVEI Perspectives 14*, University of Exeter.

Yin, RK (1984) *Case Study Research Design and Methods*, Beverly Hills: Sage.

Young, M (1961) *The Rise of the Meritocracy*, Harmondsworth, Middlesex: Penguin.

Index

Subject index

Name index